LUIGI PIRANDELLO

Luigi Pirandello, 1935
(Photograph by Edward Steichen)

LUIGI PIRANDELLO
1867-1936

———

WALTER STARKIE, Litt.D

UNIVERSITY OF CALIFORNIA PRESS

Berkeley and Los Angeles

1965

University of California Press
Berkeley and Los Angeles, California

Cambridge University Press
London, England

Third Edition, Revised and Enlarged, 1965
Library of Congress Catalog Card No. 65-11819
Manufactured in the United States of America

ALLA MEMORIA DI MIA SUOCERA
DELFINA LANDI PORCHIETTI

CONTENTS

Introduction to the Third Edition, 1965

WHEN I ARRIVED IN ITALY for the first time in 1918 during World War I Gabriele D'Annunzio had reached the pinnacle of his fame, and I hero-worshipped the poet-condottiere, but preferred to listen to his impassioned oratory in the piazza in Venice and in Rome than to his works in the theatre. Within the short space of three years (1919–1922) I was to witness the ascendance of Pirandello as a new constellation at the precise moment when the star of the Archangel (as he was known to his legionaries) was beginning to set. Luigi Pirandello was only four years younger than D'Annunzio, who was born in 1863. Both authors lived in the same spiritual atmosphere, and the publication of their works followed a parallel course. D'Annunzio had been for forty years the most celebrated of all Italian writers and a figure of world significance as poet as well as man of action, whereas Pirandello's lonely art had grown to maturity apart from the main currents of the Italian literature of his day, which followed the vogue of Carducci's cult of Pagan antiquity and D'Annunzio's Byzantinism mixed with Nietzsche and Wagner. Pirandello deliberately shunned the D'Annunzian world like the plague, and continued in his secluded life to worship Alessandro Manzoni and Giacomo Leopardi. From the author of *I Promessi Sposi* he extracted a little of the boundless tolerance of Don Abbondio, but to this he added a liberal dose of wormwood which he drew from the desolate pessimism of Leopardi. Nature in

ix

Pirandello's eyes was not the beautiful mother of mankind, but rather its stepmother, and his attitude was as stoical as that of Alfred de Vigny who addressed her saying: "On t'appelle une mère, et tu n'es qu'une tombe." Pirandello's labyrinthine soul was forever faced by a two-headed Hermes which with one face laughs and with the other weeps.

Another rival of Pirandello in the theatre in those days was the Neapolitan Roberto Bracco, the foremost Italian disciple of Ibsen, and veteran playgoers in 1918 still rhapsodized about Emma Gramatica's performance as Teresa, the pathetic heroine of *La Piccola Fonte* (1905), and Ruggero Ruggeri's interpretation of *Il Piccolo Santo* (1909). Alas, Bracco's *Teatro del Pensiero* or Drama of Ideas, with its emphasis on problems of the spirit and its tragedies of the subconscious, no longer appealed to the great Italian public of the war years, who had been exposed to the sensationalism of the "Grotesques" (*Teatro Grottesco*) with their multiple vagaries. Bracco did, however, produce one prophetic play, *I Pazzi* (1922), a Freudian interpretation of Insanity Fair, but it appeared in book form in the year of Mussolini's march on Rome and the triumph of Fascism, and was never given an opportunity on the stage. Bracco, moreover, belonged to the Aventine or Liberal party in Italian politics and was *persona non grata* to the Black Shirts, with the result that he too spent his last years in retirement and died in 1943, a forgotten figure. Pirandello, on the other hand, became a public figure through the help of the Fascist government, and in the years to come he could count on the benevolent encouragement of the Italian dictator. This help, in part, was providential, for it enabled him to press on with his revolutionary dramas. In these early days the first night of a Pirandellian play at Milan or

Rome was a combative affair: the audience would divide into two camps—the Pirandellians and the anti-Pirandellians—and between each act the drama shifted from the stage to the stalls. I can still visualize the sad, apologetic face of the bearded maestro who had conjured up this double drama of stage and auditorium. Inspired by those nights of orgiastic playgoing, I wrote my book on Pirandello, which was published in London and New York in 1926, on the eve of my departure to lecture in Sweden for the Anglo-Swedish Society. It was during this Scandinavian tour that I saw a magnificent performance of *Enrico IV* given by the celebrated Norwegian actor Anders de Wahl.

In those early days I did not know Pirandello personally, and on the occasions when I did hear him speak his voice reached me in some obscure corner of the theatre. I had listened in rapt attention at Barcelona in 1924 when he expounded his dramatic theories to the critical audience and faced, imperturbably, shrapnel epigrams fired at him by Spanish intellectuals.

Pirandello was fortunate in securing the enthusiastic support of the Italian government in 1925 for the creation in Rome of a permanent art-theatre in the Palazzo Odescalchi, and we Pirandellians felt sure that this would enable the master to lay the foundations of an Italian National theatre. The short-lived experiment in 1925 did at least serve to give a fillip to the foundation of an efficient travelling Pirandellian company, and in the following years the players visited London, Paris, and the principal European cities.

During my lecture tours in the United States in 1929 and the following two years I gave lectures in many centers on Pirandello, and discovered that he was already one of the most popular authors among the devotees of the Little Theatre movement. When at last I met Pirandello personally he had won the Nobel

Prize for Literature (in 1934) and become a world figure through the influence of Hollywood. Greta Garbo, in the jazzed-up version of his play *As You Desire Me,* had cast a Scandinavian air of mystery over his Sicilian muse. But all the spotlights of Hollywood could not dazzle the sad-eyed master. "Look at him," said an Italian critic to me: "every day he becomes more like a Buddha." A melancholy, drooping figure with wild eyes. I questioned him ceaselessly about his theatre and the world theatre today, but he would only talk of Sicily—of Catania and the literary "cénacle" in the old days of Capuana and Verga, of Martoglio, of Grasso and the Sicilian actors, of Hispano-Arabic types of female beauty around Castrogiovanni and Caltanisetta, of the innate jealousy of Sicilian men, and their ceaseless warfare against Don Juan the playboy. In response to questions of an autobiographical nature he would reply: "I have confessed myself to Nardelli." Nardelli's biography *L'Uomo Segreto* (1927) gives us a clue to the tortured mind of Pirandello, for it consists of memories of his youth in Agrigento, his sad married life, and his weary pilgrimage in this vale of tears.

In interpreting the personality of Pirandello I have attempted to explain his relationship to the other writers of the modernistic dramatic movement known as the *Teatro Grottesco.* In the theatre he led frontal attacks against the old-fashioned, bourgeois, well-made play, and against the voluptuous drama of Gabriele D'Annunzio with its supermen. The drama brought to Europe by Pirandello is intellectual, and intellectuality in his works becomes a passion. In his short stories, which as works of art may outlive his plays, his object was, as Victor Hugo said of Baudelaire, *"de créer un frisson nouveau."*

I have treated Pirandello from the Italian, the Sicilian, and the European points of view: as an Italian, a Futurist, one of the intellectual chiefs of Italy between the two wars; as a Sicilian, a regionalist, successor to Verga and Capuana; as a European, author of those remarkable plays which have made Pirandellian as expressive a word as Shavian.

On his death in 1936 I revised and enlarged my book with additional material concerning his last phase as a writer, when his plays became more subjective and even mystical, for he wished to create a series of myths for the theatre which would express his vision of the universe. In spite of his great public success and fame in many countries, we see Pirandello as a lonely exile, apart, divesting himself of all his possessions, releasing himself from all his ties, and shuffling off this mortal coil as naked as when he first came into this world.

In the present edition I have rewritten the introduction, added a new chapter (VIII: "Pirandello's Fortunes after Death"), revised the epilogue, and expanded the bibliography.

W. S.

University of California, Los Angeles
  May 10, 1964

I

Contemporary Literature in Italy

(A) THE FUTURISTS

> " Marciare non Marcire."
>
> GABRIELE D'ANNUNZIO

THIS MOTTO OF GABRIELE D'ANNUNZIO reveals in a flash the spirit of the young writers of the New Italy which is spreading its wings in the golden sunlight conscious of its great destiny. The restless energy of these young men is the restlessness of modern life with its steel and stress. " At all costs," they say, " we must advance, lest by standing still we wither away and die." With such fierceness do many of them aspire towards the future that they mind not to trample beneath their feet every relic of a superseded past. We must ascribe the causes of this restless spirit to the increase of material civilization, the electrifying of the modern world, the whizzing and whirling of its cog-wheels which allow no truce, no rest, as man dashes on grotesquely in a mad race to death that will mean final peace.

It was before the 1914 war that we noticed traces of this feverish spirit of the times in literature and art. The onset made by Marinetti in 1912, when he trumpeted flamboyantly his theories on literature, music, painting, was an exaggerated index of a new order of things, but we must go back further still if we wish to explain the origins of the Futurists. It is from Nietzsche's theory of the Superman and its application by Wagner that all these disciples of the actual draw their life-blood. The former followers of Nietzsche, Wagner, Ibsen, misunderstood their master's message. In Nietzsche they only perceived an apology for the gross materialism of the big capitalist ; in Wagner they only hearkened to the moments when his inspiration nodded. The noble message of Siegfried and Tristan fell on deaf ears. Wagnerism, remembered only by the luscious tunes and the pompous marches, engendered that cloying sentimentality which infected so much of the art pro-duced in the first twelve years of the new century. Ibsen, who had sounded the pæan of the true hero fighting against a pitiless destiny, became in the eyes of the majority a creator of obscure images and fantastic symbolism. Few saw that the true method of the Norwegian giant was realism. It was George Bernard Shaw who pointed out that Ibsen was not a creator of huge, idealistic symbols, but the great realist of modern life. " I glory in calling Ibsen suburban," he said, " for suburbanity means modern civilization. The active, germinating life in the households to-day cannot be typified by an aristocratic hero, an ingenuous heroine, a gentleman forger abetted by an Artful Dodger, and a parlourmaid who takes half-sovereigns and kisses from the male visitors."[1]

The so-called wicked 'nineties, with their pale, æsthetic Pre-Raphaelites, bequeathed to the twentieth century a subtle sentimentality which destroyed vigorous art. Gabriele D'Annunzio, another European figure who sailed into the new world on the wings of Nietzsche, was tainted at the outset by this morbid sentimentality, and for this reason he has been more misunderstood than any modern writer by those who only saw in him

[1] G. Bernard Shaw, *Dramatic Opinions and Essays*, New York, 1907, Vol. II.

an æsthete with jaded emotions. His exquisitely refined temperament prevented people from seeing the vigorous force which worked within him. The inner spirit of D'Annunzio shows a ceaseless battle between decadent self-indulgence and vigorous desire for action, and it was to himself that he repeated ceaselessly—" Marciare non Marcire." It is this struggle that makes the pages of *Il Fuoco* so poignant to read, where the spirit of Wagner floating over Venice, the scene of his death, and that of the young Italian poet Stelio, symbolize the struggle between Teutonic mysticism and the Paganism of the Renaissance.

If we examine the trend of European literature since 1900 we find an ever-increasing tendency to react against the romanticism and sentimentality of the writers of the nineteenth century.

The Futurists become exasperated opponents : they want by their uncompromising theories completely to condemn the past. Francesco Flora, a contemporary Italian critic of much acumen, shows in his book that Futurism is not a caprice or a formula : it is a spiritual atmosphere.[1] And we find that atmosphere in literature from Papini and Soffici to Kaiser and Pirandello. " Futurism," says Flora, " is to a certain degree the apex of all decadence, the final expression of Romanticism gone to seed. But that is the negative side of its character." Whereas all the former period was in opposition to Romanticism, especially during the Naturalist movement, the moderns, on the other hand, wish to complete the disruption of the edifice of Romanticism. From its ashes must rise a new will to live, a new scheme of things. The Futurists carry to a climax the tendency to look on life without any religious consciousness, and for this reason there is in their works an absence of lyricism and true passion.

[1] F. Flora, *Dal Romanticismo al Futurismo*, Milan, 1925.

The first vice that these young anarchists in art attacked was effeminacy. For them all literature was dominated by sex, and this sexual obsession was ruining the manhood of Europe. Disdain of Woman was one of their cardinal maxims, and they insisted in banishing the nude from painting and adultery from the novel. Then, from the idea of banishing sex as an artistic idea from art, they advanced still further on. They started a campaign against anything that appealed to the senses—against melodious verses, against beautiful chords and harmonies. We recall the haunting tones of D'Annunzio's prose, his evocation of æsthetic pleasure derived from gazing at the beautiful mosaics and the lace-work architecture of Venice. No, all that beauty must be destroyed, and Marinetti, the leader of the movement, exclaimed one day to his excited followers : " Burn the gondolas, those swings for fools, and erect up to the sky the rigid geometry of large metallic bridges and factories with waving train of smoke ; abolish everywhere the languishing curve of the old architecture." This remark introduces us to the positive side of the Futurist revolt. They were anarchists eager to destroy the old world so that they might rebuild a new one. Their fierce pæans of exaltation in praise of action were not purely original : we find that tumultuous force, but on a much grander scale, in Verhaeren, who in *Villes Tentaculaires* composed a symphony on modern life :

> " Par au-dessus, passent les cabs, filent les roues,
>   volent les trains, vole l'effort,
>   Jusqu'aux gares dressent telles des proues
>   immobiles, de mille en mille, un fronton d'or.
>   Les rails ramifiés, rampent sous terre
>   en des tunnels et des cratères
>   Pour reparaître en réseaux clairs d'éclairs
>   dans le vacarme et la poussière.
>   C'est la Tentaculaire."

4

All these tendencies towards Futurism were exacerbated by Marinetti when he made his tour of Europe, stirring up youth by the most militant propaganda in favour of the new art. We remember the articles in the Press which greeted his literary, musical and artistic efforts in London. But Marinetti, with his extraordinary rhythm, his discordant sounds, his play of sound, colour, smell, only exaggerated a general tendency which was sweeping over Europe just on the eve of the Great War. The War stifled the movement in art for a time because it gave youth ideals, romance, action—everything that restless humanity needed for its salvation. But the results of the War did not kill that desire which we saw manifested in artists before 1914 to destroy the last vestiges of Romanticism. The intellectual youth of to-day try increasingly to leave behind them the hallowed temples of the past. What is Romanticism, we may ask ? It is the struggle which takes place in a man's mind between the spirit of Christianity and the new, free spirit of the modern world. It might be symbolized by a double-faced bust of Hermes : one face looks back sadly to the mists of the Middle Ages, the other turns its watchful gaze towards the faint dawn of a future millennium. All through the last century the theories of Progress, and the new ideas that sprang up, found themselves clogged with the mildewed traditions of ages that had passed away. Even the Positivist movement (which fundamentally is the negation of Romanticism) is tinged with that which it is trying to react against, because it was mere opposition. And that opposition which did not start off by conquering Romanticism, ended by producing a reaction in its favour—a movement of a reaction which we call decadent romanticism or decadent mysticism, and against which Croce fulminated indignantly in his essay on the tendencies of recent literature. He looks back with regret to the heroic Paganism of Carducci which had animated the spiritual life of Italy in the preceding period from 1865 to 1885. " Nowadays," he says, " we have no more the patriot, the verist, the positivist, but the imperialist, the mystic, the æsthete, or however else they are called. The modern mystic is a Catholic, neo-Catholic, Franciscan, ascetic, but if you call him Catholic, do not question him about the fundamental ideas of Catholicism ; if he calls himself a Franciscan or an ascetic, do not let him pretend that he truly loves poverty or thinks seriously of retiring into the desert. The æsthete, if he is an artist, longs for an art that is not capable of expression in words, in lines or in colours."[1]

In those days there was one subtle philosopher of the past who gathered his pupils together all over Europe, in the solemn silence of Gothic aisles—Novalis. It was, however, not a corporeal Novalis but his ghost who was interpreted in the light of the late nineteenth century by Maeterlinck, Rimbaud and other devotees of " la chanson grise où l'indécis au précis se joint." This mysticism has but little to do with the Gothic architecture of the Middle Ages : it is a self-conscious mysticism which leads men in a quest of sensations, and breaks up the idea of one Universal God into small fragments, each one of which becomes a subject of adoration by the faithful. It is as if the human race was incapable of recognizing a great ideal : only after it has crumbled away do the faithful pick up reverently the broken fragments that once were part of a mighty structure. Perhaps Chateaubriand described the essence of decadent mysticism when he said that nothing could be beautiful or noble except mysterious things and sentiments that are somewhat confused.

[1] B. Croce, *La Litteratura della Nuova Italia*, Bari, 1914, Vol. IV, pp. 187 seq.

In our days thinking men have felt within themselves the struggle which we have described, but they have felt it more acutely because one force in the struggle, Romanticism, is all but dead, and droops inertly as a dead weight. Over its dead body the Futurists, bringing into play their will to action, seek eagerly to create theories of art that will express their experiences.

It is an age of indecision and continual doubting. The drama of Europe since the War is a mass of discordant visions : there is no unity to be found anywhere. Writers are no longer driven by great impulses to create with their own life-blood immortal works : all art, whether in drama, music, painting, limits itself to theory or to the fruitless quest of originality. If we consider Italy we find that the most-read author is Papini —a man whose spirit oscillates in time with his heart-beat between belief and disbelief, between Mammon and Christ, between reason and faith. But let us not forget that he, like so many of the moderns who write in an autobiographical style as is the fashion of the time, is able to make his experiences attractive to his readers. Consistency is not a virtue nowadays when there is no austere Inquisitor in black to point the finger of reminder. Who could be more charmingly *insouciant* than Alfredo Panzini, that idol of the cultivated bourgeoisie vacillating between poetry and prose, sentimentality and satire, but a satire that has had the chill taken out of it ? Panzini represents the transition that is taking place. One by one he thumbs his romantic books, his classical books ; he likes to play with them, but without ever letting his spirit be touched. In fact he always looks at them with a slight feeling of irritation, for he must leave them and liberate himself from their coils : they belong to the past, while he wants to catch the sensitive ear of the present.

The third writer who shows this contradictory spirit is

7

Pirandello : he is the most characteristic of Futurism's masters because he is more serious than any of the others. Pirandello's theatre has become a pulpit whence the dramatist preaches over the dead body of old literature. The plays, with their grotesquely comic masks concealing a suffering heart, have sounded a warning to the world. They recall the warning words uttered by the Oriental king's slave when his master was feasting : "Sire, remember you must die." And Pirandello has sounded the knell of the old drama.

We must not think, however, that Pirandello was the only dramatist to show the new spirit. Before the public became Pirandellian in Italy, there was a school of dramatists who called their plays grotesques, and it is these writers of the " teatro grottesco " that we shall consider now. They are small men, but they will form a crowded miniature background, setting in gigantic relief the personality of our author.

Pirandello's Contemporaries

(B) GROTESQUES IN THE THEATRE

" The grotesque is a kind of free and humorous picture produced by the ancients for the decoration of vacant spaces in some position where only things placed high up are suitable. For this purpose they fashioned monsters deformed by a freak of nature or by the whim and fancy of the workers, who in these grotesque pictures make things outside of any rule, attaching to the finest thread a weight that it cannot support, to a horse legs of leaves, to a man the legs of a crane, and similar follies and nonsense without end. He whose imagination ran the most oddly was held to be the most able."
—VASARI.[1]

[1] G. Vasari, *Introduction to the Art of Painting*. Trans. by L. S. Maclehose, London, 1907.

The initiation of the " Teatro del Grottesco " was attributed to Luigi Chiarelli, a young dramatist who in 1916 produced amid great enthusiasm *La Maschera e il Volto* (The Mask and the Face), which he had written in 1914. Chiarelli, instead of calling his play a comedy or a tragedy, called it a grotesque, and the name so appealed to the public that they applied it indiscriminately to the works of the new movement. The word " grottesco," derived from " grotta," signified a bizarre design which was to ornament spaces where a more regular picture would not have been suitable. In the quotation we have given from Vasari it is clear that the word connoted anything exaggerated and buffoon-like. No title could be better adapted to the strange productions that have crowded the Italian stage since the production of Chiarelli's play—visions, apologies, coloured adventures, fantasies, parables—all types of drama with the exception of the old well-made comedy or tragedy. The word " grotesque " not only applies to the titles and the form of these plays, but also to their spirit, their humour. The exaggerated and burlesque vein that runs through all these plays makes them an appanage to the plays of Luigi Pirandello. But Pirandello, with his strange, philosophic way of looking at life, must be considered apart : he stands like a giant amid these Lilliputians. Whereas they are merely looking to externals, he probes down deep into character. What we mean by " teatro grottesco " must really be limited to certain tricks of stage technique and play construction practised by these new writers as a reaction against the bourgeois, sentimental play which had ruled the stage for so many years. These strange burlesque experiments on the stage pleased the Italian nation, which had loved in the past glittering baroque fireworks of art, Chinese bells, acanthus leaves, ceaseless spirals that coiled away into the infinite. Capricious fantasy in

the seventeenth and eighteenth centuries was not confined to the halls of painting and sculpture : we also
find it in literary *cénacles*, where counts and countesses
lisped the conceits of Cavalier Marino, or listened en-
thralled to the *fioriture* of a Caffarelli or Farinelli : nor
was drama behindhand, for Italy had taught Europe
the fantastic intrigue play through the medium of
Pantalone Arlecchino, Pulcinella, and their merry crew.
The tradition of the " Commedia dell' arte " inspires
the modern " teatro grottesco " no less than it does
Pirandello.

Let us explain this movement in drama which critics
call a phenomenon arising from an art in decomposition,
from a society, a world in decomposition. The year
1914 marked the parting of the ways—the world was
sloughing off many of its old inventions, its effete institutions, and the War hastened the downfall of the old
order. What wonder if mental followed material chaos ?
Chiarelli, in a speech delivered at the Teatro Argentina,
Rome, fourteen years ago, stated the reasons which
prompted him to write his play *The Mask and the Face*.
" It was written," he said, " just before the outbreak of
the War. At that time Italian drama slumbered on
amid old worn-out models, especially those set out by
foreign authors. It was impossible to go to the theatre
without meeting languid, loquacious grand-daughters
of Marguerite Gautier or Rosa Bernd, or some tardy
follower of Oswald or Cyrano. The public dropped
sentimental tears and left the playhouse weighed down
in spirit. The next evening, however, it rushed in numbers to acclaim a *verte pochade* like *Le pillole d'Ercole*, in
order to re-establish its moral and social equilibrium."[1]
Chiarelli relates that such pseudo-romantic dramas made
him laugh, and from that laugh sprang *The Mask and
the Face*. The plot of the play is a grotesque caricature

[1] Published in *Comoedia*, December 15, 1923.

of the old drama. Paolo solemnly asserts before all his friends that if his honour as a husband were betrayed, he would not hesitate to kill his guilty wife Savina. Soon afterwards he finds out unexpectedly that she is guilty, and he realizes that now his friends expect him to conduct his vendetta. But on reflection it occurs to him that his rash proposal did not rise from his inner consciousness, his inner self, but from an exterior convention imposed on him by society ; and so he does not kill Savina, but sends her secretly away. By these means he satisfies his honour as a husband before society. As a consequence he is arrested and summoned before the judges, who declare him innocent. On return from prison he is received with enthusiasm by the townspeople, who delight in honouring a man who has killed his guilty wife ; bouquets are left by unknown lady admirers, municipal bands accompany him—all the clownish buffoonery of society glares grotesquely—and Paolo the primitive is so nauseated by the farcical display that he determines to rebel against it and declare his real self. By a curious coincidence a decomposed body has been found in the lake outside the house, and everybody jumps to the conclusion that it is the corpse of Savina. The funeral is arranged and Paolo braces himself up to go through the farcical ordeal. Another surprise awaits him : Savina veiled appears secretly in her husband's house. She has been in London, but hearing of his liberation from the hands of Justice she determined to try and live with him again. Paolo has felt her absence acutely : if only he could get her back ! But he dares not give up playing his self-imposed part. The following day all the friends and relatives arrive for the funeral dressed in black and showing the conventional signs of sorrow on their faces. Savina, who watches the scene of her supposed funeral, is suddenly recognized by her former lover. The game is up.

What is Paolo to do ? If he stays on he will be brought to justice for contempt of court. " As long as they believed that I had killed my wife they allowed me to go free ; now when they discover that I have not killed her they put me in prison." There is nothing left for both of them but to escape from the country. The play concludes with his words, which seem a prolongation of the Ibsenian individualists : " I refuse to render an account of my life to anyone, whether society, friends or Law." As they go off precipitately we hear strains of the town band playing the funeral march in the courtyard. The former Savina is dead, but the new one is present smiling at her own funeral, leaning on the arm of her husband.

This play, however closely it tallies with the theories of the writers of grotesques, is undeniably a well-constructed play even from the point of view of the old drama. There is perhaps a piling of chance upon chance, and we see the long arm of coincidence. It was fortunate for the development of the play that the body was found just at the right moment so as to enable Chiarelli to produce his most grotesquely humorous effect of the wife watching her own funeral. But that is not a legitimate piece of criticism to level at the modern grotesque plays, which nearly always depend on some amazing freak or prank of nature.

Let us notice the humour of the play. It is a tragedy and a comedy. It is said that Chiarelli originally meant it to be a tragedy wherein he expressed all his contempt for society and its farcical practices. " The Mask and the Face " is a title that explains the inner tragedy of Paolo, who is unable to make his mask conceal his suffering. But by looking at life as a puppet show Paolo is able to laugh bitterly, and thus we have the unifying touch which makes a mingled yarn of both laughter and tears. This mechanical puppetization is characteristic of all the productions of the Grotesque school, and at times we are reminded of the " Grand Guignol " plays. " Guignol " is derived from " Chignol," a Bolognese puppet which was naturalized in France. In the " Grand Guignol " dramas the spectators saw before them the most hair-raising melodramas, hideous in their grotesqueness. But at the end of the performances there would always be some gay buffoonery to take away the bitter taste. There is a flavour of the " Grand Guignol " about *The Mask and the Face,* and we are expected to laugh and shiver simultaneously. Italian critics have admitted that there is a certain resemblance between Chiarelli's play and the *Playboy of the Western World* by Synge, in which Christy Mahon wins renown because he has killed his " Da." The fundamental notion of Synge's play—that reality counts for nothing beside illusion—is the central problem of modern drama in Europe. The similarity between the two plays is only superficial and confined to the outer plot. Synge, who declared the measure of serious drama to be " the degree in which it gives the nourishment, not very easy to define, on which our imagination lives," breathes a rarer mountain atmosphere than Chiarelli, who is a dweller in the plain. Synge, with his power of folk-imagination, his delicate harmony of thought and phrase, stands far removed from the facile Chiarelli. Chiarelli's skill lies in parody. He is such a literary economist that he uses up his poor gifts of style to his own advantage. Instead of attempting to evolve a style of his own, he takes the ordinary bourgeois sentimental dialogue and caricatures it in order to make it tally with his cynical and disillusioned spirit. When he makes his characters, or rather puppets, for they always seem to be pulled by wires, work up a scene, he always seems to say to his audience, " Remember, I am only using this old-fashioned stuff so that you may ridicule it." *The Mask and the Face*, however, is one of the most brilliant examples of the " Teatro del Grottesco," and its triumphal success in London and the provinces and in the United States entitles it to great respect. The tendency of the performances in England, in our opinion, was to bring out the farcical elements of the play at the expense of the grotesque. We rarely felt the full force of Chiarelli's irony because the actors were too conscious of their own ridicule. They did not realize that they had to abandon the acting suitable to the Wilde and Pinero plays and assume the new style. The humour of the play is Bergsonian because life is looked upon as a repeating mechanism with reversible action and interchangeable parts. The characters weaving their society mask must play their parts unconscious of the comic effect they are producing : in that way we should get the contrast when the chief character pulls off the mask and sees his real self.

In the other plays of Chiarelli the tone of bitterness and disillusionment increases. In *The Silken Ladder* (1917) he unfolds a crowded panorama of social corruption. Beneath the veneer and polish we see cruel, remorseless cynicism and social anarchy. The play is based on the contrast existing between the upright, honest man condemned to penury, and the fatuous dancer, Désiré, to whom life offers the silken ladder which will enable him to scale without difficulty the heights of riches and power. Around these two characters revolve countless exploiters, rascals and prostitutes greedily struggling. Désiré marries the daughter of a millionaire and becomes a minister, but he remains always a dancer. The crowd that gathers underneath his windows to applaud his ministerial speech notices that though as minister he speaks of Justice and Liberty, his legs move feverishly in a continual dance.

After *Tears and Stars* (1918), which shows the reviving effect of the War on corrupt society sunk in the slough of despond, Chiarelli wrote *Chimere* (1921), wherein he plunges into the depths of pessimism. The moral of the play is that the ideals of love, virtue, honour, to which men always do lip-service, are worthless. Claudio and Marina, husband and wife, are idealists : the former claims to be a superman ; the latter imagines that her nature is incapable of a base action. Black ruin, however, sits close behind them, and there is only one hope of escape. A rich banker offers to help them out of their difficulties, provided that Marina becomes his mistress. Claudio, in spite of his superman professions, gives in—even Marina, the pure, consents to the bargain. This is the outer plot quite in the style of Jullien and his motley crew of " Grand Guignol " writers. But Chiarelli, faithful to his idea of ironically satirizing the old drama, sets as protagonist to the play a mouthpiece, cynical and malevolent, and fits him out with a full store of paradoxical aphorisms in the Wilde or Shaw style. This character goes through society, and tears off the veil hiding the grim realities : in the process he leaves but scanty covering to Claudio and Marina, and thus scene by scene the " Grand Guignol " tragedy crumbles to pieces, and we are bidden to laugh like the imp of Pirandello. The mouthpiece character adopts the same procedure as Laudisi in *Così è* of the Sicilian dramatist : the plot falls to pieces like that which the Six Characters try to express.

In his next play, *La Morte degli Amanti* (The Death of the Lovers), 1923, he turns to love as it was considered by the Romantic and the Bourgeois sentimental dramatists, and pulls it to pieces. This he does by exactly the same method as in *Chimere* : on one side he sets the loving pair, on the other the paradoxical chorus character. However, instead of performing the mild

15

functions of the chorus, this demon pours acid. No play could be better adapted for satirizing the obese self-satisfaction of the nascent playwright enraptured by his own turgid bombast and sentimental pretentiousness. Eleanora longs for a love that will make her wear the buskin of tragedy, but in these prosaic days her quest is in vain. At last she hopes to realize her aim by telling her husband that Alfredo is her lover. She then proposes a death pact to the latter, and though he had been the ironical, realistic character of the play, he consents to die with her. They enjoy their last meal together, and when it is over, turn the gas tap on. The husband, however, arrives just in time to save them before the curtain drops. Thus this play too ends as a farce, and we are forced to the conclusion that Chiarelli is not so much a dramatist as a dramatic juggler. In one of his later plays *Fuochi d'Artificio* (Fireworks), 1923, however, there is a nearer approach to genuine comedy. Chiarelli does not abandon the fundamental idea of all his plays, that this world is nothing but sound and fury signifying nothing. The hero of the play seems to have strayed out of the theatre of Capus, the master of the " Déclassés." His name is Scaramanzia, and nobody more *insouciant* could be imagined. He is a descendant of the gay Picaresque knaves of Spain who were able to live without thought for the morrow. Scaramanzia with his friend Gerardo arrive from America without a sou in the world and put up at an hotel. Gerardo meditates grimly on suicide, but Scaramanzia gaily receives friends who have come to welcome the return of the former. They all take him for a secretary : " Well, what has Gerardo done in America—has he made his pile ? He must be a millionaire." Scaramanzia does not deny, and so they all spread the news that a great rich man has arrived. The whole play thus works out as a very pleasant comedy in the best

Chiarellian manner. As usual, the long arm of coincidence is stretched out to aid the author, but we must
remember that in the universe of the Grotesque theatre
any vagary of chance is allowed. The world that its
authors show us is not ruled by any reasoning deity and
so anything is possible. Let us do obeisance to the
Deus ex machinâ! In spite of his realistic touches, his
attention to the details of modern life, the world of
Chiarelli's characters seems fantastic and unreal.

In Luigi Antonelli the grotesque becomes still more
fantastic. The main idea at the basis of *L'Uomo che
incontrò se stesso* (The Man who met Himself), 1918, is
the same as *Dear Brutus* by Barrie. Luciano, the hero,
bewails his fate because he has not got a second chance
of arranging his life. Married to a beautiful girl whom
he passionately adores, one day he finds her in the arms
of her lover, and so his illusion breaks to pieces. The
first act of the play shows us an enchanted island whither
Luciano arrives after the foundering of his ship. In
this island by virtue of spells cast over him Luciano sees
himself as he was twenty years before, and also his wife
Sonia. Again he sees the false Don Juanesque friend
approach, and in vain he warns his wife against the
peril that threatens her—she falls just as readily into the
deceiver's arms. Thus the enchanted island does not
bring any more happiness to Luciano than the Lob's
wood on St. John's Eve does to Dearth : nay, less, for at
the end of Antonelli's play we are left with a madman.
The central idea is the same in both plays—

> " The fault, dear Brutus, is not in our stars,
> But in ourselves that we are underlings."

What a difference in the working out of both plays. At
the close of *Dear Brutus* we are left with a ray of hope
that Dearth will benefit by his strange experience and

will save the remnant of his broken life. In Antonelli's play we seem to see a moral in the words : " Let us look to the future, not to the past, if we truly want to live." But there is no pathos to kindle the life of the spirit.

Antonelli has not been able to treat his subject in the way it deserved. He fails altogether to preserve, as Barrie has done, the contrast between reality and fantasy. In *Mary Rose*, where the heroine is conveyed away to the land of the fairies, we have another example of fantastic drama and we see how carefully the author works out the details of each world—the world of reality and the world of the spirit. In Antonelli's enchanted island there is no air of mystery, no wonderland ; it is a replica of our own dull vesture of decay, and so the play never becomes transfigured and perishes as a farce. His other plays, though written in the manner of grotesques with the ever-present central cynical character who tries to draw philosophical generalizations, yet never succeed in arousing the interest of the audience. In *La Fiaba dei Tre Maghi* (The Fable of the Three Magicians) he treats the abstract subject of poetry. " It must never," he says, " submit to the overmastering will of Truth or Justice ; nay, it must soar unfettered to the skies and bring back a message of peace for humanity." In *L'Isola delle Scimmie* (The Island of the Monkeys) he follows Anatole France, but from afar ; there is not one sparkle of the irony that makes *L'Ile des Pingouins* immortal. Under the leadership of men, monkeys abandon their primeval state of innocence and adopt the civilization of man with all its corruption. He recalls more closely Pio Baroja's brilliant novel, *Paradox the King*, where the moral is that civilization destroys everything it undertakes. While Paradox rules, the natives are happy and contented, but when official civilization arrives, it brings evil with it— drunkenness, syphilis and vice of all sorts.

Antonelli's plays have all the faults of the abstract. He does not give his characters flesh and bone, and so they flit about uncertainly in our consciousness. A dramatist must write out of an abundance of emotional or intellectual excitement. The old school dramatists mostly wrote when under the impulse of emotional excitement. The moderns, on the other hand, are excited by the intellectual, and we can gauge the success of the new theatre by the extent in which it makes us think passionately. But in order that we may think, it is not enough for the author to breathe his views into our ear, he must create characters who feel passionately the consuming fire within them. And so we find two qualities that are necessary to the modern dramatist : he must create men possessed of brain as well as muscle, and kick them on to the stage to struggle there by themselves.

Of greater interest for its contrast between reality and illusion is Ernesto Cavacchioli's play, *La Danza del Ventre* (1920). It is a symbolical play wherein the hero Nadir personifies the life of the ideal, but he is a eunuch dancer and he has the misfortune to fall in love with Pupa, who symbolizes brutal instinct and feverish desire. Nadir, in order to satisfy her craving lusts, gives her to Harlequin, the slave who is body without soul, hoping that she will return to love him spiritually after satiety. But instead Pupa falls in love with Harlequin, and the latter rebels against his master of the spirit. Then Nadir commits suicide, and Harlequin, who only lived through radiance from the spirit of Nadir, loses the love of Pupa, who disappears.

In this play, though at times it awakens emotion in us, specially in the scenes between Nadir and Pupa, yet has the same defect as we noticed in Antonelli. It floats in the sea between reality and fantasy without

ever attaining either shore. The author is never completely convinced in his own mind what he wants to
create—whether real men of this world or Ariel spirits
who inhabit gossamer kingdoms. If we take a play
like *A Midsummer Night's Dream*, we find that Shakespeare
keeps definitely separate the two ideas of reality and
illusion. Bottom and his merry men live for us as men
of our own stature. On the other hand, Oberon and
Titania are set in the higher plane of our imagination
where dwell " the little people." In *L'Uccello del
Paradiso* (The Bird of Paradise), 1919, Cavacchioli takes
a morbid " Grand Guignolesque " subject, and instead
of making his grotesque mouthpiece character a cynical
man of the world like Laudisi in Pirandello's *Così è*, he
introduces a fantastic ghost character who is called
" He " by the awestruck people. In the play " He "
defines his characteristics thus : " You believe that I
am speaking to you. It is not true : you simply translate
into reality a suggestion made by your spirit. You give
me voice and clothes and human semblance. I think,
but I do not exist. The answers which I make to your
arguments are formulated by your own imagination.
I do not exist for you or for anyone else. If I were
acting a play in a theatre I should not exist for the public
otherwise than as a simple abstraction." As critics have
shown, such a character derives directly from the *Life
of Man* by Andreev (1906), where " the Being in Grey,"
who symbolizes fate, guides man in his weary journey.
But there is a great difference in treatment between
Andreev's *Theatre of the Soul*, with its passionate seriousness and sincerity, and Cavacchioli's disillusioned puppet
play. " He " is simply a garrulous manipulator of
these puppets and never strikes our imagination. The
rest of the play is the usual banal, sordid story that
resembles slightly Roberto Bracco's play *Nellina*, treated
in the sentimental manner of the former Bourgeois

drama. Anna, the faithless wife who has left her husband, gives herself up to the life of a *demi-mondaine*, and
even persuades her young daughter to follow her example.
Then the catastrophe takes place : Anna's lover falls in
love with her fresh young daughter : the latter is about
to throw herself into his arms when the mother just in
the nick of time saves her by confessing the truth. Then
we see Anna at the end suffering from heart disease and
awaiting death. We have thus come back again to the
old drama, and Cavacchioli has not got Chiarelli's
skill in so parodying the old tragedy that a fresh new
comedy springs to life. At times he is able to create a
queer original character in relief against the sordid
backgrounds, and there is a certain poetical fantasy in
his work.

It is to the works of Rosso di San Secondo we must go
if we wish to find greater poetry than in the other writers
of the Grotesque school : in fact he always gives us the
impression of having strayed into our tumultuous century
by a mischance. Modern life with its steel and stress
harasses his sensibilities, and hence we find him for
ever trying to gaze back through the mists to a more
radiantly happy world. Signor Tilgher, in his extremely
interesting essay on Rosso di San Secondo,[1] says that
all his work is based on the contrast between North and
South : the South where lie the lands of brilliant sunlight and blue skies and seas, the North with its grey
climes, its snows, its livid, darkening seas. In the
North, men have disciplined and organized, nay, even
willed their existence : in the South, life is all instinct
and passion. All the men of the North and the South
are stupefied because they have emigrated from a
celestial paradise where they lived before birth—the

[1] A. Tilgher, *Studî sul teatro contemporaneo*, Roma, 1923, pp.
139 seq.

paradise of the unborn children in the *Blue Bird* of Maeterlinck. But the men of the North, living amid their snowy drifts and thickening mists, have so dominated their own natures and lulled their primeval longings for the paradise that they feel no more the homesickness. On the contrary, those in the South live in a perpetual state of semi-consciousness which does not allow them to accommodate themselves fully to this earth nor to turn back to the paradise they came from. There is thus a profound sentiment of pity underlying all Rosso di San Secondo's work. If we take one of his most characteristic plays, *Marionette che Passione* (What Passion, ye Marionettes), we find the same tendency as in the other grotesque writers to puppetize his characters, but he does not grin sardonically at them or make them stand on their head ; he just shows them to us in their ordinary everyday life with all its sickening disillusion and hopelessness. The scene in the first act is laid in a telegraph office on Sunday, one of those hopelessly wet Sundays that would be more characteristic of our northern climes. Against this background the author shows us three persons, each suffering in himself from some mental anguish. The three enter the office as strangers to one another, and try to write their telegrams, but chance brings them together and they tear off their masks. There is a young lady wearing blue fox who has fled from her lover because he beat her and treated her most cruelly ; the man in mourning wears it because his wife has deserted him ; the man in grey is more ironic than the rest and he scorns the other two when he sees them beginning to feel the mutual attraction that sympathy in affliction always brings. But he carries within him some still more painful secret which he will not reveal. At last the three separate, but the man in grey follows the woman of the blue fox, and so does the man in mourning. An altercation ensues ; insults are bandied about ; then follow sighs and reconciliation, then frenzied dancing. They both agree to meet the lady at a restaurant. But the man in grey has arranged another table near their own with chairs reserved for the three who will not come. The dinner is as funereal as any Borgian meal. Suddenly there arrives one " who was not to come "—he is the lady's lover. He rushes furiously to carry her off and she resignedly submits to her destiny. Thus the two men are left face to face. The man in grey pulls out a packet of poison, pours the contents into the water and drinks it. Then he says good-bye to his friend, telling him to salute the fair-haired lady who may arrive, and he goes away to liberation. The man in mourning is left alone sobbing and the curtain falls. The play, though characteristic of the Grotesque theatre, shows all the faults of Rosso di San Secondo as dramatist ; though the setting of the scenes resembles Antoine's stage in modest austerity, the characters are shadows which seem to flit through a hideous nightmare. Their passions in consequence never move us profoundly.

In *La Bella Addormentata* (The Sleeping Beauty), 1919, we find more poetry as the author tries to express his meaning by symbols. It is called a " play in colours," and these fleeting colours symbolize the fantastic inconsistency of life. The characters are not puppets this time but colours, and they move about in a world of gross materialism. In the midst of them all lies the Sleeping Beauty—the prostitute of the town. She resembles closely Sonia Sarowska, the heroine of Bracco's play, *I Pazzi* (1922), in that she is entirely a-moral. She is the sleeping beauty in this hideous world, and thus there is a halo of idealism and illusion round her. At last, when she becomes a mother, her personality awakes and at least for a time she ceases to be the placid animal. Rosso di San Secondo, in spite of his originality, uses in this play the pivotal character, the Zany, always so dear to the writers of the " Commedia dell' arte." In fact this central character, who is supposed to be the author himself, is the old mouthpiece character that we used to meet in Dumas Fils or Brieux. He ironically undertakes to rescue the Sleeping Beauty ; he makes her first seducer promise to marry her though she has lived as a prostitute with other men. This play has many poetical qualities, for it moves in a rarer atmosphere than that of real life—a world of lyrical symbols. All life is considered an adventure in colours ; nothing matters but colours, which are symbols of man's tortured destiny : the yellow sulphur, the blue skies, the white clouds, that change to sombre hue when they ride the tempest, the green fields that fade before the blasting rays of the sun. The poetical symbolism of the play is developed by the author in *intermezzi* which act as prefaces to each act and envelop the whole work in an atmosphere of fantasy. The fantastic element is also to be found in the temperament of the Sleeping Beauty herself. She never quite comes within our ken. In the earlier part of the play, when she is a woman of the town, she lives as it were in a trance ; her vice is not voluntary as her soul sleeps. Then the magic influence of maternity awakens in her the desire for purity, but it is at the end, for she dies at once. As usual we meet the central character who interprets the play ; he is called " the black man from the sulphur mines," and we can see by his irony and sentiment that he is the author himself.

In the dramas we have considered Rosso di San Secondo does not conceal his bitter disillusionment ; for ever he seems to mourn a golden age that has passed. He resembles Adam standing disconsolate in the shadow near the gates of Paradise, guarded by the angel, sword in hand, and gazing at the sunlit loveliness that once

was his. In *Marionette che Passione* his bitter humour
dissolves the mean aspirations of those sad bourgeois
puppets ; in *La Bella Addormentata* all life has no more
reality than the interplay of various colours and sounds ;
it becomes in fact *música celestial*, which is the Spaniard's
equivalent for nonsense. In *La Roccia e i Monumenti*
(Rough Marble and the Sculptured Monuments), 1923,
he has ceased to be abysmally pessimistic and becomes
constructive. The whole play rests on the contrast
between the rough unhewn stone in its primitive, brutal
state, and the sculptured monuments which men carve
with chisel, directed by brain and will-power. The
subject is treated in an Ibsenian manner, and we see
the struggle between two heroic individuals each
becoming a symbol of their respective ideas. The scene
of the play is not laid in our grey, dingy world, but up
above Carrara on the marble slopes of the Apennines,
where is the house of Ilario Del Roco, the owner of a
great marble works where the rough stone is turned
into the elegant statue. To Ilario's house comes Isabella,
a great-hearted young woman who has devoted her
life to her aged and blind husband, Gabriele the scientist.
Isabella has a tragedy in her life ; she is in reality
attracted towards Brunetto Lartesca, a young ex-service
man who has fought heroically in the late war. Brunetto
is one of the primitives in life ; he is the unhewn marble
and he finds it impossible to return to the monotonous
round of everyday life. He is engaged to Nada, the
daughter of Ilario Del Roco, but he abandons her for
Isabella, whom he knows instinctively to possess a
similar temperament to his own. Isabella, however, is
no less heroic than Brunetto ; she derives her heroism
from her noble power of self-domination, her will
triumphant. The strong scene of the play comes in
Act II, where the two fight the battle of instinct versus
restraint.

BRUNETTO.

" I now know what it means to pay respect to the instinct which keeps us alive ; it means that we must not bend the knee to anyone, but belabour the craven hearts and brand the poor wretches who drag their slow length along by dint of manufactured arrangements. Let us shout our own woes when we are alone in the mountain ravines, but never ask men to pity us ; better for us to be scapegraces than hypocrites and cowards."

ISABELLA.

" Oh ! Brunetto, why, the whole history of man has been one glorious struggle to bring the savage impulses of our primeval nature under the domination of the higher laws of reason and intellect : it is a gradual conquest of ourselves carried out with the greatest sacrifice and the most painful renunciation, by means of our will."

Brunetto in vain tries to break down the resistance of Isabella : she loves him and she alone can make him happy. But Isabella stands firm. She will remain beside her blind husband not through pity for him, but because she cannot now return to her primeval state. She explains her state in the last words of the play she utters to her husband : " We cannot become again rough unhewn stone after the chisel of man's will has laboured us."

Brunetto dashes out into the tempestuous night to perish amid the thunderbolts on the crests of the mountains.

This drama is worked out on a larger scale than the other plays of Rosso di San Secondo. There are, however, certain faults which were more properly common to

the old drama.   There are passages that are full of pompous rhetoric : the scene between the two protagonists
does not excite in us great emotion, because the symbolism
of the two characters is too apparent : they are, in fact,
symbols, not men and women who possess a personality
of their own.   Rosso adopts just the opposite course to
that of Pirandello in *The Six Characters*.   He first of all
finds his thesis and he insists on making characters that
will obey every word of that thesis.   They must not
have a different existence outside, but must be ready to
submit to the author always.   The Six Characters of
Pirandello refuse thus to be dominated : they have
their own reality which must be respected.   If the
contrast between Life and Form is too evident, there
is also too much simplicity about Brunetto's character :
he does not go through any evolution in his personality or show any of those complexities that are to be
found in the characteristic modern drama.   So that the
criticism we might pass on this play is just the reverse of
our criticism of the others : instead of being obscure and
complex, it is too clear and simple, and the art of Rosso
di San Secondo loses thereby.   Let him remember
Mallarmé's admonition : " Il doit y avoir toujours
énigme en poésie :   Nommer un objet c'est supprimer
les trois quarts de la puissance du poème qui est fait du
bonheur de deviner peu à peu ; le suggérer, voilà le rêve."
It is indeed but rarely that we can accuse Rosso di San
Secondo of simplicity ; his works are nearly always
obscure.   He possesses the characteristic modern European temperament, refined and disillusioned, sensitive to
every pulsation of modern life.   But he shuns the clear,
crystalline qualities of mind and prefers to lurk in a
limbo of nebulous fancies.   We must admire his seriousness as an artist, his poetical charm, but he does not
draw us after him in panting chase like Pirandello.   In
one of his later works, *L'Avventura Terrestre* (The Terres-

trial Adventure), he asks himself the questions : Why do we exist ? What are we ? Whence do we come ? Where are we going ? As Montaigne said, " Que sais-je ? " Living and dying is all an adventure. When we talk of house, family, home, we speak of meaningless things. We are simply inhabitants of the earth—our home. It is all nonsense to talk of Latins or Northerns, Britons or Japanese, Zulus or Hottentots. We participate in this adventure on earth like explorers who do not know where destiny will carry them. Rosso di San Secondo tells us not to construct marble palaces, not to strike our roots deep in the earth ; rather must we live like the nomadic tribes who sowed the fields for one year's harvest before they moved on to the next region. Again he admonishes us against raising the barriers of nationality ; we must not complain of being strangers to one another as long as we are strangers to ourselves. Here we have reached the nadir of pessimism. What have we to guide us ? Nothing. We are shadows that flit about uncertainly, swept on by the irresistible Life Force which overwhelms us unmercifully.

When we look back on the writers we have examined as characteristic of the Grotesque school we are struck by the uniformly pessimistic attitude towards life—an attitude which contrasts with the Futuristic slogan— " Marciare non Marcire." Rosso di San Secondo and his companions seem to cry out the despair of a wearied race that endured five years of the most Mammoth War the world has ever seen. They do not put hopes in action, for their soul is weary. Ibsen wrought heroes of Shakespearean stature because he showed energy of will defying Fate, and Brand planting his church up in the snows. But amid these moderns the only Ibsenian hero, Brunetto, perishes without even defying the Fate that is striking him down.

The true function of these grotesque dramatists was to

prepare the way for a new drama which would combine the tendencies of the Futurist followers of Marinetti with the relics of the past. One of the most striking features of the European theatre to-day is the use of drama to express the struggle between the partisans of the old and the new idea of the Machine. Is the Machine to be Master or Slave of humanity, destroyer or constructor? In the Grotesque dramatists we saw the tendency to treat human beings as puppets or else cogwheels in an immense engine-driven world. As Mr. Huntly Carter says, " They see Man of to-day being more and more absorbed by the machine, broken up into minute subdivisions to feed it, and Man of the future entirely disappearing under its dominion and the increased production of mechanical contrivances."[1] Then ideas reach a paroxysm in the German plays, such as Toller's play, *The Machine Wreckers*, where the devil—or is it our familiar puppet manipulator?—is agent of destruction, or else Kaiser's *Gas*, where the Machine is looked upon as an inhuman monster. The same tendency is seen in Capek's *R.U.R.*, where the efficient Robots, like the slaves in ancient Athens, give men leisure for their freedom. Here we are nearer to the Marinetti disciples who glorify the Machine which will lead man out of the nebulous chaos into glorious light. " The Machine," they cry, " if you administer it wisely will become the champion of liberty instead of being the champion of slavery. With such an engine will man win world-power to his service."[1] This is the moral of Marinetti's series of ten poems called " Le démon de la vitesse," which a critic calls " a kind of railway journey of the modern soul." The poet dashes madly on in his course across the " delirium of space," eager to sacrifice his life as a manifestation of the speed

[1] Huntly Carter, *The New Spirit in the European Theatre*, London, 1925.

and vital impulse of our century. To such a man motors, aeroplanes, engines of all sorts symbolize the attempt that is being made to redeem mankind, and as such they become objects of beauty in our modern geometric civilization. In the theatre the Futurists try to educate people up to appreciate the beauties of the Machine which contains all the finer qualities of man.

Rudolfo de Angeles with his Futurist theatre, the ballets decorated by Depero for *Anikam de l'an* 2000 by Franco Casavola, and *The Psychology of Machines* by Silvio Mix were all characteristic of the new movement which spread over the Italian peninsula from Milan throbbing with its motor engines. Plays like *Il Tamburo di Fuoco* (Fire-Drum) by Marinetti or *Sensualità* by Fillia were exaggerations of the same fundamental tendencies which created the vogue of the Grotesques with their uncertain vacillation between the new and the old theatre. Let us look at the whole matter from a more philosophical point of view. In reality if we fix our attention too closely on Marinetti and his followers we shall only find the external symptoms of the movement. It is not physical velocity which modifies modern life, but ideal velocity—that is to say, criticism. Futurism is essentially critical in its attitude towards modern life and art : it does not hesitate to set up its philosophy against the philosophy of the past. And this modern philosophy is the romantic exaltation of the artist who alone knows his world. He is the great-grandson of Don Quixote, who saw giants where other men saw only windmills, and Mambrino's helmet where others saw only a barber's basin. And thus we have arrived at a point far removed from the problems which used to agitate the dramatists of the last century. In those days the theatre slumbered on amid well-defined problems of social and moral order, and rarely did the dramatist issue forth from the narrow circle of a well-ordered society. Nowadays all is chaos : man has destroyed the Valhalla of his old beliefs, and his mind is torn this way and that by conflicting passionate opinions. No more can he gaze with the calm serenity of his father or grandfather to whom the mind appeared as simply two-dimensional. The modern mind might be compared to an inextricable maze which many a writer has tried to thread, but in vain. To Pirandello belongs the credit of having more than any Italian writer explored this maze and stated clearly the problems of the moderns. Through his instrumentality the ideas of the Grotesque theatre together with those of the Futurists have extended their sphere of influence over Europe, nay, even over the whole theatrical world, and we have witnessed in every country the death of the bourgeois, well-made play with its vestiges of Romanticism, and the rise of a new critical drama which was to be an expression of the modern active mentality.

II

Luigi Pirandello:
Master of the Grotesques

" I see, as it were, a labyrinth where our soul wanders through countless, conflicting paths, without ever finding a way out. In this labyrinth I see a two-headed Hermes which with one face laughs and with the other weeps ; it laughs with one face at the other face's weeping."

THESE WORDS, WHICH PIRANDELLO set as the motto of one of his works, may be taken as a symbol of his literary personality. In the inextricable maze of contemporary life his soul wanders ceaselessly, changing, chameleon-like, from weeping sadness to strident laughter. In former Italian dramatists, such as Butti and Bracco, with their sensitive powers of mental dissection, there is but little of that true spirit of Humour that can rise above the world and look down, humanly malign, on struggling mortals. Bracco, a poet of the tragic conflict in our lives, could not change his mournful countenance to the slim feasting smile of High Comedy. When he descends from the tragic to the comic stage he lets his features relax into the broad laughter of farce—where the *gros sel* of the ancient *novella* is tempered by modern Latin subtle wit. With Pirandello we advance a stage further on, where the tragic sense combines with the comic sense and produces the spirit of humour. Former dramatists were psychological, following the example of Ibsen. The drama of Pirandello is a prolongation of those psychological tendencies to their logical conclusion, and we might follow some critics who say that the true protagonist of the Pirandellian theatre is King Thought, whom Edgar Allan Poe saw sitting in crowned state on a throne of suffering in an enchanted palace.

It was not difficult to investigate Pirandello's views about the fundamentals of the dramatist's calling, for he wandered over the face of the globe, proclaiming them and resisting the tumultuous onslaught of questions fired at him from well-stacked audiences. At Barcelona in 1924 we listened with interest to Pirandello's answers on the subject of his theatre. To one of his interlocutors he answered, " People say that my drama is obscure and they call it cerebral drama. The new drama possesses a distinct character from the old : whereas the latter had as its basis passion, the former is the expression of the intellect. One of the novelties that I have given to modern drama consists in converting the intellect into passion. The public formerly were carried away only by plays of passion, whereas now they rush to see intellectual works." In other dramatists emotions are allowed free play and thought follows close behind, acting as a slight reactionary force, but in Pirandello the intellect is the fundamental cause of the drama. His characters justify, condemn, criticize themselves, and think of themselves in the act of living, suffering and tormenting themselves. They not only feel, but they reason out their feelings, and by reasoning they transfer them to a higher plane of complexity. In Pirandello dialectic becomes poetry. What the word Shavian means to the English theatre the word Pirandellian means to the Italian. Dramatic critics, in the past, at any rate, were never wearied of attacking Shaw for artificiality and for insisting on making the theatre a place for social propaganda. The same critics might now turn and attack Pirandello for artificially dramatizing metaphysical conceptions. Never was a playwright less inspired in the conventional sense of the term. Visions come to our mind of the traditional dramatist writing in furious indignation in order to attack some long-enduring abuse in society. The ghost of Dumas fils appears struggling with the French code, the long line of social playwrights such as Brieux, Galsworthy, Toller recur to our memory. In fact it would be almost true to say that the modern theatre until recently has been almost entirely devoted to the social preacher, and Shaw has not been ashamed to call himself a social preacher dressed up as a mountebank. Pirandello has no messages for humanity, no slogans of progress. He runs counter to all those writers who attempt to approach as nearly as possible to the representation of real life in all its details on the stage. Very often in his plays he describes situations that seem impossible even to those accustomed to reddest old Adelphi melodrama. But when Pirandello has set on the stage his incredible characters with their far-fetched situations, he delights in resolving the problems in accordance with all his brilliant metaphysical devices. To understand his delight in this tricky unravelling of the intellect, we should remember that Pirandello belongs to the race that in the past taught Europe how to play by means of the traditional "Commedia dell' arte." The writers of the *scenarî* for the masked players loved to construct the most fantastic plots with amazing situations and embroil them to such an extent that the unravelling would seem well-nigh impossible. The public in the theatres used to enjoy watching the piling up of Pelion upon Ossa of improbability. Then, hey presto ! when the climax is reached, all must become normal again. Andrea Perrucci, an actor who wrote at the end of the seventeenth century a book on stage improvising, shows that the object aimed at by the actor-dramatist was to awaken surprise in the audience by every means, and embroil the intrigue in the most puzzling fashion ; then at the end must come the unravelling. The lost children must be found by their parents ; the young heroine must marry the hero ; the villain must be shown up in order that the public may go home contented with their evening's amusement. Pirandello has elevated such plays on to a higher plane and applied their mechanism to the intellect. The pleasure that his plays give the public is an intellectual counterpart of the pleasure given by Flamino Scala, Alberto Ganassa and their actors. We can see the truth of the comparison between the two types of play when we consider the importance of acting. The " Commedia dell' arte " was essentially an actor's drama : the author only wrote out a skeleton plot and left the actor to fill in the parts. Each actor had always acted a particular mask part, whether Pantaloon's, Harlequin's or Pulcinella's, and so he had all his stock phrases, stock actions. Nowadays in Pirandello's plays the actors are of prime importance, and one of the reasons why the master's plays fail to produce an impression on the public when done by amateur companies is that the acting is insufficient. We have seen performances of *The Six Characters in Search of an Author* and *Henry IV* that left us cold. Why did those plays seem dull when their qualities as revealed by Ruggeri or Pitoeff and his company had given us such delight ? The answer is that these plays, with their tortuous reasoning, require all the skill of the trained actor to elucidate their difficulties. The modern actor for the Pirandello plays must not be an actor by instinct or impulse : he must for ever be ready to analyse coldly his own feelings. He must be ever ready to see the character he is representing, from without, as it were, in a mirror. In the plays there is fluidity, and the actor's performance must be plastic. And this plasticity, the

35

result of complete self-control, can only be found in the cerebral actor. Not only the actions, the facial expression must be reasoned out, but also the diction. Pirandello's queer jerky style, so ugly from the point of view of literature, becomes an admirable medium for the stage. It requires the most subtle attention possible on the part of the actors. It is interesting to recall the stress laid on diction by the ancient " Commedia dell' arte " actors such as Riccoboni. The counsels contained in his history of the Italian theatre would apply admirably to the art of Ruggeri or Lyda Borelli to-day. Pirandello realized fully the importance of training a new school of actors, and for this reason founded an art theatre in Rome. His actors, by dint of practising their art, were capable of producing any new play in five or six days. In that theatre there was a slight return to the " Commedia dell' arte," for sometimes the scenario was printed on a sheet of paper in the wings, and the actors were trained so as to be able to develop the theme out of their own skill in improvisation.

Another reason for the necessity of evolving a brilliant school of actors trained to the Pirandello idiom becomes evident when we consider the characters of the plays. Unlike the characters of other authors, those of Pirandello have but few distinctive traits : they are always the same poor puppets worked by wires who obey their author's fancy in all cases except in *The Six Characters*, where they pluck up courage and rush out to seek another author who will complete them. It requires extremely clever actors to introduce variety into these puppets which are as rigid as Harlequin and Brighella of old. The characters of Pirandello, instead of being various and manifold, appear to be one and the same character set amid conditions that are ever different and yet identical. Every play fits in like a mosaic in a huge ornamental pattern which symbolizes his vision of the world. When we watch these characters harshly grimacing on the stage, grotesquely exhibiting their tortured, writhing personalities, it is difficult to avoid thinking of the village puppet show where the roughly painted marionettes are moved by coarse threads visible to the audience. Their mental process seems rigid, like the stiff walk of the doll in the *Tales of Hoffman*, In all the plays, however, there is one moment when those queer, rigid puppets seem to wake to life and assume human semblance. We are reminded of a Spanish grotesque, *Los Intereses Creados*, wherein Benavente sums up thus : " In our play, as in life's comedy, you have seen puppets like human beings moved by thick strings that are their interests, their passions, their deceits, and all the miseries of their condition : some are pulled by their feet and driven to sad wandering ; others are pulled by their hands, work by the sweat of their brow, fight fiercely, hoard skilfully, commit dread murders. But amongst all of them at times there descends from heaven a fine thread, woven as it were of sun and moonlight, the thread of love which makes yon puppets that are human in appearance seem divine ; and it lights up our brow with the splendour of dawn ; adds wings to our heart, and tells us that not all is make-believe, for there is in our life something divine, an eternal truth which cannot end when the play ends."[1] In every play of Pirandello we must look for that great *scène à faire* wherein those puny creatures of his fancy, whether they be bourgeois fathers, boarding-house drudges, village schoolmasters, painted prostitutes, assume noble bearing and become gigantic symbols of the author's philosophy. The effect is always a continuous crescendo, and we see the puppet gradually rising in stature. G. K. Chesterton has said that really every play of Bernard Shaw is the dialogue of a conver-

[1] W. Starkie, J. Benavente, Oxford, 1924, p. 161.

sion. This remark is true of Pirandello if we reverse its significance. Shaw delights in tearing off one by one the veils of illusions which cover the eyes of his characters until he makes them gaze with his own normal gaze on the rational. Pirandello, on the other hand, takes a malign pleasure in making his characters start from the rational and gradually descend until they secure the triumph of the irrational. The irrational may be entirely logical : what we call reason is only one of the many possible forms, one of the many reasons possible. Let us take a characteristic play of the author which shows the triumph of the logic of the irrational. In *Pensaci Giacomino* we meet Professor Toti, an old Government teacher in a small town in Sicily, who for many years has patiently carried the burden of his underpaid drudgery without any promotion. At last he decides to revolt and, old as he is, take a young wife. In this way he will compel the Government to pay for many years a pension to his widow. He does, in fact, marry the young daughter of the school beadle, but just before so doing he finds out that she is expecting to become a mother by a young man of the village, Giacomino. This announcement does not deter the old Professor : he calmly argues out that all will be for the best and he will be able to do even more good to those around him. It is impossible for his young wife to betray him as husband, as he is only to be a benefactor and father, not a husband. As for Giacomino, the girl's lover, he finds him a good post in a bank. He also arranges that after his death all the money will be settled on both of them and their child. Giacomino, however, is unable to bear up against the scandal which throbs in the Sicilian village, and determines to abandon this *ménage à trois* and thus end an intolerable situation. The Professor then rises up in all his indignation and threatens the youth with exposure if he refuses to return to the mother of his child. He tells him that he has no right to break up the family and destroy the lives of three persons. In the end he gains his point and Giacomino accepts the irrational. It would be difficult to discover more irrational situations than we find in this play, where a husband forces his wife's lover to return to her. To find any parallel we can only recall Crommelynck's *pochade, Le Cocu Magnifique.* One of the extraordinary points about such a play is that when we see it performed or when we read it, we gradually assume Pirandello's queer logic and cease to consider it as irrational. We feel powerless before the old Professor's arguments : he is right to act as he does. Pirandello is always able in such cases to extract emotion from the situation. The Professor ceases to be a ridiculous figure, and tears, as it were, the mask from his face. When he appears at Giacomino's house in the last scene, leading the little child by the hand, he awakens our sympathy, and the harsh, satirical laugh dies away on our lips.

The fact that Pirandello shows us that there is no one logic, no one reason, but as many as there are individuals, leads us to consider the fundamental problem of the Pirandellian theatre. The soul of Pirandello has always been obsessed by the problem of personality. As G. A. Borgese says, it is an exaggeration to say that all religions were liquidated at the end of the nineteenth century, for one at least remained burning with all the fire of fanaticism—the religion which gave divine semblance to the rights and power of the individual and made every phenomenon of the world submit to his criticism.[1] In Ibsen we see the struggle between this new religion and the others. His heroes, gifted with superhuman powers of reasoning, see the results of the contradictory arguments, but they always choose the more difficult

[1] G. A. Borgese, *Tempo di Edificare*, Milano, 1923, p. 225.

path which will lead them to the complete expression of their individuality. Thus Brand resists even the claims of the family in order that he may set his church above in the snows. He knows that he may never reach his ideal, and that even at the start he is dogged by defeat, but he struggles on fiercely against overwhelming odds. It is this temperament which makes Nora leave her husband and children in order that she may grow up in the modern world ; it is this that produces the subtle complexities in Hedda Gabbler and in Ellida the lady from the sea. Those characters are not possessed of one solid, unvarying personality, but of many personalities, and the drama shows us how this multiplicity is affected when it comes in contact with the fixed laws and conventions of society. Owing chiefly to Ibsen's influence, the drama of man's multiple personality has been continued by contemporary dramatists in Europe, whether we turn to Roberto Bracco in Italy, Shaw in England, François de Curel in France, or Andreev in Russia. The task of the modern dramatist has been to penetrate farther and farther into the recesses of man's mind. The problem of personality is an old, philosophical one, but it becomes an artistic one when it is suffered, and it may be stated at once that no modern author gives the impression of having suffered this obsession like Pirandello. For Ibsen it was still possible to imagine one big individual with many facets, but the moment Pirandello looks at the individual, he sees him in double, in triple, in multiple forms until his head reels and the ground yawns beneath his feet. Owing to this ever-present obsession, it was never possible for Pirandello to create characters of flesh and blood such as modern literature and drama especially have always required. In Ibsen's plays we see the representation of complete and homogeneous men and women : Rebecca West, Hedda Gabbler, Gabriel

Borkmann, Dr. Stockmann, all live before us and become acquaintances. We see them with our inner eye even down to the second button on their jackets. In Pirandello there is none of this homogeneity, for there is no fixed personality. An Individual is only one of the indefinite personalities, which has for the moment the upper hand over all the others. In every human creature there lurks a mass of contradictory sentiments, and we are reminded of nothing so much as a volcano. Every now and then there is an eruption, caused by one of those latent personalities, which is trying to force its way into the outer air. In *Il Giuoco delle Parti*, Pirandello gives an interesting description of the multiple personality. Leone is speaking about his wife Silia to Guido—

" Perhaps you do not know all the riches she possesses in her character ; certain traits that you would swear were not hers, because you don't pay attention to them, . . . you only see her as she exists for you. To give an example : some mornings you would never believe it possible that she should hum so freely . . . and yet she does hum. I heard her some mornings from one room to another—yes, in a quavering voice like a child. I tell you she was another person—another person, and yet you do not know it. She is just a child who lives one moment and hums to herself when you are absent. I'd like you to see her at other times—when she has a far-away look in her eyes, while unconsciously she strokes with two fingers the curls on the back of her neck. Could you tell me who she is when she acts thus ? It is another personality of hers, and she cannot make it live, because it is unknown to her and because no one has ever said to her, ' I want you to be so : you must be so.' . . . There is always the risk that she will then ask you, ' How ? ' And you would answer, ' Oh, just as you were just now.' And then she would ask again, ' What was I doing ? ' ' You were singing.' . . . .

' Singing ? ' ' Yes, you were stroking the curls on the back of your neck like that. . . . ' She denies it and tells you that she was doing nothing of the sort. She does not recognize herself at all in the image which you give her as you saw her a little time before, for you always see her in a particular light, and that is all about it. What a pity, my friend ! Look at what a charming possible personality she possesses in herself and that goes to waste."[1]

In nearly all the plays we find references to this torturing problem, but it is in *The Six Characters in Search of an Author* that we find the most dramatic representation of the delusion of personality. The guilty father says : " With different persons, we may be quite a different individual ; we cling, however, to the illusion that we remain identical for all persons and in every situation. Nothing could be more false than this illusion, as we realize when suddenly surprised in the midst of some particular action. We know that we are not wholly committed and expressed in this action, and that it would be a cruel injustice if a man were judged solely upon the strength of it, pinned down perpetually to this particular moment as if the whole of his life were thereby summarized and made manifest."

The characters who were called to life by an author and then cast aside unfinished have an immutable reality which is for ever attached to the degrading scene which the author had in his mind. On the other hand, men have an ever-changing reality which is ruled by time. It is a fugitive and passing thing which to-day may be one thing and to-morrow something else, always at the mercy of chance. As the author says, a character in a play comes to life just as a tree, as a stone, as water, as a butterfly, as a woman. And he who has the fortune to be born a character can afford to jeer even at death, for he will never die. And to live for ever needs no

[1] *Il Giuoco delle Parti*, Act I.

miracle-working. Who was Sancho Panza ? Who was Don Abbondio ? And yet they live on eternally as live germs—because they had the good luck to find a fertilizing womb, a fantasy which knows how to bring them up and nourish them so that they might live for ever.

In such a play Pirandello produces his greatest effects by antithesis. He is as eager a searcher after antithesis in his philosophical farces as ever Victor Hugo was in his grisly melodramas with their juxtaposition of the ugly and the beautiful. Bernard Shaw is always being told that he stands on his head by those who forget, as Chesterton says, that all romance and all religion consist in making the whole universe stand on its head. How much truer the accusation is of Pirandello and his followers of the *teatro grottesco*. Pirandello delights in reversing the conventions of society, and we do not feel that he belongs, as Shaw does, to that ten per cent of humanity gifted with clearness of vision. Many are the examples of this topsy-turvydom : in one play it is the lover who brings his mistress back to her husband ; in another a man marries for a joke in order to avoid the perils of marriage in earnest ; in another a husband insists on his wife's lover returning to her. It is as if all those characters had a slight mental disorder which made them pursue an abnormal course in life, but according to the most lucid logic. We must, however, look on them all as being the symbols of the torturing doubts in Pirandello's mind—doubts which he has derived from his profound meditation over philosophers from Kant to Einstein.

All modern philosophy is based on a profound intuition of the dualism which exists between Life which is absolute spontaneity, creative activity, and the forms which tend to restrict and enclose Life. The Life Force, like an inexorable tide, dashes up against those forms created by man ; it breaks down barriers which impede its triumphal progress. It is from this point of view we must start off to criticize Pirandello. With him it ceases to be an abstract philosophical theory and becomes dramatic—dramatic because it appeals to him with such intensity and assumes such mortal semblance that it causes him to suffer. To him the struggle between the Life Force and the masks with which men try to cover it becomes the material for tragic drama. In this respect we might say of Pirandello what Shaw says of himself, " I have always been a Puritan in my attitude towards art." The essence of Puritanism is intellectual earnestness, always ready to probe dogmas and dissect institutions, and in both authors we see that love of logical consistency which makes them avoid the sensual. It is interesting, though, to contrast the two authors in their attitude towards sexual questions. Shaw sees in sexual love the chief means of climbing up towards the superman. In *Man and Superman*, Tanner, symbolizing the thoughtful man, struggles against snares of marriage and responsibility. He fears that the snare of sex will hinder his development. But then the Life Force comes along and entraps him, and prevents him from outsoaring the race and thus defeating his own purpose. In *Back to Methuselah* he develops this idea and preaches the religion of the future which will depend on the human will acting through the medium of creative evolution— a religion which will be the gospel of redemption for humanity. Pirandello does not make use of sex in the Shavian manner. He looks on sex as one of the great manifestations of the Life Force, but he does not construct with it : rather does he use it as a weapon for his mordant irony. Women in his plays are not as they are in Shaw, symbols of a better state of things in the world. He makes them represent unrestrained instinct, the exact antithesis to clear reason. In Shaw's plays we meet light open-air characters like Vivie Warren or

Anne, who have the temperaments of young Valkyries and are a justification of the advance of civilization. Pirandello's women are creatures of instinct, neurasthenic and ever hovering between madness and hysteria. All of them have unhealthy, hectic madness painted on their countenances and are far removed from the healthy Shavian women, who are like harbingers of a new dawn.

If women are creatures of instinct, lacking any reasoning power, it is to man that the duty of analysis falls. Very often it is to a character not intimately concerned with the action of the play that the author entrusts the task of explaining the point of the play. Such a character performs the part of the ancient chorus or else the confidante of French comedy. A good example is to be found in that most popular play *Cosi è (se vi pare)*. The plot centres in Signor Ponza and his mother-in-law, Signora Frola. Ponza lodges his wife and his mother-in-law in separate houses and refuses to let them meet. The whole town seethes with curiosity, and at last the curious make the two speak. Signor Ponza says that Signora Frola is mad and her madness consists in believing that he is forbidding her to see her daughter. The daughter, he says, died in the earthquake some years before. But afterwards Signora Frola says that Ponza is mad and his delusion consists in believing that his wife had died. He will not recognize her and believes that she is his second wife, married a few years after the death of the former. Both the husband and the mother-in-law uphold their case with the most lucid reasons, and the townspeople do not know what to do in order to discover the truth. The earthquake has destroyed the documents which could have given the proof. There is only one thing to do : call up the wife, Signora Ponza. But she will not satisfy their curiosity, and the play ends with her words, " I am the daughter of

Signora Frola, and the second wife of Signor Ponza. As for myself, I am nobody." That play, with its dramatization of the philosophic theme *esse est percipi*, is explained to the audience by Laudisi, who adopts the rôle of scoffer at the ill-timed curiosity of the townspeople. His sarcastic sallies show us that Pirandello wished primarily to contrast vulgar curiosity and demand for truth with the illusions of the Ponza family. In each scene of the drama, as the townspeople become more and more puzzled, Laudisi is there to point the finger of scorn at them. When there is eager talk about the production of documents which will clear up the mystery, he says, "You want documentary proofs in order to affirm or deny ! I have no use for them, for, in my opinion, reality does not lie in these, but in the mind of those two persons into which I cannot enter unless by that evidence which they themselves give me." As he shows, the documents would be of no avail, because they have been annulled in the minds of the two concerned. "And no document could ever destroy that reality of theirs, because they breathe within it, they see it and touch it—the only use of a document would be to allay your idiotic curiosity." Thus Laudisi sums up the central parable—"What is truth ? Truth does not exist : truth we have in ourselves : truth is the representation that each of us makes of it." This idea does not differ from the gospel of Don Quixote. The knight of the sorrowful countenance was possessed of such a faith that he could dissolve all the exterior, hostile world and create another world in accordance with the beautiful and extravagant fancies with which his mind was filled. Don Quixote sees giants, whereas Sancho only sees windmills : the helmet of Mambrino instead of a barber's brass basin, Dulcinea instead of a kitchen wench, Maritornes. But are we to believe that Don Quixote is raving and Sancho is telling the truth ?

The giants which Don Quixote sees are as real to him as the windmills are to Sancho. In the words of Unamuno, the problem may be summed up thus : " What we call reality, is it anything more than an illusion which drives us on to action and produces works ? The practical effect is the only worthy criterion of the truth of any vision." This quotation from Unamuno, one of the masters of European contemporary thought, will explain how the problem of the difference between reality and illusion is obsessing modern writers. Whereas the dramatists of the nineteenth century were occupied in trying to reconcile ethical heaven with positive earth, Pirandello, Chiarelli, Rosso di San Secondo and the New School for ever seek the solution of the problem that had preoccupied the mind of Cervantes and Calderón. Pirandello explains the problem again by one of his characters, " Cartesius, examining our consciousness of reality, had one of the most terrible thoughts that ever occurred to the human mind—to wit, that if dreams appeared regularly, we should not be able to distinguish dreaming from wakefulness. Have you ever remarked how strangely you are affected if a dream occurs several times ? It becomes well-nigh impossible to doubt the presence of reality. For all our consciousness of the world is suspended on this finest of threads—the regularity of our experiences."

Pirandello leads us beyond the objective stage to an inner subjective theatre, where we see, as in a reflection, the shadowy prolongation of the puppet show on the real stage. Our discovery of that inner subjective stage fills us with the surprise that Alice felt when she climbed up on the mantelpiece and walked through the mirror into the Looking-Glass World. A new world of fantasy whose existence we had long unsuspected opens before us and makes us forget for a time the commonplace materialism of our daily lives. And Pirandello is able to be our *cicerone,* because he throws off the philosopher's thinking cap and assumes the cap and bells of the writer of comedy. He looks at life squarely and makes no attempt to conceal or to magnify its grossness. It is when he leads us beyond, in quest of deeper realities, that we feel how unstable are the foundations of our city in which we have lived from time immemorial. Well has Pirandello termed his theatre *teatro dello specchio* —that inner theatre is in the looking-glass world, a world which deforms our shapes so that we cannot recognize our own image. It is in these moments of internal silence when our soul divests itself of all our customary figments and our eyes become more acute and pene-trating : we see ourselves in life and life in itself, as though we were stark naked ; we feel a strange impression creep over us, as if in a flash a fresh reality was lit up for us, different to the one we normally see, a supreme reality that transcends human vision and human reason. With supreme effort we attempt then to regain normal consciousness of things, reconnect our ideas and feel ourselves alive in the usual way. We can no longer lend faith to that normal consciousness, to those connected ideas, to that customary view of life, because we know henceforth that they are only an illusion created by us in order to live, and that beneath there is something else which man may not face except at the cost of death or madness.[1] It is not because Pirandello is a thinker that we are subjugated by him. Woe to him if he had tried to create a system of philosophy and out-Hegel Hegel. It is the dramatic struggle in his mind between the phantoms of his reason and his fantasy that arouses our emotions and make us throng to his theatre. He does not dictate, he only discusses and suffers. And this suffering in Pirandello we discover more easily in the short stories of his earlier career than in the later plays

[1] Pirandello, *Umorismo,* pp. 215, 216. Firenze, 1920.

where he tries to captivate his audience by feasts of dialectic. In some of those sad little tales of Sicily we might call him poet, using the term in the way that Croce applied it to Guy de Maupassant. An analysis of Pirandello writer of *novelle* will clear away many difficulties that we feel with regard to an author against whom there is a perpetual charge that he is naught but a cerebral writer. In the following chapters we shall study Pirandello's literary development through his novels, his short stories, his plays. And when we have examined the master's works, it behoves us to study him as a humorist, for however much the fickle fashions of the stage may change as generation succeeds generation, there will always be some who will remember Pirandello the humorist, and his humour will have a deep historical value as symbolizing the trend of our days. As De Sanctis says, humour is an artistic form which signifies the destruction of limitations with the consciousness of that destruction. It appears at moments of social upheaval, and it never has had so rich or so serious a development as in our times. What limit remains any more ? What about religion ? The eighteenth century and Voltaire have passed over it. What about philosophy ? One system pays no attention to the other. What about literature ? Romanticism barks at classicism—all affirmatives, all negations have destroyed one another in turn. All that remains is a limitless void, the feeling that nothing is true or serious, that each opinion is worth the other. In literature humour corresponds to this state of mind. Humour has contradiction as its essence, and thus we find people making and unmaking, destroying with one hand what they are constructing with the other. And Pirandello, in one of his works, compares the spirit of humour to an imp which loves to pull the heart to pieces as if it were a piece of machinery, in order to see how it is made.

49

III

Pirandello the Sicilian

" I Siciliani che fur già primi."
PETRARCH.

" L'ISOLA DI FUOCO," THE island of fire, as Dante called
Sicily, has on many occasions in the world's history
shone out as a beacon of progress. The truth of
Petrarch's saying is borne out by the number of famous
Sicilian writers who enriched the Italian language
ever since the dim ages when the dramatic Canzone
di Ciullo di Alcamo became the pediment of Italian
literature. Sicily was the meeting place between East
and West. The Greeks had sailed into its roadsteads in
quest of romance and adventure, and had peopled its
mountains and rocky coasts with supernatural beings
whose influences swayed the whole world. The
Carthaginian disputed its rich granaries with the
Roman. Then afterwards came the Arabs and the
Normans to add their still richer legends to its history.
The Normans, with their Germanic chivalry, brought
their crusaders and ladies fair and built their mediæval
castles to be the bulwarks of feudalism. Arabs added
the fantastic imagination, the voluptuous colours of
Oriental life. And the recollection of those great
races has never faded away from Sicily. More than in
any other part of Italy do we still find in its folklore

50

traces of those far-off days of romance. For many a century they remembered the stories of Godfrey and Saladin, or else the brilliant court of William II the Norman or Frederick II with his troubadours, when, as Dante tells us, all writers called themselves Sicilians. It was a short-lived period of brilliance, but in later centuries we meet such poets as Pietro Fullone, and the Anacreontic Giovanni Meli, musicians such as Scarlatti and Bellini, all of whom testify to the skill of the Sicilians as innovators in Art.

Nor were the islanders lacking in practical energy : in the nineteenth century they played a great part in the Drama of the Risorgimento, not only in the Garibaldian campaigns, but also in the events which have succeeded that heroic epoch. In literature the naturalist movement, called in Italy Verism, was led by two Sicilians, Verga and Capuana, who expressed in their most characteristic works the life of the folk of the island. Pirandello in many respects must be considered a transmitter of traditions handed down to him by those two writers. To understand his origins as novelist and dramatist we should go back to his fathers in literature —to Capuana and Verga, leaders of the Verist movement. The early novels of Pirandello, as we shall see, are but prolongations of the psychological method of Capuana. The *novelle* or short stories are an attempt to reconcile the direct regional art of Verga with a morbid and tortuous self-analysis which is natural to our author.

In considering, then, these writers, one question comes to our mind : Is there any unity in Italian literature ? This question will assume greater significance when we compare Italian with French or English literature. In France, Paris has always dominated the world of literature ever since the days of François I. The tendency has always been for the provincial young man of letters to emigrate to Paris and work his salvation out, whether in the *salons* of great ladies or the *mansardes* of the Bohemian quarter. His one thought is Paris, and the greatness of his country is reflected for him in the greatness of his capital city. In England we observe the same tendency even in early times. London is the centre of the literary man's aspirations. There is but little decentralization or regionalism in English literature, and so the question as to whether such and such a writer is a Yorkshireman or a Devonshire man is only of secondary importance, because English is an entirely unified language and London is the literary as well as the political capital of the country. Even a writer such as Thomas Hardy was not altogether a regional writer. His novels all deal with characters of his native province, Wessex, but they are written by a man who is first of all an Englishman and then a Wessex man. In Italy there is a great difference of point of view. In spite of the great political unifying work done by the Risorgimento and carried to such a pitch of perfection by Mussolini and Fascism, Italy is the country of the city state, its unity, however apparent politically, is not to be found in its literature or art. The greatness of Italian art and literature lies in this very regional variability. The Italian is first of all man of his city, then man of his province, and then Italian. Goldoni's best plays are not those written in classical Italian, but those written in the vernacular of his native Venice. Manzoni in aspirations was always a Lombard, Carducci a man of the Maremma Toscana, D'Annunzio a son of the Abruzzi. In Italy drama has never been a flourishing plant, just because writers did not realize this regional peculiarity of the nation. At the time of the Renaissance dramatists followed the model of Seneca in tragedy and Plautus and Terence in comedy. Thus a rigidity set in on national drama, barely relieved by such great works as the *Mandragola* of Machiavelli.

The people then created as a contrast their masked, improvised comedy which was to burlesque the academic drama, and please the people of each region. In the "Commedia dell' arte," as it was called, Arlecchino and Brighella spoke the dialect of Bergamo, their place of origin, Pantalone spoke Venetian and the Doctor lisped in Bolognese. In the Neapolitan region Pulcinella roared his *lazzi* in Neapolitan, the Captain swaggered *à l'espagnole* and Coviello in Calabrese. In the nineteenth century, with the rise of democracy in literature when Grub Street invaded the perfumed *salons* of nobility, a great change came about. In the modern Italian, as in the modern Spanish novel, we seek local colour, and it was the naturalists who made writers open their eyes to their own surroundings. In the case of Capuana, Verga and Pirandello the immediate surroundings were those of their native Sicily. Let us first of all examine the two former writers separately, so that we may be able to appreciate more clearly the position of Pirandello. They should really be considered together, for if Verga is the artistic conscience of the Italian Verist movement, Capuana is its intellectual conscience.

LUIGI CAPUANA.

Many of Capuana's novels lie dust-ridden and forlorn on book-shelves of the past, but as a critic he arouses interest still. It was his proclamation of the theories of the new movement that drew the attention of the public. According to him art in its evolution should fuse with science, and thus Verism, as the Naturalist movement was called in Italy, was in his eyes an ideal that responded to the spirit of his time. "The art of our times," he says, "while still remaining art, must submit to all the exigencies of natural science and the modern analytical method." "Art," he says again, "should be impersonal, and the artist must subordinate himself completely to his work." And again : "We must start from human documents in order to reconstruct the psychological process which has taken place." And in Capuana's novels there is always present the shadow of a naturalist who analyses minutely the other characters and studies them coldly. In his novel *Giacinta* (afterwards dramatized in 1888) the doctor Follini studies the heroine with the dispassionate curiosity of a scientist who has before his eyes an interesting case.

In the end Capuana wearies us by his perpetual dissections : nearly all his novels, and his short stories begin with the clear exposition of an abnormal pathological case. In *Giacinta* the problem deals with the heroine's strange, morbid love for the man who has outraged her innocence. Fearing, however, that one day her ravisher, Andrea Geraci, may reproach her for her past weakness, she marries Count Grippa, a weak-minded man whom she does not love, and reserves for Andrea the post of lover. Andrea, after seven years of this *ménage à trois*, becomes wearied and abandons Giacinta, whereupon the morbid girl, in despair at his departure, commits suicide before his eyes. In this drama of cynicism and jealous passion we search in vain for any charm of feeling or poetry. It is all worked out with implacable logic of analysis. Giacinta, though she comes of the Sicilian bourgeoisie, is full of the morbid self-questionings of the Bourget heroine. Her slight education has released her from all the prejudices of religion or morality and taught her to dissect every emotion, every thought. In the short stories dealing with peasant life, Capuana has many pages of humour, but it is not a humour that bubbles over unconsciously, and it lacks spontaneity. What Flaubert said of History is true of Capuana, "Quand donc consentira-t-on à faire de l'histoire comme on fait du roman, c'est à dire sans amour et sans haine pour les personnages en jeu, au point de vue d'une blague supérieure, exactement comme le bon Dieu voit les choses d'en haut ? " And often the Sicilian tried to shake off the passionate qualities of his race and look down coldly on the creatures of his fancy. Like Flaubert he also corrected and recorrected, trying to achieve an art that dominates torrential passion by purity of form. But living later in a century of material progress, he was less able to cling to what Flaubert called his *mysticisme esthétique*.[1] When Capuana could forget the theories of the naturalists and his own critical writings, he was able to create characters that will live as vivid presentations of Sicilian personality. In *Il Marchese di Roccaverdina* the personality of Agrippina Solmo resembles the finest creation of Verga. Agrippina, the poor peasant girl, has been made the mistress of her master, the Marquis, and hearkens in humble submissiveness to every desire of his, without any thought of her own individuality. Even her own heart she does not allow to speak, and thus she agrees to marry the husband chosen for her by the Marquis, who thinks that with a *mari complaisant* his intrigue will be more effectively protected. Later, when the Marquis, who has become jealous of the husband's prerogatives, kills him, Agrippina still does not rebel. Afterwards, haunted by his guilty conscience, he lets her get married again and go away, but never a word of reproach crosses her lips, and at the end of the story we see her performing the most intimate duties for him, as he has lapsed into dotage. The creation of types in this novel shows us a warmer Capuana—a Capuana who resembles very closely Verga by that sense of dramatic representation of character. In fact, as dramatist Capuana is of greater

[1] Cf. B. Croce, *Poesia e non-Poesia*. Bari, 1923. Essay on " Flaubert."

interest to us, not only on account of his original plays, but also because he gave great impetus to the Sicilian dialect drama.

In the preface to his volume of plays in Sicilian dialect he wrote the following words, which sum up what we have said about regionalism in Italian literature : " I believe that we must pass through dialect drama if we wish to arrive at national drama. People will answer that we refuse to take into account the levelling of the middle classes, which are no longer Italian, French, English, German, but European. This is not true. The levelling is more apparent than real, more in the external customs than in the depths of the soul, whither our authors do not direct their attention. Not only are there enormous differences between the Italian, the French, the English and the German bourgeois, but there are perhaps just as many between the Roman, the Neapolitan, the Sicilian, the Lombard bourgeois."[1]

Capuana's remarks were destined to bear fruit in Sicily, and in 1903 Sicilian dialect repertory companies were formed under the influence of a young writer from Catania, Giovanni Martoglio. Great success attended the actors in their efforts and they speedily acquired fame all over Europe. It was interesting to note the effect produced by these dialect actors on audiences in other countries. There was no need to understand the language, so convincing were the gestures of those frenzied players. Their playing was characterized by extreme rapidity of movement. In fact, their dramas seem to dash furiously on to the inevitable tragic conclusion. All Capuana's plays written for that company are set in Sicilian villages. *Malia* (The Spell) is one of the most characteristic, with its brutal gusts of passion. Jana, though betrothed to Ninu, falls in love with Cola, the husband of her sister

[1] L. Capuana, *Teatro Dialettale Siciliano.* Palermo, 1912.

Nedda. Like all the Sicilian heroines of Capuana, Verga or even Pirandello, she is like one possessed by a demon. She gives herself to Cola in spite of the entreaties, the kindly endeavour of Ninu to dispossess her of the demon. In the end there is a struggle between the two men and Cola's throat is cut by his rival. " Ora, sì, è rotta la magaria " (Now at last the spell is broken), says the murderer, looking at the corpse. *Cumparaticu* (The Godfather) is another play characteristic of this Sicilian theatre, but more interesting than the last owing to its greater subtlety of psychological treatment. It is a tale of jealousy—that fierce passion so natural to the Sicilian where his womenfolk are concerned. The husband struggles with this overpowering feeling. All around him everyone is sure of his wife's shame, but he dares not believe it. At last the storm breaks out : he has final proofs, and he slays his wife before her frightened lover's eyes. In these two plays of Capuana there is a wealth of picturesque details, a grandeur of tragedy which never fails to move the public. Nobody seeing such plays can fail to notice the salient features of Sicilian art—the rapidity and incisive qualities of the dialogue, which are still more characteristic of Verga than Capuana. Capuana in his novels belonged to the Naturalist movement and worked out all its theories. He was irresistibly attracted towards human beings of strange and tortuous psychology and his books suffer from prolixity. In his plays he allowed himself to look on life with greater simplicity because he was not describing subjectively his own bourgeoisie, but objectively the lives of the poor folk of Sicily. We are thus forced to a conclusion that the best dramatist is not he who puts himself into his plays and describes his own self-questionings, but he who observes closely the people round him and sets forth objectively their struggles.

GIOVANNI VERGA.

In the early works of Verga there is little that foretells the later Sicilian scenes. In *Una Peccatrice* (1866), *Eva* (1873), *Tigre reale* (1873) the scenes are all laid amid luxurious surroundings, and the heroines are brilliant, dangerously attractive women whose caprices drive their admirers to furious passion. Verga in those years was living at Catania, Milan, Florence, and was drinking deep of the attractions of the big cities. " Verga the provincial," as his biographer says of him, " was dazzled by luxury, by stage love affairs, by duelling, by that innate curiosity in healthy natures which drives them to love by contrast all that is exquisite and morbid."[1] Gradually a change came over his literary personality, helped on by the naturalist literary criticism of his day. As Croce says, " Under the outer layer formed by the customs of the great cities, the love affairs of the smart world, there lurked in him vivid, immediate impressions and recollections of the native countryside where he had spent his youth."[2] Instead of perfumed ladies and starched fops of the city, there appear before our eyes humble folk of the tiny hamlets, tragic figures whose monotonous lives are broken here and there by violent outbursts of pent-up passion. In the short story *Nedda*[3] we can see the initiation of this new style of Verga. Nedda is a fresh young girl living amid the crowd of peasants who are engaged in their country tasks. She is the hard-working Sicilian woman who has to go out and work manually in order to prevent herself and her poor sick mother from dying of starva-

[1] L. Russo, *Giovanni Verga.* Napoli, 1920.
[2] B. Croce, *Lett. della Nuova Italia*, Vol. III. Essay on " Verga."
[3] G. Verga, *Novelle.* Milano, 1887.

tion. On return from one of her expeditions she arrives just in time to hear the last words of her dying mother, and forthwith she continues resignedly her heavy, weary life, saving her spare money in order to make herself a trousseau. Misfortune follows close on the footsteps of the poor Nedda—her lover dies just on the eve of marriage and she finds that she is *enceinte*. She cannot nourish sufficiently the child, for work is harder to get when a girl has an illegitimate baby. At last the weak child dies, and Nedda, after laying the little body on the bed where her mother had died, kneels down and cries out, " Blessed you that are dead—blessed you, Virgin Mary, who have taken away my little one, so that it may not suffer as I do." The pathos of the little story *Nedda* is characteristic of Verga at his very best. Unlike Capuana, he was not moved by any theoretical ideas. As Croce says, " The formula and the example of Verism had only the effect of striking off his fetters and giving him his liberty."[1] He ill tolerated the labels of Naturalist and Verist which were affixed to him by his contemporaries. " Words, mere words," he would say to his friends and enemies. Naturalism, psychologism— there is room for the lot, and from all of them the work of art may rise. The important thing is that it should rise."[2]

Vita Dei Campi, 1880, and *Novelle Rusticane*, 1883, are the two principal volumes which include Verga's Sicilian tales. In nearly all these stories we see terrible scenes of jealousy and sexual passion, culminating in the use of the knife. In the celebrated *Cavalleria Rusticana* Turiddu comes back from military service and finds that Lola, whom he used to love, is married to another. Out of spite he pays court to Santuzza, and Lola, piqued and jealous, tempts him to her side

[1] B. Croce, *op. cit.*
[2] L. Russo, *op. cit.*, p.9.

and yields to his advances. Santuzza, mad with jealousy, seeing that her lover has deserted her, reveals the whole story to Lola's husband, and as a result the two men challenge one another to fight. Turiddu, who feels that he himself is guilty, would be disposed to allow his rival to kill him, were it not for the thought of his aged mother, who depends on him. In the fight, however, Turiddu is on the point of winning when his rival picks up a handful of dust and throws it in his enemy's eyes, and thus blinded, the latter is an easy prey to the cruel blade. In *La Lupa* the plot centres round a sensual woman, no longer young, who follows ceaselessly on the track of a young man whom she desires, and in order to gain access to him makes him marry her daughter. The youth tries to liberate himself from her nefarious influence, but in vain. " Kill me," she answers, " I don't care ; but without you I will not live." At last he determines to put his threat into practice. They were working in the fields, and seeing her afar off, he took the axe from the tree. The woman saw him coming, pale and crazy-looking, with the axe shining in the sunlight. She did not retrace her steps nor did she lower her eyes, but continued walking straight towards him with her hands full of red poppies, devouring him all the while with her black eyes. " A curse on your soul," gasps Nanni as he strikes her down with the hatchet.

The strongest quality of these scenes is the brevity of description. There are no long-drawn-out periods full of bombastic phrases. There is in these little masterpieces complete restraint. Not only is there parsimony of words in Verga, but also a kind of modesty characteristic of the Sicilian. In *Cavalleria Rusticana* the characters avoid using the gross word referring to Turiddu's sin with Lola. " Turiddu comprese che compare Alfio era venuto per quell'affare " (Turiddu

understood that Alfio had come about that business).
And Alfio afterwards, when he meets his enemy Turiddu,
says, " Era un pezzo che non vi vedevo e volevo parlarvi
di quella cosa che sapete voi." This modest simplicity of Verga's style explains his relations with
regard to the Verist movement. He himself related
that one day he found a sea-captain's diary written
during a voyage, and the perusal of that ungarnished
document inspired him to throw off the trappings of
rhetoric. In all this let us render due praise to Verga's
friend Capuana, who encouraged him and led him in
the path of artistic truth. In Verga's art there are
infinite details of subtlety, which set him far above
Capuana as an artist. Whereas the latter attempts to
describe in all their fullness the stormy passions of the
Sicilian, passions that seem to have been inherited from
the mingled blood of different races, Verga ever suggests
by light touches here and there. He shows in stories
like *Nedda* the resignation, the fatalism of the peasant
conquered by life. What can Nedda do ? She is so
poor, so destitute. She can only bow her head before
the cruelty of humanity. And all the time Verga,
though he does not drop tears, shows us all the philosophy
of suffering—a deep philosophy, because it never takes
away from the dignity of the sufferer. And this sadness
of Verga must not let us forget his humour—a curious
type of humour characteristic of his country. As one
of his biographers has said, " Humour in Verga is always
passion : it is passion which, in face of sad renunciation,
has still the power to smile, because it understands
life and sympathizes with its vicissitudes."[1] The
humour of Verga is based on his largeness of compre-
hension, his understanding. He judges his characters,
but with sympathy. He is like one who has been a
long time away from his country and who one day in

[1] L. Russo, *op. cit.*, p. 94.

after life revisits the scenes of his youth. He does not look at his village folk with the photographic eyes of the present : he looks at them as inheritors of the life of the past. He does not confine himself to outer appearances like the modern realistic novelist, but as a poet pierces beneath the surface to the essence, the kernel, so that his realism is of things recollected.

In the majority of Sicilian plays we are struck by the impression of frenzied rapidity which they give to us, men of the North whose heart-beat is slower. There is something grotesque in this rapidity, these ceaseless gestures, these contortions of countenance which give us the impression that men wear masks. Verga, however, always corrects the grotesque : his humour is a balm. Whenever he stresses an emotion he does not raise the opposite emotion to it in violent antithesis : rather does he soften the rigid outlines.

We notice the same sober tendency in Nino Martoglio, another brilliant writer for the dialect theatre of Sicily. Martoglio goes still further than Verga towards eliminating the brutal elements from the drama. Indeed, it may be said of him that he is the one creator of joyous Sicilian comedy in his play *S. Giuvanni decullato*, with its shoemaker hero. His later play *L'aria del Continente* (The Air of the Mainland) deserves to be studied by all those who love Sicily, because of the interesting contrast between the Sicilians and the Italians of the peninsula. It is useless for the Sicilian who has spent some years away from his island to come back and show new ideas. He will always remain a Sicilian in his heart.

LUIGI PIRANDELLO.

Born in 1867 at Girgenti, one of the most historic and picturesque spots in the island, Pirandello was steeped in its traditions and folklore. Federico Nardelli in his biography *L'Uomo Secreto* (The Unknown Man) has recorded the master's recollections of childhood. Pirandello's father Stefano—a rich proprietor of sulphur mines—was a man of heroic character. More than once he had driven off the thugs of the secret Mafia when they demanded money with threats. He trusted to his fists rather than to his gun, but this did not prevent him from being ambushed and wounded. Pirandello's mother Caterina was the opposite to her husband—a timid, resigned soul, whereas he was violent and overbearing.

At the age of sixteen Luigi began to lisp in numbers. The poems of youth were collected and published under the title *Mal Giocondo*. Many resembled Carducci's in form, but the subject matter was romantic. The youthful Pirandello preferred to take his stand by the young scientists and democrats who voiced the claims of the workers. *Mal Giocondo* may thus be called a poetical diary of young Pirandello.[1] It was followed at intervals by various other volumes of verse, such as *Pasqua di Gea* (1891), *Elegie Renane* (written in Germany), *Zampogna* (1901), *Scamandro* (1909), and *Fuori di Chiave* (1912). Those volumes are of interest to the critic of Pirandello in so far as they show how naturally a Sicilian turns to lyricism in expressing his emotions. The title *Fuori di Chiave* (Out of Tune) is significant, for it explains Pirandello's failure as a poet. It was, he said, his destiny to be out of tune with the world. His peculiar quality of humour, springing from antithesis between laughter and tears, was discordant instead of harmonious. The nine maidens from the smiling slopes of Parnassus began to wither beneath so frosty a humour and took to their heels. At eighteen years of age Pirandello was sent to the University of Rome, where, according to his confessor, Nardelli, he

[1] F. Pasini, *Luigi Pirandello* (come mi pare), Trieste, 1927.

quarrelled with some of his professors and advocated revolutionary methods of teaching. Through the help of the famous philologist Monaci, Pirandello was sent off to Bonn to study for his doctor's degree. As a result he produced a learned treatise *Laute und Lauten-wicklung der mundart von Girgenti*—an exhaustive study of the Sicilian dialect of his native town. That work was useful to him later on when he wrote plays in dialect.

On his return from Germany he went to live in Rome, where he became a member of a "cénacle" including well-known men of letters. In those days the highest star in the literary firmament was Gabriele D'Annunzio, who was preaching to the great public his theories on the Nietzchean superman. Pirandello all his life was a bitter opponent of D'Annunzio : he rejected with scorn the Nietzchean theories and all the trailing robes and languid harmonies of the voluptuous poet-dramatist. He shunned the D'Annunzian rhetoric like the plague and dwelt, in consequence, in Grub Street for many years. Luigi Capuana it was who first encouraged Pirandello to devote himself to short stories and novels.

In 1894 he married Antonietta Portulano in obedience to his father's wishes. In Sicily it was the custom for parents to arrange the marriages of their sons and daughters, and Pirandello had never seen the girl before the wedding day. It was a marriage of family interests, for Antonietta's father was a partner of Stefano in the sulphur mines. The first years of married life were spent prosperously in Rome, but then came the disaster. Floods ruined the sulphur mines, the family fortune was engulfed, and Luigi Pirandello had to become a school-teacher—a drudge like Professor Toti of his play *Pensaci Giacomino*. He was appointed Professor of Italian Literature at the Female Institute of Teaching in Rome. But financial disaster was the least of the crosses Pirandello had to bear. Worry and anxiety affected the mind of Donna Antonietta, and drove her into insane hysteria. Her madness took the form of violent, unreasoning jealousy : she tortured Pirandello unceasingly, accusing him of treachery and unfaithfulness. Day by day, as he lived through his inferno, he began to doubt of his own sanity. Which was his real personality—the one he had lived with heretofore, or the mean, deceitful phantom created by his insane wife ? From 1904 to her death in 1918 Pirandello endured a life of increasing torment. He gave up visiting his friends in order to devote himself to her, and handed over to her every penny he earned. Some of his friends advised him to put her into an asylum, but out of compassion he chose to keep her at home and endure her terrible fits of fury. It was thus that he withdrew into his own thoughts and sought relief in the tenuous world of the imagination. Such is the terrifying background to the short stories, novels and dramas. They all constitute an interminable " danse macabre "—a mighty tragedy in a hundred acts played against a crowded chorus of bewildered humanity. The stage is lashed by contrary winds : clouds scurry across and sinister shadows flit here and there. But through the storm and chaos we see, from time to time, a tiny glimpse of blue sky—the sky of Sicily, whose elemental beauty pacifies momentarily the restless soul of Luigi Pirandello.

His first novel was *L'Esclusa* (The Outcast), which was written in the early 'nineties and published in 1901. It is characteristically Sicilian, and seems to be a continuation of Capuana's work in style and in matter. The plot centres in a girl who is cast aside by her husband for motives of insane jealousy. Marta, the heroine, is fated to be unhappy. Every attempt she makes to re-establish herself in life fails in the little Sicilian provincial town, where everyone shuns her as one tainted. Marta stores up in her heart a mountain of bitterness against her husband and against the hypocrisy of society. With all the skill of the psychologist, Pirandello studies her tortured mentality. She is innocent, but such is her hatred that she wishes to be considered guilty. In Sicily the dishonour of a wife falls like a blight on her whole family, and Marta's father dies broken in spirit. After his death begins the decline of the family : the business languishes and falls into bad hands ; there is a sense of helplessness in the lives of Marta, her mother and her sister Maria. Marta, to remedy matters, becomes a school-teacher, but her reputation follows her there, and it is with difficulty that she can endure the taunts and jeers of the students or the grotesque leers of men professors who admire her good looks. Her old admirer, who had been the cause of the rupture with her husband, contrives to approach her again and renew his attentions. But Gregorio Alvignani, as he is called, is the Don Juan of the story, and only looks on Marta as prey for the moment : he has no intention of spoiling his brilliant political career by marrying her. By one of those lucky coincidences that happen frequently in the world of stage or novel, Marta, who is hidden in the next room, hears her betrayer's confidences and saves herself in time from his clutches. In the end, after thoughts of suicide, she becomes reconciled to her husband by the bedside of his dying mother. The story, though characteristic owing to the psychological treatment of the heroine's personality, is full of strange coincidences and romantic prolixities which weary the reader. The book is of greater interest if we consider it as a description of Sicilian life among the bourgeoisie. If we set aside Marta, who is enclosed within a dark cloud of fatality, there are many secondary characters that recall Capuana : the schoolmaster Matteo Falcone, whose bestial ugliness is relieved by his intelligence ; Anna Veronica, the religious Sicilian woman ; old Mother Pentagora, who believed in witches. Pirandello shows how deep-rooted are the traditional superstitions in the country people. Old Mother Pentagora was supposed by the neighbourhood to see " the Maidens," and on windy nights they used to whistle her name down the blast. In her little house she had an altar on which she stood three dried ears of corn surrounded by scarlet bags of salt. " My tiny soul," she says, " has round, round eyes, red, as live as live can be ; aye, and a long tail and a black beak. There is a swallow's nest hung on a tower, up near the chimes. It's there my little soul is at home. Ding Dong, Ding Dong Dang ! Out runs an old mouse, out run little mice from their holes and start playing with a pebble on the balustrade of the tower. The chimes peal, the chimes yawn at heaven, for their tongues are hanging out. They are hungry for wind, the bells are." She is a Meg Merrilies character, and it is a pity that Pirandello does not make greater use of her in the novel. Sicily is a land of tradition, and in these novels we look for original descriptions. Where Pirandello is at his best is not in the development of the story according to the analytical methods of the Naturalists, but in the exact Verist description of village scenes. In one chapter he de-scribes the Feast of the Saints of the town. Saint Cosimo and Saint Damiano were the two saints, but the people considered them as one saint in two persons. In that chapter Pirandello vies with Verga for the representation of the vivid scene. The images of the two saints were carried through the streets of the town at break-neck speed, for they were the saints of health, the protectors against epidemics of cholera. And so on rushed the statues, borne aloft by perspiring youths intoxicated with excitement and with the wine which they gulped down every now and then in order to satisfy their thirst. From the thronged balconies women threw down slices of black bread out of devotion on to the procession. And there was a struggle to catch the pieces as they fell —hundreds of excited red faces dashed in between the shafts of the bier on which the saints were carried : there was nothing but a tangled mass of bare, sinewy arms, torn shirts, perspiring faces, grunts and groans of anguish, shoulders crushed beneath the weight of the shafts, as knotted hands fiercely grasped hold of them. And each one of those excited men, though ready to sink beneath the terrible load, became filled with a mad desire for the saints, and tried to pull to himself the bier. Thus the saints, pushed this way and that, passed on through the shouting, gesticulating crowd. Sometimes the saints seemed to be of miraculous lightness, and the bier passed on at a brisk pace amidst the acclamations of the crowd. At other times they became an intolerable burden, as if they did not care to go on. Then there were accidents : someone was sure to be trampled on by the crowd. But after a moment's panic there were shouts of " Viva Saint Cosimo and Damiano," and everything was forgotten. Many other passages are there in this novel which show the skill of Pirandello as a descriptive artist of his Sicilian compatriots. He has the same eye for the vivid scene as Verga, though not his simplicity. His style also is more jerky and disjointed than that of Verga or Capuana and more complicated. In Pirandello right from the outset we notice the tendency towards dialogue. All his characters, when they are not speaking to their neighbours, are carrying on an everlasting dialogue with themselves.

In another early work, *Il Turno* (His Turn), which appeared in 1902, Pirandello shows greater advance in his powers as a novelist. It is a very interesting novel, owing to its local colour, its analysis of the strange personalities we meet in a small Sicilian town—in this case, the author's birthplace, Girgenti. To those who have read deeply the works of Verga, *Il Turno* will form a welcome addition. It is, so to speak, the other side of the picture. Verga in all his stories leaves us with an intense feeling of sadness : Pirandello never lets us become sad, because he is always grinning sardonically at his countrymen. The story centres in a certain old man, Diego Alcozer, who has buried four wives and is about to marry a fifth—a young girl who does not care a rap for him, but her father wants to have his money. Stellina, the young wife, is to be married off to the old man in true Sicilian fashion. Her father does not ask her whether she cares for the old man : girls in Sicily, at any rate in those days, were not asked for their opinion. In this, Don Marcantonio, the father, considers that he has made a very good stroke of business, for Don Diego is very rich and he surely will not live long. Every day the old fiancé sends a present to the girl—one day a bracelet, the next a watch and chain, then a ring with pearls and diamonds or else a pair of ear-rings. " Alcozer did not spend a sou : not that he was a miser, but because he had so many jewels left belonging to his late wives. What was he to do with them ? So he kept on sending them to his new fiancée, after getting them polished at the jeweller's and put into new cases."

Stellina did not look any more kindly on the aged suitor for all his presents : she shut herself up in her room and threatened to throw herself out of the window if they married her to Don Diego. However, after the mother had shown her the ear-rings and bracelets, she used secretly to put them on and look at herself in the looking-glass. " Curiosity was stronger than her sense of repulsion against the old suitor." The wedding at last took place, and Don Diego found married life this time a veritable torment, for Stellina would leave him no peace. She carried on the most outrageous flirtations with the young men of the town right under the nose of her spouse. Duels were fought for her, and confusion reigned everywhere. Eventually she leaves Don Diego and goes off with the nearest approach to a cave-man she can find—Ciro Coppa. Ciro Coppa was not considered a woman's man, but when he was struck by the charms of Stellina, there was no denial possible : he all but carried her off, as if he had been a Saracen of old. After winning the case for the annulment of Stellina's marriage with Don Diego on the grounds of non-consummation, he settles down to live with her in a little house outside the town. But Ciro Coppa is one of those men who are very familiar to readers of Verga and Capuana. He has all that restless violence that seems to be characteristic of many Sicilians—and all that gnawing jealousy. He is unable to be happy or contented owing to the thought that Stellina has once been the wife of Don Diego. " He had determined never to enter the city any more, at least while Alcozer was alive. He felt unable to stand the sight of that mummy, who had seen in intimacy the woman that now belonged to him." The peace of the countryside did not calm his fevered brow. He became entirely absorbed in this terrible passion. To take his thoughts off the one problem, he bought twenty Tunisian horses and set himself to break them in, tame them like a circus trainer, and lash at them with all the fury of a hundred devils within him. But there was no rest possible for his weary heart. Pirandello, in an extremely subtle way, analyses the character and personality of this Sicilian. And because he is an abnormal character, Pirandello describes his personality with great success. In Verga's stories and Capuana's novels there are many queer, frenzied characters such as " La Lupa " or Giacinta, but they are described objectively. Pirandello starts off to describe Ciro Coppa objectively, but then, when jealousy enters the heart of the man, he becomes excited and interested in the personality. It is then that his best pages are written. Then there ceases to be mere psychological analysis and there is poetry. The best pages of the novel are at the end, leading up in a quick crescendo to the death of Ciro by apoplexy.

It is interesting to compare scenes of such novels as *Maestro Don Gesualdo* and *Il Marchese di Roccaverdina* with these two Sicilian novels of Pirandello. In Pirandello we do not obtain such a complete description of the great virtues of the Sicilian—his obedience, his attachment to the soil, his fatalism. Pirandello rather looks at his countrymen from another angle : he watches the queer and distorted types and makes them revolve logically in accordance with their own temperament. Very often, as in *L'Esclusa*, there is a lack of spontaneity, so closely does he try to analyse. Such a novel ends by wearying us, because there is no architectural construction. *Il Turno* is much more interesting, because the author tries to observe more closely the surroundings of his characters without attempting to delve too deeply into their subconscious minds.

Now that we have considered examples of Pirandello's early Sicilian novels, let us turn to some of his *novelle* or short stories which deal with Sicilian life. All through the countless volumes published by him, there are many stories which might be called prolongations of the *novelle rusticane* of Verga. We shall limit ourselves to the consideration of isolated examples, for our intention in this chapter is merely to show Pirandello in Sicilian garb. In these stories we get to know the life in the countryside or else in the towns of the island,

and it is all the more interesting because we see at work the struggle between old feudal customs and modern life. Pirandello never fails to let us see the struggle, owing to his desire to produce at all costs in the minds of his readers that antithesis which he calls humour.

In the collection *Terzetti* (1912) we find some characteristic stories. In " La Giara " we read a vivid description of the olive harvest. Don Lollo Zirafa had a fine quantity of olive trees planted in his *podere* or farm, and during the harvest-time, when the fruit was being picked, he was in a state of great excitement. As the five old jars were not sufficient to contain the produce of this exceptional year, he bought a sixth, which was to be, as he said, " the abbess " of the other five. That jar excited astonishment in the district : no one had ever seen one so big : it would hold two hundred litres ! One day, however, the workers noticed with horror that a great piece had been broken off the side of the jar. Don Lollo when he saw the damage nearly went out of his mind, and it was all his workmen could do to calm his fury. At last they called in old Zima Licasi, who possessed a particular putty of his own invention. After much parleying Zima got into the jar and started mending it, grumbling all the while against the crusty old Don Lollo. When he had finished the work with putty and with stitches he tried to get out of the vat, but as he was of corpulent build, try as he might, he could not extricate himself from the narrow neck. The workmen, instead of helping him, could not restrain their laughter. Amidst the pandemonium caused by Zima's infuriated roars and the workmen's laughter, Don Lollo arrived on the scene. After realizing the position of the unfortunate Zima, who was now speechless with impotent fury, he said : " This is a new case, my friend, and must be settled by a lawyer : I can't take the responsibility on myself." And so saying, he went off on his mule to consult the lawyer, after giving orders for food to be brought to Zima. To the lawyer he exposed his case : Zima had sewed himself up in his jar, and what was he to do ? Was he to keep him there or let him out and so break his jar ? "But if you keep him there," said the lawyer, " you are guilty of sequestering his person." " Sequestering," answered Don Lollo. " But what fault is it of mine if he has sequestered himself ? " At last the lawyer settled that all would be well if Zima paid the price of the jar. But when Don Lollo stated the terms to Zima, the latter refused point blank : " I pay ? You must be joking ! I'd sooner become worm-eaten in here." No threats could prevail on Zima, and Don Lollo had to retire for the night baffled. In the middle of the night he was awakened by an infernal din in the courtyard. In the moonlight he saw what he took to be a herd of devils gesticulating. The farm labourers, all drunk, were joining hands and dancing around the jar ; and Zima within, with his head sticking out, was roaring out ribald songs. Don Lollo could not bear it any longer, and in a sudden fit of rage, he rushed down and gave such a huge kick to the jar that it smashed in bits, and old Zima won the day.

This story is very brilliantly written in Pirandello's most incisive and dramatic style. Sometimes the style is so vivid that it ceases to be a *novella* and becomes a little play :

" ' Let me out ' (shouted Zima). ' In the name of fortune, I want to get out ; hurry up—help me ! ' Don Lollo at first paused as if stunned : he couldn't believe his senses.

" ' What ? Is he in there ? You don't mean to tell me he has stitched himself up inside the jar ? '

" Then he went over to the jar and cried out to the old man : ' Is it help you want ? What help can I give you, you old idiot ? Why didn't you take the measurements first ? Come on, put your arm out, try . . . that's the way—then your head . . . come . . . no . . . go easy . . . down . . . wait a bit : not that way . . . down, down. . . . How did you get into this ? What about the jar now ? Now be calm, be calm.' He went on telling all and sundry to be calm as if the others, not he himself, were going to become excited."

We could imagine such a scene performed by the Sicilian actors, with their mobile gestures and *lazzi*. It is interesting to note that the author has recently dramatized this story and produced a most effective one-act piece.

In " La Lega disciolta " (The Dissolution of the League), another story contained in *Terzetti*, we get a glimpse of a more sinister side of Sicilian life—the " Mafia." Often the crafty Sicilian peasant in league with the Mafia is able to hoodwink his simple neighbours and make them slaves. 'Nzulu Bummulu, with his little Turkish fez, administered justice to the countryside from his accustomed seat in the café. All the farmers whose cattle were stolen—and in Sicily this was a frequent occurrence—came to 'Nzulu and begged him as a favour to interest himself in their recovery. After a sum of money had been paid to him, off he went to his companions of the League, and in that conclave the question of restoring the cattle was debated. Everyone did obeisance to the grotesque little man, poor and rich alike ; shopkeepers looked up to him, peasants bowed down to him, noble landowners visited him. 'Nzulu, of course, had his own code of morality : he dispensed his own justice and his arbitration was (as he assured all) absolutely disinterested.

Such a character, with its subtle irony, shows Pirandello at his best. In describing such types he is the superior of Verga or Capuana, for he wields a more delicate rapier. It is sad to think that 'Nzulu Bummulu and his crew will not inspire Sicilian novelists any more : in 1926 the Fascist Government undertook to rid the island of the Mafian brigands. It is said that the women of Monreale burnt candles to the Fascist Prefect entrusted with the task when he was ill, and many welcomed him as a second Garibaldi. The dissolution of the Mafia has modernized Sicily more than anything else. There are no more picturesque bandits such as Ferravallo or " Cagnaccia," who, in their disregard of the logic of modern civilization, resembled some of the characters in those Pirandellian stories. The Mafia in Sicily is divided by many authorities into two types, classic and baroque Mafia. The first rose out of an exaggerated cult for personal courage and physical force, and was not bereft of chivalry, though the Mafioso might scorn all social laws. To this grand type belonged Ferravallo and even 'Nzulu Bummulu, with his code of honour. We may ask the question whether it will ever be possible to free Sicily of the Mafia. Professor Pitré, the great Sicilian folklore scholar, said that it was impossible to eradicate the Mafia, because it was not an organized association, as many people thought, but a sentiment, a point of view, as it were, born and bred in the bone.[1]

In another story Pirandello describes life in the little town of Nisia on the Southern coast. It is a squalid little town, and the houses of the inhabitants resemble dens of beasts rather than human dwellings. The men work like beasts of burden unloading ships ; the women feel the position of their husbands acutely and seem to have gone mad in consequence. Their madness appears to consist in bringing countless children into the world. Out of their countless children, the majority die of inanition, but those unfortunate ones by their deaths

[1] *Observer*, March 21, 1926, article on the " Mafia."

75

assist the three or four survivors ; for every woman, after the death of one of her children, runs to the Foundling Hospital and chooses one to rear, in return for which she gets six lire a month for several years, and the name is entered in a little red book. These red books are the property of Maltese business men who do great business at Nisia. To each woman whose name is entered in these red books as a foster-mother to the foundlings the Maltese give a trousseau to the value of two hundred lire. The girls at Nisia all get their marriage trousseaux in this way—by means of the little red books of the foundlings whom the foster-mothers should in return feed and bring up.

In all these stories Pirandello does not conceal his bitter, sarcastic grin. He has no illusions about the beauties of country life or the pure innocence of the peasant ; in fact, his pessimism sinks as deep as that of Brinsley McNamara in *The Valley of the Squinting Windows*. It is interesting to contrast his personality with those of Verga and Capuana. Verga, in spite of his blood-stained art and his passionate heroes, can become at will a humorist. His humour is a poetic quality that appears in all his work. Humour with him, as an Italian critic has said, is always passion—passion that renounces and makes huge sacrifices always with a smile. Verga through all his work is the Sicilian *filius terræ* who has refined his nature by education and has raised himself spiritually. He does not weep hot tears over his characters with that *sensiblerie* of Sterne or Richardson, but he judges and justifies them. Pirandello, on the other hand, treats his characters as if they were poor devils ; he seems to be a disinterested spectator watching the writhings of the wretch who is performing before him. His attitude does not resemble that of the Homeric gods who sat on their mountain and smiled sweetly at the crowded misfortunes of men. Verga gives the impression of having lived away for years from his native countryside and then of having suddenly returned to it, when all its beauty, that had lain hidden in his soul since his youthful days, returned with redoubled strength. Pirandello can never resist the temptations of that malignant spirit of humour within him which for ever commands him to analyse ruthlessly the conventions, the beliefs and superstitions of his Sicilian compatriots. In this respect he resembles rather Capuana, whom some call an Italian Paul Bourget, but Pirandello has carried logic still further, for analysis with him is a passion. Unlike Capuana, the naturalist, who put down objectively with scrupulous accuracy his descriptions of places and people, Pirandello irresistibly is driven to interpret and criticize his descriptions. If we take Capuana's novel *Giacinta* we notice that the author has described minutely the strange, morbid passion of the heroine for her enemy. In Pirandello we notice the same mania for subtle dissections of morbid neurasthenics, but whereas Capuana looks at his heroine objectively and allows her to possess a mentality of her own, Pirandello imparts a twist to his heroines at times and makes them puppets or symbols of his self-questionings. Let us take as an example the story " Leonora Addio " out of the collection *Terzetti*, in which he studies again the jealousy characteristic of the Sicilian. In the story a Sicilian officer in the Italian army married Mommina, one of the daughters of Don Palmiro, a citizen of a village where his battalion was billeted. The Palmiro girls were exceedingly hospitable to the officers : and in fact, their reputation in the district was lurid, for, owing to their desire to do as the up-to-date people on the mainland do, they threw the conventions of Mrs. Grundy to the winds when in the company of the young men. Only one of the men was in earnest, and he became Mommina's husband. As

soon as he had married her, he shut her up in a lofty
house outside the village on a windy hill and devised
every scheme imaginable for closing her in hermetic-
ally. Locks were ordered from Germany, servants
were not allowed near her, and every day the husband
did the household shopping himself. To such extents
did his fierce jealousy go that he would not even let
her care for her person : he would not allow her to
comb her hair or wear a corset. It seems grotesque to
imagine how a man could feel jealous on account of
such a woman, whose shoulders were bent, whose body
had advanced to fleshy protuberance, whose legs
scarcely upheld its weight. But he saw her always
as she had been years before, when his fellow officers
had courted her in her father's house. Poor woman,
imprisoned at the behest of this madman ! even her
children were never allowed out of the house. One
day in a coat which her husband had thrown aside she
found a leaflet announcing a coming performance of
the opera *La Forza del Destino*. Then all the scales fell
from her eyes, and she saw her past life, when she used
to go to the theatre with her sisters and their friends,
and when the evenings were spent in mirthful hilarity.
Then she remembered her singing, and even the arias
of the opera came back to her mind. To her daughters
she insisted on singing, right through, the songs of the
operas she had heard. One day the husband came in
and heard someone singing the " Miserere " from *Il
Trovatore*. He rushed up the stairs into the bedroom,
and there he saw outstretched on the ground the
enormous body of his wife. She had on her head a big
hat with feathers in it. Near her were seated the two
little girls, open-mouthed, terrified, waiting for their
mother to continue her performance. But Pirandello
does not even then spare our sensibilities. He termin-
ates the story thus : " Rico Verri, with a mad roar,

rushed up to the outstretched body of his wife and stirred it with his foot. She was dead."

There are many morbid touches in this story, both in the description of the madly jealous Rico Verri and the pathetic lackadaisical wife. Not at any time do these characters assume mortal form ; they are exaggerated caricatures, symbols of Pirandello's warped manner of looking at the world. He takes the characteristics of the Sicilian as shown by Verga and exaggerates them till the characters become like the caricatures of Dickens. But he has not got the humanity, the pity, that we find in the English writer ; we always feel that he looks on these creatures with contempt, and for that reason he does not scruple to show us Rico Verri kicking the dead body of his wife. We must, however, give credit to Pirandello for his description of the customs of the Sicilians. In all the novels and plays we get a comprehensive panorama of life in that part of the world where modern civilization is entering slowly and driving out the last remaining vestiges of feudalism. For Pirandello has well learned his lesson in the naturalist school of his predecessors ; he describes objectively, even to the minutest details, the life and surroundings of his characters. In " Alla Zappa " (contained in the collection *Erma Bifronte*) he relates a story that is Irish in its peasant flavour. In Sicily, as in Ireland, the farmers always hope to be able to dedicate one of their sons, generally the delicate one who has taste for books, to the career of the Church. " Though old Siroli needed many hands for his land, he had wished to give one of his sons as a present to God. It was the dream of many peasants to have a son as priest ; and he had managed to fulfil his dream, not for ambition, but just to win merit by such an action in the eyes of God. By dint of scraping together savings and enduring privations of every kind, he had been able to keep his

79

son for many years at the seminary of the neighbouring city." The atmosphere in this story recalls to us very forcibly the moving play of T. C. Murray called *Maurice Harte* (1912), where the mother insists on making her son a priest. In both cases the parents are doomed to bitter disillusion : in the Irish play Maurice Harte goes mad, in Pirandello's story the young priest is guilty of an unspeakable crime against orphans entrusted to his care. Afterwards the matter is hushed up and the bishop arranges to send the culprit away to another district, where, unknown, he may expiate his sin. But the father will have none of this : " Monsignor may pardon, but I will not," he cries, and then he rushes to his guilty son and orders him to take off his priest's habit. Then when he had done so he orders him to take up a hoe and go back to the land, though he is unworthy even of that labour. " Your brothers hoe," he says, " and you may not stand near them. Even your toiling will become accursed in God's eyes." The moral of this sad little story is the same as that of *Maurice Harte* and might be expressed by the homely Spanish proverb—" Cada oveja con su pareja." This is the nemesis of the desire in parents of educating their sons above their capabilities and making them set their eyes on professions that are too high for them. But whereas T. C. Murray in his play lays stress on the ambition of the mother that her son should be a priest, and thus shifts the sympathy from her to the victim son, Pirandello leaves all the sympathy for the poor old father, who had not sent his son into the priest-hood from any feelings of ambitious pride. He has also intensified tragedy by laying stress on the fatalistic temperaments of these Sicilians, who live, as old Siroli does, in a malaria-infested district. The poor man feels that now there is no hope for his house ; after such disgrace the curse of God will rest for ever on the wretched family. Very characteristic of the Sicilian peasant is the austere idea of honour, and Pirandello sets it up in antithesis against the facile method of compromise with sin which is followed by the bishop. The bishop holds that after a few years of expiation, when the scandal has faded away, the son will be able to return to his native district and perhaps become a priest again. Old Siroli, in characteristic fashion, rejects this plea. For him his son is dead, and Pirandello ends the story with a touch of pathos that recalls the exquisite sense of humanity of Guy de Maupassant : " Siroli was all alone. He took the tunic, brushed it and folded it carefully and kissed it ; he picked up off the ground the silver brooch and kissed it ; he picked up the cap from the ground and kissed it. Then he went and opened a long old chest of pine which looked like a coffin, where he religiously kept the clothes of the two sons who had died, and making the sign of the cross over them, he added those of his son the priest— he too was dead."

For once Pirandello has cast aside the mask of grim humour. There is no grimace in this story, and we imagine him writing it with tears in his eyes. In the space of about ten pages he has managed to interpret the Sicilian people to us. In most of the stories we have quoted there is not much feeling for humanity ; Pirandello's pessimism does not distil pity. We live with him through sorrowful experiences, but he rarely lifts us up with any message of pity which would impart a sense of poetry to his creations. In this story, however, there is pity and there is poetry. At the end we feel that there is no hope left to these peasants of the malaria-infested district. Old Siroli had worked for forty years on his little farm and had managed to bring up a family, though some of the children had died. But yet somehow or other he had won the battle against the terrible disease, and it was to be hoped that the family were now immune. Then comes the terrible blow and dishonour to his name, and we take leave of the story with the feeling that there is no God to help struggling humanity. Man wanders about aimlessly in life : he clutches at everything he sees to try to stay the current which is sweeping him on. All effort is vain, for life is only ruled by chance. Pirandello makes us feel the pathos of his conception of life when he allows his creatures full scope for their development, but when he looks on them merely as symbols of some hallucination that is inwardly devouring him, they become merely grotesque and arouse no emotion in us except sometimes horror.

Those who are accustomed to the strains of the Sicilian Greek poets, or the folk-poets of more modern times, such as Pietro Fullone or Giovanni Meli, long to find traces of that poetical nature in the modern inhabitant of the island. No country is richer in folk-poems than Sicily, and from the collections of *Canzuni* and *Ciuri* that have come down to us we should infer that every Sicilian was a budding Meli. Pirandello sometimes shows this poetical and idealistic nature in his country-men. Let us take as an example the first play he ever produced, *Lumie di Sicilia* (Limes of Sicily), a little comedy in one act.[1] The hero of the play is a poor musician from Sicily, Micuccio Bonavino, who arrives in Italy at the house of a celebrated prima donna, Sina Marnis. Sina Marnis originally came from Micuccio's village, and when she was a young girl it was he who discovered her voice, and as her father was dead, he sold some of his land to give her money to go away to Italy to get trained for opera. As she was going away she made a pact with him that when she had made

[1] This play is dramatised from a *novella* contained in the collection *Quand' ero Matto* (When I was Mad), 1902.

her way in her career, he was to come and claim her in marriage. Now some years have elapsed and Sina has become famous, but she has forgotten her poor shabby little lover of former days. When Micuccio arrives she is having a dinner-party and is surrounded by the smartest young dandies in the city. Micuccio sees her dressed in a brilliant modern dress, with low neck, and covered with flashing jewels, and he realizes that she can never be his any more. His rustic sense of modesty is shocked by the nudity of this exotic woman, and he departs from her for ever. But before going he pulls from his pocket a bunch of limes and showing them to her says : " Look at them. You must not touch them nor even gaze at them from afar : smell the scent of our country." Such a play is characteristic, not so much of Pirandello, for it has not got enough psychological experiment in it, but of all the former Sicilian writers. It is a profound description of that *nostalgie* so acutely felt by all Sicilians far from home.

Occasionally Pirandello allows his sadness to disappear when describing his countrymen. In *Liolà*, which most critics consider his best play in Sicilian dialect, we might even apply the epithet " breezy " to his satire. It is interesting to compare the play with the dialect plays of Luigi Capuana and Nino Martoglio. In most of the plays of the two authors the same types pass before our eyes—the calculating, miserly old man who, like the ancient Pantaloon, falls in love with a young girl and is hoodwinked by her lusty lover : the good and bad brother, always in contrast, but both loving the same girl ; the rustic Don Juan who sings as he works and accepts the love of all the girls of the countryside as his due. But whereas Capuana and Martoglio try to be strictly faithful to the customs of their native regions, Pirandello in this play tries to be the humorist who produces his humour by reflection. Guido

Ruberti analyses his style thus : " The character of these plays is not frankly comic or essentially dramatic, not gay or sad, but smiling and sad at the same time, both simple and involved, superficial and profound. We find, in a word, that humour which pervades every work of the celebrated Sicilian novelist and loses none of its personal and suggestive power when brought on the stage."[1]

Pirandello is for ever standing beside the scales, and this perpetual attempt at antithesis makes him look at his characters from without. He never lets blaze up the unrestrained passion which inspires plays like *Malia* or *Cumparaticu*, and thus he never reaches the heights of tragedy. The culminating scene of the former play, when the two men fight for possession of the heroine, and Nina cuts the throat of his rival Cola, saying the words : " Ora, sì, è rutta la magaria, don Sciaveriu," does not find an echo in the sarcastic Pirandello, who resembles a modern Machiavelli in whom the broad laugh of the sixteenth century has tempered to the slim, feasting smile of the twentieth century, but with a trace of bitterness. In *Liolà*, though the characters are rustic, there is a refined subtlety of presentation that contrasts with the rough giants of Capuana. The hero resembles the traditional Spanish Don Juan—the eternal *burlador* who sings, like Chantecler, after every contest. He is as characteristic of the fields of Sicily as of the *patios* of Sevilla, for he derives his origin from Eastern civilization, which swept over both countries. In contrast to Western civilization, which has followed Dante's words, " Donne ch'avete intelletto d'amore," and set up woman as the ideal of beauty, the Oriental has led in the strutting Don Juan to whom women are offered in sacrifice. Liolà, like Feliciano in Benavente's rustic Spanish play, *Señora Ama* (produced 1908), has driven

[1] G. Ruberti, *Il Teatro Contemp. in Europa.* Bologna, 1920.

all the girls of the neighbourhood distracted by his charms. The countryside resounds with tales of his adventures, but Liolà, as a consequence of his fickle temperament, cannot get a girl to marry him. " Amuri è cecu e nun vidi lu veru," runs the Sicilian proverb, but in this case the girls, for all their love, have no bandage across their eyes. Even Tuzza, one of his victims, who has the misfortune to be *enceinte* as a result of his attentions, refuses to marry him. But she has a plan in her mind which will get her out of trouble. Old Simone, who is married to a young wife, Donna Mita, longs to have a son who may be his heir, but his wishes so far have met with no success. He therefore agrees to a bargain with Tuzza ; he will proclaim himself father of the child to which she will give birth, provided that she will let him adopt it. Naturally Donna Mita, when she hears of the old man's plan, falls into the utmost consternation and looks about for help in her affliction. Meanwhile Liolà, the village gallant, always ready for a new adventure, bethinks him that now is a superb chance of revenging himself on Tuzza, who had rejected him. He is attracted by the beauty of Donna Mita, and reflects that if she bears a son, all Tuzza's calculations will fail ; for Simone, thinking that the child is his, will welcome the fulfilment of his long-deferred wish and renounce his former intention of adopting, and Tuzza will be left grinding her teeth in hopeless dismay.

The play recalls by its plot Guy de Maupassant's piquant story, *L'Héritage*, where the good services of a friend to the family are requisitioned in order that an heir may be found to the long-desired inheritance. The satire of Pirandello, with its biting saline basis, recalls the French author, and just as Guy de Maupassant in that *conte* tosses the *gros sel* of his artistic ancestor La Fontaine, so Pirandello in this play, which finishes with the gross, red-faced laughter of the rustics, shows his legitimate descendance from Machiavelli and Aretino. And just as Machiavelli in *La Mandragola* showed up mercilessly the corruption of society in the sixteenth century—its venality and superstitious ignorance—so Pirandello, with even less illusions, laughs stridently at the vices of the peasant of to-day. In Machiavelli's day, *La Mandragola* caused indignation in Germany and provoked the Reformation, but in Italy it caused laughter, and among the first to laugh at it was the Pope. De Sanctis says of that laughter : " All laughed. But the laughter of all was buffoonery, pastime. In the laughter of Machiavelli there is a sadness and seriousness which pass beyond caricature and impure art. Evidently the poet did not exchange confidences with Frate Timoteo ; he does not place him as he does Nicia, nor does he enjoy him, but stands away from him, as if he felt repulsion."[1] Pirandello also seems to be detached from his characters, as if he despised them utterly, with the exception of Liolà, whom he makes dangerously attractive. When we examine the manifestation of the comic spirit in this play, we see a contrast to the rest of the works of Pirandello : the laugh is much broader and heartier, as if it tried to rival the ancient spirit of the sixteenth century. It is a return to that classic humour which Alberto Cantoni, the humorist, symbolized in the form of a fine old man, rosy and jovial, whose impressions could have been the plot of a *novella* by Boccaccio or Bandello.

In *Liolà*, Pirandello, with the greatest glee, shows the innate shrewdness of the Sicilian peasant, who is always able to make a bargain for himself. Sometimes we find these peasants exploiting the credulity of their

[1] F. De Sanctis, *Storia della Lett. ital.* Milano, 1912. Vol. II, p. 81.

fellows and drawing money from superstitions. In *La Patente*, a one-act comedy, he satirizes the sinister superstition, so rife in southern Italy, of the *Jettatura*. Chiarchiaro appears before the judge in his district with a sad story to tell. Everyone believes that he has got the evil-eye, and they make all the customary signs when they pass him in the street. As a result of being considered to be possessed of the evil-eye, Chiarchiaro loses his means of subsistence : no one in that superstitious countryside will give him a job. Nothing remains for him but to resign himself to his fate and make the best of the evil powers thus thrust upon him. And so he sets about taking up seriously the profession of a *Jettatore*,[1] with all its consequent emoluments. And very big emoluments they are in Sicily, if we believe the story which Chiarchiaro tells the judge when he is summoned before him.

" Ah yes, sir ! you obstinately refuse to believe in my powers. But luckily the rest of the people believe in them. Everyone believes, and that is my fortune. There are lots of gaming-houses in our village ! It's enough for me to show myself. There's no need to say a word. The manager of the house and the gamblers all grease my palm to make me clear out. Then I start buzzing like a bumble bee around the factories ; or else I stand in front of a shop here or a shop there. Look ! there's a jeweller. Well, I stand like this in front of his shop and I begin to scrutinize the people thus . . . and who's going to enter that shop and buy a jewel, or even look at the window ? The owner comes out and puts three or four lire in my hand to make me go

---

[1] A. Panzini, Dizionario Moderno, who says that a " jettatore " is one who by his presence or by his words is supposed to bring evil luck : a species of innocent and passive sorcerer. A jettatore, like a poet, is born, not made.

off and stand in front of his rival's shop. Do you understand ? It will be a kind of tax which henceforth I shall start exacting."

THE JUDGE

" The tax on ignorance."

" Ignorance ? No, my dear sir ! The tax on safety ! For I have accumulated so much hatred and so much bile against all the filthy human race that I'm convinced, your Worship, I have in these eyes of mine the power to make an entire city crumble."

Such a passage is most characteristic of Pirandello, not only for the ironic sentiments it expresses, but also for the literary style in which it is written. Pirandello's style is always full of jerks and jolts. His characters all seem to stutter and stammer in their eagerness to speak. They rush on sometimes with a flood of words, then suddenly they stop short with some parentheses. Pirandello's mind is full of parentheses, because he is always questioning every idea, every sentiment. This jerky style is Sicilian, because we find it, though in much lesser degree, in all the other Sicilian writers. Chiarchiaro is a true Sicilian, but in his hatred of the " filthy human race," he is a rhetorical Pirandellian.

We have examined in detail Pirandello as a painter of his native folk and their customs and superstitions, and we have shown him as successor to the inheritance left by his literary predecessors. But he has written another work wherein he tries to combine in a harmonious construction the history of modern Sicily. The work is called *I Vecchi e i Giovani* (The Old and the Young), and was published in 1913. In this two-volume work Pirandello has painted on a broad canvas the history

of the generations of the Sicilian people since the time
of the Garibaldian expeditions ; in addition, he has
exposed through the mouths of his characters his own
social and philosophical views.

It is a very interesting book for the general reader, not
on account of its descriptions of battles, boss systems,
intrigues, but on account of its painting of characters.
Here Pirandello has not given way so frequently to his
mania for deformation : he has allowed himself to
describe the folk of Sicily without so much aid from that
sarcastic little imp who treads on his shadow.

The whole work shows three phases—the setting sun
of the old world, the present generation, and the dawn
of the future. Through these pages we see the result of
the glorious Risorgimento set up by a race of supermen, then the consequent miseries of Parliamentary
intrigue, the disorderly demonstrations of a people that
remembered the great heroes of the past, and was therefore determined not to go on enduring patiently the
rule of meaner descendants.

To the student of Sicilian History, Pirandello's work
will be of the greatest interest, for in it we see the final
evolution of the Trinacrian land from feudalism and
ancient beliefs into the modern world. The old ills
of Sicilian government find their expression in bribery,
corruption, Mafia, brigands, bureaucracy, incompetent
officialdom, and all converge and produce class revolution. The greatest difficulty of the author was to represent in human form each of the different forces at work
in this period of Italy's history and make all of them
combine into a harmony in which romantic fiction and
historical truth might balance each other. The great
generation that had given men of every class in society
to fight for Italian liberty, is symbolized in a survivor,
Francesco d'Atri, who had started life as a humble man
of the people, but becomes head of the Government.

He is a noble example of the generation which produced Carducci and Arrigo Boito.

Roberto Auriti, the son of Stefano, who was killed in heroic circumstances at Milazzo, has lived at Rome, the centre of all intrigue and trafficking, and becomes a victim through his own honesty. He sacrifices himself to cover up the dishonesty of Corrado Selmi, who symbolizes political graft and back-stairs intrigue. Prince Ippolito Laurentano is the representation of the Bourbon régime—the old traditional ideas of feudal times—but his son is the supporter of the Socialist Fascists in the island. Behind the maze of crowded events—assassinations, battles, intrigues—that form the outer plot of this modern historical novel, we can descry the sad, ironical smile of Pirandello and the inner philosophical idea. There is the same dualism between the mask which we wear and the every-varying life. It is thus that Cosmo Laurentano, lonely philosopher, analyses the vanity of human wishes when he comforts the political refugees who are hiding in his villa : " There is one sad thing, my friends—to have understood the game ! I mean the game of that scoffing little demon we all have within us, which amuses itself in showing us as reality what soon afterwards it makes out to be only our illusion. It derides us for all the anxieties we have borne on account of that illusion and derides us also because we did not know how to delude ourselves, since outside those illusions there is no other reality. Do not then torture yourselves ! Whatever anxious thoughts you may have, do not imagine that all this cannot end. If it does not end, it is a sign that it is not fated to do so and to seek a conclusion is vain. We must live in illusion and let the scoffing little demon play within us until it wearies of the game—and think that all this will pass away."

Many critics call *I Vecchi i Giovani* the central work of

Pirandello, because it is based on a larger idea than any
of his other works. It is of interest to those who consider Pirandello one of the most characteristic writers
of our present epoch. In this novel, in which he
attempts to reconcile history and fiction, we should note
especially the dramatic method by which he describes
the crumbling of the heroic generation of the Risorgimento, which had created Italian freedom, as a result
of all the wretched Parliamentary struggles and intrigues.
Pirandello describes the political corruption that set
in after 1885 in the same way that Croce describes it
in his article on the character of recent literature.[1]
Pirandello, like Croce, exposes the hypocrisy, the insincerity of the leaders and shows the gradual awakening
of the people to a consciousness of their destiny. Then
the masses confusedly evolve towards a class revolution.
Each generation in this big work is represented by a
special type, and this produces a feeling of artificiality in
the whole work. In many cases these symbols do not
acquire a life of their own : they are abstractions—and
we become wearied at their prolixities. The whole
book gives one the impression of having been written
by the author in a burst of sadness at seeing the district
around his beloved Girgenti—the traditional Agrigen-
tum—expand into a modern port. There is in all
those descriptions of tradition yielding to modern
civilization, the nostalgia of the Sicilian who looks on
his island with eyes of the past. Many are the typical
characters which strike us in the book, such as Mauro
Mortara, the humble servant yet glorious in his idealism
as a former Garibaldian, or else the grotesque Captain
Placido Sciaralla, the tattered aide-de-camp of His
Excellency Don Ippolito Laurentano. Many of these
characters resemble those twisted trunks of olive trees
which may be seen abroad ; their contortions show the

[1] B. Croce, *Litt. della Nuova. Italia*, Vol IV, p. 187, *seq.*

struggle they have waged against ceaseless buffetings of time. So too in the case of those Sicilians : they are grotesque survivors of a past age and they have no sympathy with present civilization. But they obstinately refuse to bow their heads to the storm. Donna Caterina Auriti-Laurentano, the mother of Roberto Auriti, is one of those characteristic Sicilians of the old stock. She had endured every torment, even hunger, for her principles. After being reared in a Prince's house, she had to suffer the revolution of 1848 and go into exile with Roberto. Then, after having all her goods confiscated, she had to beg alms for her son. Tall and rigid in stature, dressed in widow's weeds, her face in its waxen pallor gave the impression of being a mask of terrible suffering. Her hair, which had remained black and shining, served but to mark the contrast with her features and to disprove the common belief that sorrow makes the hair turn white. She in her rigid mask of the past is as petrified as Mauro Mortara thinking of his dear master the General Mauro Mortara, however, has the faith of Don Quixote : he can retire within himself. No matter what happens to Sicily, he knows that all the country belongs to him, because he won it in the past from the enemy who held it in slavery. Now at seventy-eight years of age he has not got a sou in the world, nothing except the medals on his breast, and yet he can laugh at all :—

" What do I care ? I . . . I . . . Sicily. . . . Oh, Mother of God ! I tell you Sicily . . . if it were not for Sicily. . . . If Sicily did not wish it. . . . Sicily started and said to Italy : ' Here I am : I am with you. Come down from Piedmont with your King. I shall set out with Garibaldi, and we shall both join together at Rome. Let us see who will be first.' Who would have been first ? Holy Mother, I know : Aspromonte, reasons of State, I know. But Sicily wanted to be first

—always Sicily. And now four rascals have wished to dishonour her. But Sicily is here with me—Sicily never lets herself be dishonoured : she is here with me."

Such a passage will go far towards explaining the character of the Sicilian—his extraordinary love for his island. We find the same love for the earth in the peasants of Verga and Capuana, but more rarely in Pirandello. There is no doubt, however, that Pirandello, when describing the history of Sicily and its people, becomes more tragic. His procedure is to describe some queer abnormal character generally afflicted with some bodily imperfection. But then, when he has described that character in all its grotesqueness as a puppet, he allows it to come to life and reveal a personality to us. And like his predecessors, Pirandello is always able to suggest the Sicilian background to his characters, because he is so devoted to his country. It is just this subtle patriotism which makes us value so highly the Sicilian stories and plays of Pirandello.

IV

Pirandello, Novelist and Short-Story Writer

IN THE PRECEDING CHAPTER we considered Pirandello as a regional writer interpreting and expressing the customs and mode of life of the inhabitants of his native Sicily. But Pirandello was not fated to continue treading the path of Verga or even Capuana. He soon turned away from describing the folk and its primitive passions, and began to examine morbid psychological problems such as present themselves in the crowded lives of our soul-tormented twentieth century. The rural communities of Sicily with their simple village life did not give Pirandello the opportunity which he ceaselessly demands, of expressing his own torturing doubts and fears ; he was not satisfied, as Verga was, with the objective description of character. Pirandello regards each of his characters as a symbol ready to express the distracting ideas that agitate his mentality. He seems perpetually to ask the question, " What is character ? Does it exist ? " When he looks at an individual he sees him in duple, triple or quadruple, and so he tells us that character, as writers have considered it up to this, is a pure illusion. In reality every man bears within himself two, three, four men, each of which, at a given time, dominates the others and determines an act. Pirandello in many of his stories shows the multiplicity of the individual and how unjust it is to judge a man only from the point of view

94

of one out of his many personalities. And this idea of the multiplicity of the individual does not appeal to Pirandello as an abstract philosophical problem : it is an agonizing obsession which tortures him so unceasingly that each little story, each play, becomes a piece of self-expression undertaken in order to give relief to himself. No writer has ever been so obsessed by this problem as Pirandello, and it is the sense of inner conflict which causes these works to produce such a vivid impression on readers. It is absurd to see in Pirandello the philosopher whose works must be considered manuals for the student. Nothing could be farther from the truth : he might well say to the public who have listened to his plays what a famous actress once said of her enthusiastic audience : " They do well to applaud me, for I have given them my life." In his descriptions of morbid soul-torture Pirandello has given us his life and exposed every corner of his complex personality. It we look on his work in this light, we shall not disturb ourselves at the manifold contradictions that arise in every manifestation of his genius. So far from ascending to the higher ether of philosophical speculation, the Pirandellian threads his weary way through inextricable maze and chaos. He is driven this way and that by his notions of reality and illusion, and yet in the depths of his mind he believes positively in Life. We shall thus be able to explain why Pirandello in his novels does not stop short at communicating his complexities : he goes still farther, and makes his puppets analyse and criticize themselves. Many critics condemn him for the long-winded self-analysis of his characters and their arguments ; but we should remember that Pirandello, though he regards his characters as puppets, yet allows them to come to life at the end and argue- out their own case even against the author. And what often happens is that these characters annihilate themselves by their self-criticism just at the very moment when they are about to become artistically realized.

How different Pirandello is to the great masters of creative art ! We imagine Beethoven in the act of writing the *Fifth Symphony* or Wagner writing the drama of *Tristan and Isolde*—both of them entirely absorbed by their subject. It never comes into their mind to doubt the reality of their idea, for it is at the moment the one reality of their life, and their problem is how they may attain complete self-expression. Look, on the other hand, at Pirandello : as soon as his imaginative brain seizes an idea and he begins to revel in its fantasy, then there appears that malicious little imp who follows him like his shadow, breathing the chill breath of doubt, and thus most of the fantasy withers as beneath a shrivelling frost. Francesco Flora in his study of the author states the case : " Pirandello constructs men from one set idea. After having constructed them, he does his best to make them live. He distributes abroad false syllogisms dressed up as men. All the characters of Pirandello theorize on their own life : they are pseudo-philosophers, every man and woman of them."[1]

I NOVELS

If we would seek the origins of Pirandello's grotesque spirit that revels in complicated inversions, we should examine the novel *Il Fu Mattia Pascal* (The Late Mattia Pascal), which appeared in 1904. It is the centre from which radiate all his other characteristic works, whether short stories or plays. Like so many modern novels, from *Jean Christophe* of Romain Rolland to *Ulysses* of James Joyce, *Il Fu Mattia Pascal* is set in quasi-auto-

[1] F. Flora, *op. cit.*

biographical form. Mattia Pascal in jerky style tells us the history of his own personality. He comes of a respectable Sicilian family, but owing to the death of his father, the unworldly character of his mother, the swindling of neighbours, his patrimony is swallowed up and he is forced to eke out a wretched existence as village librarian. Mattia Pascal had also been so foolish as to marry a woman of the neighbourhood, who with her villainous mother made life a hell for him. Eventually Mattia cannot endure it any longer and goes away from them to commence a wandering life. They all think that he has committed suicide, and their suspicions are confirmed when a putrefied corpse is recovered from the mill race. This can be no other than poor Mattia Pascal, and so due honours are paid to what they think is his corpse, and notices of the funeral are put in the papers. In the meantime Mattia has gone to Monte Carlo and has won a big sum of money at the gaming-tables. He is startled to read his own obituary notice in the papers, and at first determines to return to his native township and with his money relieve his wife and family. But on reflecting he decides against that course : what cause had he for believing that they would be glad to see him ? His wife had always been of execrable humour towards him, in which she was efficiently helped by the curmudgeon mother-in-law. No, a much better course was to let them go on believing that he was dead, and so he would start life afresh—a life of freedom released from the commonplace, hide-bound conventions. Henceforth he would be able to look at life as a spectator from without. And so he changed his name to Adriano Meis, a name taken haphazard, and started off again on a wandering tour. But troubles arise at once. It is a difficult task to have to create afresh all one's life. " What a number of substantial and minute things our

invention needs if we are to become again a real person."
And Mattia gradually becomes intensely wearied of his
lonely, friendless life, travelling from one hotel to
another. At last he lodges with a family in Rome and
allows himself to cultivate their acquaintance. With
subtle touches Pirandello describes old Paleari, his
daughter Adriana and the rest of the family. Mattia
Pascal, though he seeks solitude, cannot help taking
interest in them, especially in Adriana. In spite of all
his efforts he becomes more human, and at one of the
séances of spiritualism held in the evenings in the old
man's house he declares his love. But he realizes that
life is becoming more and more impossible for him since
he left his roving habits. It was easy for him to live a
solitary life as Adriano Meis, for no one paid any
attention to him ; but the moment he tried to enter
society and claim his share in its joys and sorrows, he
saw that he had no right to anything. As Mattia
Pascal he had died and his corpse lay in the cemetery
of his village in Sicily : as Adriano Meis he had no
existence. It was so difficult to answer Adriana's questions
concerning his past life. There was the ceaseless fear
of meeting in Rome somebody who would remember
him as Mattia Pascal.

" What could I do ? Contradict him ? How ?
No, nothing ! I could do absolutely nothing ! "

He also felt that he had yielded to the lure of his
senses, and by making love to Adriana had raised hopes
in the poor girl which he could never fulfil. He saw
then in all its sadness the falsity of his illusion that he
was free to live again.

He had imagined that he could become another man
and live another life, forgetting that this was possible
only on condition that he did nothing :—

" What sort of a man was I then ? A shadow of a
man. And what life was mine ? As long as I contented

myself with remaining self-centred, watching the others live, yes, I was able to save my illusion that I was living another life ; but when I entered life to the extent of kissing two dear lips, I had to draw back in horror as if I had kissed Adriana with the lips of a corpse, a corpse that could never come to life for her."

His trials did not end even there. One day he finds that most of his money, which he kept in his room, has been stolen. He knows for certain who the thief is, but when on the point of calling in the police, he draws back in horror, realizing that it is impossible for him to accuse anybody.

" I saw I could do nothing ! I knew the thief and I could not denounce him. What right had I to the protection of the law ? I was outside any law. Who was I ? Nobody ! I did not exist for the law, and anybody henceforth could rob me, whilst I should have to remain silent."

The only solution for him is to go away, renouncing his love for Adriana. Mattia Pascal as Adriano Meis was but a shadow, but that shadow had a heart and yet might not love ; that shadow had goods and yet anyone might rob them ; that shadow had a head, but only for thinking and understanding that it was the head of a shadow. After mature deliberation he determines not to commit suicide, but to come back to life as Mattia Pascal. " Yes, I must kill that mad, absurd fiction which has tortured me for two years—that Adriano Meis who has been condemned as a cowardly lying wretch." In this way he would give the only possible satisfaction to poor Adriana for the wrong he had done her in trifling with her affections. With this object in view he left on the parapet of one of the bridges over the Tiber his hat and stick, and within the hat he wrote the name Adriano Meis. Thus Adriano Meis committed suicide by drowning, and

Mattia Pascal alive again fled through the night from Rome, back to his old life—back to his slatternly wife and cantankerous mother-in-law. This was going to be his revenge on them. But Mattia is destined to another setback ; he may not come back so easily from the dead. From his brother he finds out that his wife has married again, a wealthy husband this time, and has a child by the second marriage. And thus the book ends with the grand climax of the late Mattia Pascal's appearance before his frightened family, who had thought him safely buried two years before.

The whole book is a brilliant *tour de force* of logical argument, and the subject is developed in a most dramatic way. The argument becomes more and more intricate, climax of reasoning follows climax until at the end the whole puzzle is unravelled.

It is all like the high, complicated intrigue plays of the " Commedia dell' Arte " by Flaminio Scala or Loccatelli, but raised up to the plane of high psychology. Pirandello resembles the servant of those plays who weaves ingenious mental *lazzi*. He might even be called the Pulcinella or Brighella of dialectic.

In *Il Fu Mattia Pascal* we get the first complete presentation of the Pirandello phenomenon. Pirandello has that quality with G. K. Chesterton found in G. B. Shaw—" a queer clearness of the intellect, like the hard clearness of a crystal." And this hard clearness at times prevents him from creating human beings possessed of a heart and emotions.

The characters of *Il Fu Mattia Pascal* seem to clang their skeletons before us, until we long for some flesh and blood. They are abstractions that only rarely enter upon our real life. In the description of Mattia's home and village, however, there are many subtle touches : old Aunt Scolastica and Widow Pescatore, rivals in tongue and nails, Romitelli, the old librarian,

Pomino—all are characteristic of Sicilian life, and we meet their fellows in Verga, Capuana or De Roberto. But when Mattia leaves his native province and goes to Monte Carlo to initiate his wanderings, the book develops slowly. None of the characters interests us : the house of Paleari at Rome, the endless discussions on *le Plan Astral* and spiritualism weary us. Even Mattia's phantom of a love affair does not awaken much interest, because Adriana never becomes a complete personality : she is like one of the Six Characters, still in search of an author to complete her artistic individuality. The real interest arises towards the end of the book when the illusion begins to crumble away ; then Mattia becomes for a while a tragic character. He had hoped to enjoy life in all its infinite liberty, releasing himself as far as possible from all forms, from all masks which society, history and the events of each particular existence have fashioned. But he was doomed to disappointment. He learnt that by liberating himself from society and its forms, he was only able to watch the life of its members as a spectator and stranger, without any possibility of taking part in that life and enjoying it in all its fullness.

It is only possible to emancipate oneself from the forms of life on condition that we renounce living. In this respect Pirandello works out to a fuller conclusion the problems that had agitated Ibsen and his disciples. Ibsen had shown the tragedy of the modern superman who tries to reach a noble life of liberty, far away from the narrowing conventions of a society supported by pillars of falsehood and hypocrisy. He makes them all struggle like Titans against that force of society which ends by trampling them underfoot. What use is it that Brand should follow out to the bitter end his motto of " All or nothing " and let his son die, soon to be followed by the broken-hearted mother ? All those Ibsenian supermen, living on their snow-capped peaks, can only look down on the mortals who live in society on the plains, but they never enter their lowly lives. Pirandello, writing in the present miniature age, far from supermen and valkyries, looks at the problem from a purely logical point of view. Mattia Pascal does not set out a hero to rebel against society : his attitude towards life resembles rather that of the characters of Alfred Capus in plays like *La Veine*, who wait patiently for the turn of the wheel of fortune—and various in the extreme are the fortunes their opportunism brings them : at one moment they are millionaries, the next they are paupers. In the lives of Pirandello's characters the unexpected always happens, and perhaps this is not strange in a country where earthquakes and volcanoes make life a gamble.

Pirandello is a characteristic novelist of modern times. Unlike so many Latin writers, he fears the traditional rhetoric as he would the plague, and there is very little attempt in any of his writings to yield to beauty of form. Like Pio Baroja, that " arch European " of modern Spanish literature, he cultivates a jerky, disconnected style that lacks beauty as our fathers understood it. We have shown in our analysis of Capuana and Verga that this jerky style is true to the Sicilian, but in Pirandello this tendency becomes European. The dialogue in *Il Fu Mattia Pascal* does not read like the dialogue of a novel : it has none of that sensitive rhythm that we hear in Proust. Like Baroja, Pirandello is also a repressed sentimentalist, but the reasons are different. Baroja, as Salvador de Madariaga[1] says, refuses to show his feeling, partly from pride, partly from timidity, partly from a self-conscious fear of the ridicule attracted to sentiment in a country in which fire is more prized than water. Pirandello,

[1] S. de Madariaga, *The Genius of Spain*. Oxford, 1923.

on the other hand, comes from the warm lands of the South, where sentiment is prized and where the peasant or fisher boys are troubadours. He seems to repress his sentimentality from a desire to attain a European mind—that is to say, an inquiring mind which seeks ceaselessly to interpret the universe in terms of its own individuality. If we consider literary artists like D'Annunzio, we find that their most conspicuous quality is a subtle, sensitive harmony which makes them interpret the world according to their own sensibility. No better examples of that sensibility could be found than *Il Fuoco* or *La Città Morta*. Again, if we compare the works of Bracco with those of Pirandello we shall see a great difference between two modern writers. The former for ever looks on the sad scenes of life with tears in his eyes, and his art, as one of his biographers says, is meditation and suffering, brain and heart, thought and sentiment. The latter when looking at those scenes of sadness turns away his head and lets his features contract into a bitter grin of hatred against a world that can allow such things to happen. He does not want to feel sorrow or joy, but with every little work he makes an additional scientific experiment in his mental laboratory with the object of eliciting truth. There is one law which regulates the life of the greatest as well as the smallest of men : the uselessness of everything. Every human experience ends in impossibility. "We forget," he says, "that we are infinitesimal atoms which should respect and admire one another mutually : we are ready to come to blows for a little piece of land or become grieved at certain events, whereas if we really understood what we are, they ought to seem to us incalculably paltry and petty."

In all Pirandello's novels we find that deep pessimism, and there is no author who is able to impart a greater sense of terror at the instability and the vanity of human wishes. And yet his method of producing that sensation of terror in us is not based on sympathy or emotion, as in other novelists of the past. There are love scenes, scenes of passionate jealousy, scenes of death and suffering in his works, but they all seem to be described *en passant*. Pirandello does not excite himself when describing them : he always seems to look at them from without. The scenes of love must be skipped over quickly by the author so that we may arrive at the discussions about them. The author looks on humanity always like Mattia Pascal when he arrived back home to his village :—

" ' Now,' I said to myself, ' where shall I go ? ' I wandered about, looking at the passers-by. But not one of them recognized me ! And yet I was the same. All those who saw me might at least have thought to themselves : ' Look at that stranger over there. What a resemblance he bears to poor Mattia Pascal ! If his eye was a little crooked, you'd swear it was he.' Nobody recognized me, because nobody thought about me any more. I aroused no curiosity, not even the slightest surprise. . . . And I had imagined such an outbreak, such tumult the moment I showed myself in the streets ! "

Mattia Pascal, like all the Pirandellian heroes, is a weak man, always struggling between opposite ideas. His mind has no rest, because he reasons out everything and argues to himself about everything. In an age of action which we summed up in the words of D'Annunzio *marciare non marcire*, he is inactive because reason has killed his powers of action. At the very first struggle with reality he relates to us his experiences and tells us that there is no help but to leave oneself at the mercy of Fate without making any attempt to resist.

Pirandello and Cinema

The next work in which we see a continuation of the ideas of *Il Fu Mattia Pascal* is in *Si Gira*, a novel published in 1916, and which has been re-published under the title *Quaderni di Serafino Gubbio Operatore* (The Diary of Serafino Gubbio, Cinema Operator). In this novel, which is the description of the life of a cinema operator at Rome, Pirandello has infinite opportunities of studying his favourite problems. Serafino Gubbio is not an ordinary cinema operator, as we find out very soon ; he is a Pirandellian *acharné* and describes his function thus :—

" I study people in their ordinary walks of life with an ever-awakened curiosity and deep attention, to see if I can discover in other men what I lack in everything I do : the certainty that they understand what they are doing." People appear to be so certain of themselves. They salute an author, they run hither and thither, they puff and blow with excitement over their affairs, their caprices. Ah, they must be sure of themselves ! But then, when Serafino begins to examine them with his inner eye, all certainty vanishes, and he sees that they are floating about in a surging tide of perplexities. The reason of all this uncertainty, all this torturing anxiety, is that the earth is not made for man so much as for animals. " Nature," he says, " has given animals just enough to live on under certain conditions. But to man she has given too much, and this superfluity is the cause of his unending torture, because it never allows him to be satisfied with his existence." All men are in the same state as a poor farmer's son who has been sent to a city school where he has to consort with the sons of city magnates and gentlemen. When he returns to his farmyard he finds that his varnished manners have unfitted him for the life of simple rusticity. He is discontented because he looks with other eyes at his former life. So it is with the human beings in Pirandello's novels : they have imbibed a fatal dose of modern sophistries and it allows them no truce. In *Si Gira* Pirandello affects us even more deeply than *Il Fu Mattia Pascal*, because he has chosen surroundings that bear out his theories. The tales we read in the papers of cinema stars and their fantastic life make us prepared for the Pirandellian puppets darting hither and thither. We understand how characteristic our author is of this machine-made age and the Futurist theories of art which have sprung therefrom. The motor, the cinema, the aeroplane, all symbolize the cult of speed in our modern life—a speed that is not so much a sign of vigour as of decadence. It is like the hectic glow on the face of a consumptive person—excitement which demands more and more excitement until the patient wastes away exhausted. All those film actors and actresses have their motor cars. They have them free, for the establishment pays for them. And so they dash along at a furious pace without seeing anything except the white road and confused objects flying past : thus they try to satisfy their insatiable desire for speed. Serafino Gubbio, the operator, is a man of the past. He goes along slowly in a horse-driven car because one by one he can admire the trees by the roadside with their shady nooks and the country around in its calm beauty. And thus we arrive at the contradiction in Pirandello's nature. He is not altogether a Futurist : he is not a worshipper of speed and machinery like Marinetti and his followers. He feels every now and again nostalgia for the country around Girgenti—the fresh grass sod, the far-off, wandering sounds of the country, the silence, broken only here and there by the hoarse croak of some frog when it rains, and the pools of water reflecting the starlit sky. Instead of that, nothing all day but a cloud of motors, carriages, cars, bicycles, operators, actors, engineers, workmen, and the sound of hammers, saws, pickaxes, and floating over all the petrol-scented dust.

Pirandello frequently in the course of the book makes references to this mechanism of modern life : " Life which has been swallowed by machines lies there in those big tape-worms : I mean to say, in the films ready rolled up in cloth. We have to fix this life which is not life any more, in order that another machine may give it movement. . . . We are, as it were, in a belly in which monstrous, mechanical gestation is taking place."

And when Serafino goes into that atmosphere of machines all his superfluity vanishes, and he watches himself compelled to become a hand and nothing else.

Few authors have given such subtle impressions of the horror of our civilization, where man has become a mere cog-wheel in a gigantic engine. And this engine is growing every year in size, and man is becoming more and more absorbed by it in minute subdivisions. According to many authors, the man of the future will be entirely dominated by mechanical contrivances.

If the man of 2000 loses his mass of mechanical aids, such as motor cars, typewriters, wireless sets, gramophones, aeroplanes, he will cease to exist. The development of the machine is the revolution bringing in man's servitude and helplessness. In Italy the Futurists hold the opposite view. They claim that the machine, if controlled properly, will become the champion of liberty. Pirandello accepts the rule of the machine, but he cannot help comparing our present feverish age with former ages when Individuality had freer play. Pirandello shows the contrast in the case of famous actors who yield to the temptation of becoming film actors. They consent to act for films contrary to their conscience. The only reason why they do so is because they are paid more money and because there is no intellectual effort needed in their acting. They hate the cinema, not only for the senseless, mute work it condemns them to do, but especially because they are separated from that direct intercourse with the public which is the artist's greatest recompense and satisfaction :—

" Here they feel, as it were, in exile. In exile, not only from the stage, but from themselves. For their action, the living action of their living body, exists no more on the cinematographer's screen : all that exists there is their image, caught in a moment in a gesture, in an expression which flashes and then disappears."

Their feeling of anger extends to our friend Gubbio, who stands with the black cloth over his head : it is he who despoils them of their reality and gives it as pabulum to the machine—it is he who reduces their body to shadow. Serafino Gubbio tries hard to be the impassive spectator, but try as he may, he cannot prevent himself from taking interest in the puppets that move before him. He cannot help becoming interested in that exotic actress La Nestoroff, who had driven men to suicide for love of her. He is interested also in a young girl who comes to play her first scene. For a good part of the book he forgets his notes, so eager is he to follow this girl in her family story—one of these characteristically bourgeois stories where there is a weak, conventional husband and a voluble and strident wife. Luisetta the girl in the end becomes Ibsenian and leaves her home. But she is afflicted with the Pirandellian disease, and she is not able to become a true revolutionary. So too her father, who tries to revolt. " He will come back again when he is tired of running and when again the shadow of his tragi-comic destiny, or rather his conscience, will appear before him."

Pirandello shows all the hopelessness of these lives : he makes us weep for them, because they have no powers of revolt in them. They never struggle against Fate, because they are so possessed of the demon of self-criticism that every step becomes an impossibility. Pirandello asks himself the question, Why should they revolt ?

" I think their life might be comfortably spent in peace and tranquillity. The mother has a dowry : Cavalena is a decent fellow and might quietly follow his profession. . . . Signorina Luisetta might gracefully cultivate, as if they were flowers, the fairest dreams of youth and innocence."

Instead, those poor creatures insist on torturing one another remorselessly, and Pirandello chides them for their lack of reason as though they were naughty children. It is with savage irony that he ends the book with the great scene of the tiger which one of the actors is to shoot while Gubbio clicks his film machine. The tiger unfortunately seizes the actor and crushes him to death : Gubbio is speechless with horror, but his hand continues mechanically to turn the handle. Thus the terrible scene is reproduced and becomes the rage of the cinema world. Serafino Gubbio has lost his voice for ever in that scene owing to shock, but he has now become a perfect being, enclosed in his own silence. No more is he afflicted with that superfluity which distinguishes man from the beast. Besides, he has become rich with the royalties on that scene which he filmed.

There is no doubt that *Il Fu Mattia Pascal* and *Serafino Gubbio* are among the most interesting works of Pirandello, because they give us such a clue to the understanding of his complex personality. They seem also to sum up the qualities of the contemporary novel which is simply a conversation carried on by an author with himself.

The most subjective novel of Pirandello is *Uno*

Nessuno e Centomila (One, No one and a Hundred Thousand), which was begun as far back as 1910, but did not appear until 1925. The hero, Vitangelo Moscarda, is the son of a banker, who leaves him heir to a considerable sum of money. Vitangelo, however, pays no attention to his money interests and prefers to leave them to be administrated by two friends of his late father. They carry out their duties with such efficiency that public opinion gives Vitangelo the reputation of being an arrant usurer. Vitangelo, when he realizes what the world thinks of him, determines to prove that they have misjudged his real personality. He therefore sets about playing havoc with his savings : he gives away houses and money ; he ill-treats his wife and drives her from the house. The friends and relations then determine to have him declared insane and locked up. Meanwhile Vitangelo pays court to a friend of his wife called Anna Rosa, but the latter after a passionate scene in which she succumbs to his caresses, suddenly, in a fit of remorse, pulls out a revolver and fires at him point-blank, wounding him gravely. The ensuing scandal brings the chaotic novel to a close. Vitangelo Moscarda becomes converted and mutters Dante's " Incipit Vita Nova." When Anna Rosa is brought up in court he manages to get her liberated by making everyone believe that he is a madman. Then when the question of his money affairs is debated he appeals to the Church for help. If the priests will only help him to get back his money, he will employ every penny of it in works of charity. The priests naturally persuade the court to have him declared sane and responsible for his actions. At the end of the book Vitangelo Moscarda founds an asylum and becomes the first inmate. As for his friends and relations, they remain outside in the cold, and he has the final laugh. Vitangelo has reached his bliss, for he has broken every link with his past life. Henceforth they will not be able to nail him to one form which was not true to all his nature. Most readers of the general public who started to read *Uno Nessuno e Centomila* soon gave up in despair, because the book had all the appearance of being a pedantic treatise on psychology. The story of Vitangelo Moscarda is hidden away in a chaotic medley of psychological dialogues between various personalities of the author. Fernando Pasini in his subtle analysis of the book compares Vitangelo's conversion with that of Saint Francis. But whereas Saint Francis became converted through love for humanity, Vitangelo becomes converted through spite, and the author gleefully at the end makes Vitangelo " cock snooks " at the whole world in general.

In summing up the peculiarities of Pirandello's style as a novelist we should lay stress on his rambling method of composing. The main object is to give in semidialogue the conversation between the hero and his other ego, but then suddenly some external character interests the author, and then we get a long parenthesis before he brings us back to the main story. The expedient is not a new one, as we find it is used with wonderful success in *Tristram Shandy*. Sterne has often been taken to task by professional critics for loose syntax, slang and slovenly style. His style, however, did not drift into dashes and stars out of mere trickery to puzzle his readers : they stood for real pauses and suppressions in a narrative which aimed at reproducing the illusion of his natural speech, with all its easy flow, warmth and colour. To read Sterne was like listening to him. The wit, humour and pathos of his conversation made his readers delight in the frequent parentheses interrupting the narrative, because they were able to go off in company with Uncle Toby to Namur or else listen to Corporal Trim. In Pirandello we see a return to the Sterne method of novel construction. A sudden remark, a sudden epigram, leads the author off in a long digression involving metaphysical issues. Some new character appears on the horizon ; he may have no connection with the central theme, but his personality fascinates the author and so he monopolizes our attention and draws it away into a side issue. Then suddenly we slip back to the original story again. Compared with Sterne's humour, with its mixture of kindness, sentimentality and *espièglerie*, Pirandello seems arid in the novels. He leads us on, nevertheless, fascinated after him, and his path is always an ascent to some bare mountain-top whence we may look down on the dwellers in the plain.

II. SHORT STORIES

Now that we have considered our author in his two most important novels, let us examine some examples from his great output of short stories or *novelle*, as they are traditionally called in Italy. Italy is the country *par excellence* for the short story, and from Boccaccio to Pirandello, Italian authors have always known how to adapt their inspiration to this most difficult form of literature. English writers have never been able to make a complete success of the short-story form. The neatness of finish, the lightness of touch, the vivid style, seem far truer to the genius of Latin peoples, whose qualities are of the spontaneous kind. Northern nations produce novel writers in abundance, because in the North men brood over their sorrows and there is calculation even in their joy. Just as their lives in sunless climes are governed by will-power, so their literature is above all things an expression of their inner thoughts, an analysis of their passions. In the South, where the sun shines and where men's passions rise high, happiness, as Nietzsche once said, is short, sudden and without reprieve. There is less calculation and analysis, and more spontaneity. There is less sustained effort, but more frequent flashes of inspiration. This is especially true of Pirandello. In his longer novels there are many prolix passages which fatigue even the most hardened Pirandellian. In his short stories, on the other hand, Pirandello is rarely prolix, and he has a variety of methods of treatment worthy of Guy de Maupassant. But it is only the outer technique that resembles the Parisian writer : whereas Maupassant the malicious and sarcastic novelist deserves, according to Croce, the name of ingenuous poet, Pirandello must not be considered thus. The adjective " ingenuous " is the antithesis to his self-conscious art. Maupassant suffers and rejoices with his characters—he is all sensibility. Pirandello rarely shows any pity openly. The pity we feel for his characters is derived from our sense of pain at the heartlessness of the author. Both authors are profoundly pessimistic and a-religious. God is absent from both, and we have a sense of desolation and sadness. Guy de Maupassant watches the sad destiny of humanity with pity and with composed serenity ; Pirandello is never serene, because he suffers ceaselessly in himself. He is more egotistical than Maupassant and thinks for ever of his own woes, not of those of his characters. Every short story of Pirandello is, as it were, a myth in the Platonic sense, to explain his subjective philosophy. And this philosophy is the philosophy of the individual, because Pirandello, like most of the moderns, would deny that there is a real world of things and persons, existing by itself outside the spirit which knows it. Like Maupassant, Pirandello would refuse to be called a realist, saying that " the great artists are those who display to other men their illusion," but he would go farther in his statement. For him the world is only a dream, a mirage, a phenomenon, an image created by our spirit. There are no such things as fixed characters, for life is ever changing, ever ebbing and flowing. Thus we find it very difficult to seize hold of these characters : they often resemble those modernist pictures wherein the painter has tried to paint the subjects in motion. It is for this reason that Pirandello is a symbol of all our present age : his fantastic stories are symbols of the struggle that goes on ceaselessly in all the minds of modern men. There is no dolorous serenity in his work, because the mind of to-day cannot rest : there are few men of flesh and bone in his novels, because flesh and bone are of no account. The world of Pirandello resembles that of Lucretius : shimmering myriads of atoms that combine by chance with one another and produce now a tree, now a man, now a beast—all according to the rules of chance.

Pirandello has been unceasing in his production of short stories ever since the first years of the present century. In these stories we can see his evolution as an artist. In the earlier collection, such as *Quand'ero matto* (1902), *Bianche e Nere* (1904), *Erma Bifronte* (1906), *La Vita Nuda* and *Terzetti*, many of these stories are, as we have seen, Sicilian. They are in many cases simple and unaffected in style and purged of rhetoric, as if he had attempted to cultivate the short rhythmic style of Maupassant. Gradually then we notice a tendency to prolixity and rhetoric—towards dialogue which announced the future dramatist. In many of the later volumes of stories, such as *Berecche e la guerra* (1919) and *Il carnevale dei Morti* (1919), the story is the merest excuse for long pieces of tortuous sophistry. The early editions of the Pirandellian *novelle* are difficult to obtain, and it is very fortunate that Bemporad the Florentine publisher undertook the task of issuing a complete collection under the title of *Novelle per un anno*, or a " Stories for Every Day in the Year."

Death and the Maiden

First of all let us consider some stories in the earlier editions which might seem to reappear again and again with slight variations through the author's entire production. One of his favourite plots for his short stories is to show how " the best-laid plans of mice and men gang aft agley." In *La Vita Nuda* (Life in its Nakedness), a story which has given its name to a volume, a young girl whose fiancé on the eve of the wedding has died suddenly, visits a sculptor to order a memorial in honour of the dead man. Stricken with grief, her one thought is to symbolize eternally her sorrows by representing Life in the form of a young girl resigning herself to the embraces of Death, represented as a skeleton holding out the bridal ring. At first, under the influence of sorrow, the lady insists, contrary to the wishes of the sculptor, that the figure of Life should be clothed, but later on, when she falls in love with the sculptor's friend and her recollection of the dead fiancé has begun to fade, she insists that Life should be shown in its symbolic nakedness resisting the contact of Death.

On other occasions Pirandello takes the opposite course, and makes his characters lament over the past that will never return. In *Prima Notte* (from the first volume of *Novelle per un Anno*), he describes the marriage between Lisi Chirico and Marastella, village folk of Sicily. Lisi was a widower, and Marastella had been in love with a youth who perished in a shipwreck. The bridal couple spend their first night in the graveyard ; she weeps over the tomb of her lost love, he calls on his dead wife by name : " The moon gazed from heaven down on the little graveyard in the uplands. She alone on that fragrant April night saw these two black shadows on the yellow little path near two tombs. Don Lisi, bending over the grave of his first wife, sobbed : ' Nunzia, Nunzia, do you hear me ? ' "

Such a story, in spite of the morbid and rather unnatural thesis it develops, is a good illustration of Pirandello's power. More than most modern authors he is able to convey to his readers a haunting sensation of sadness that does not leave us even when we have laid aside the book. Lisi Chirico and Marastella are not normal human beings : they are too neurotic, too highly strung for country folk ; but so subtly does the author paint the background that they stand out in bold relief. And this skill of the author in drawing his background does not appear by direct touches, after the manner of a Thomas Hardy. Except for the last few lines which we have quoted there is no pictorial description. We infer the setting of the story from the dialogue bandied about by the characters. Pirandello's skill in producing the atmosphere he requires for his story or drama recalls the methods adopted by Jacinto Benavente, another master of the indirect description. As in the case of Benavente, too, if we probe deeply the mind of our Pirandello, we reach sentimentality—a modern sentimentality which hides away from the light of day and erects a structure of irony and cynicism as a barrier to protect its sensitiveness. The last story we treated showed traces of the sentimental, but perhaps the most characteristic example occurs in the story, " Il lume dell' altra casa," from the collection *Terzetti*. Tullio Butti, the hero, like eighty per cent of the Pirandello heroes, is a queer, grotesque fellow. It is a good thing that the world of Pirandello is the stuff of dreams : what a miserable state real life would be if all men were like Mattia Pascal or Tullio Butti ! Tullio Butti seemed to have a feeling of rancour against life. Nobody was ever able to make him take any interest in anything or relax his sullen, introspective gaze. Even his talkative landlady and her daughter were unable to humanize him. From the window of his room Tullio could see into the house at the opposite side of the street. In the evening, looking out at the windows of the house, he saw a family sitting round the dinner-table, and at the head sat the father and mother. The children were waiting in eager impatience for their food to be served. All were laughing gaily, and the mother and father laughed too. Every evening Tullio sat in darkness and gazed at the lighted window opposite, and it became his one joy in life. But the inquisitive daughter of his landlady, noticing that he used to remain hours in his room without a light, did a very excusable thing under the circumstances : she looked through the keyhole and saw Tullio standing gazing at the lit-up window. And forthwith she rushed off in hot haste to her mother to relate that he was in love with Margherita Masci, the lady opposite. Soon afterwards Tullio saw with surprise his own landlady enter the room opposite when the husband was not there and talk to the lady. The same evening, as a result of that conversation, the lady came to the window and whispered across to him good night. From that day onwards Tullio did not wait eagerly in his room for the illumination of the window opposite : nay, he waited impatiently until that light should be extinguished. With terrible suddenness the passion of love raged in the heart of that man who had been for so long a stranger to life. He left his lodgings, and on the same day as he left, the tidings came that the lady opposite had abandoned her husband and three children. Tullio's room remained empty for some months, but one evening he returned bringing the lady with him. She begged for leave to stand at the window and look across at the other house, where sat the sad father surrounded by the three downcast children. In this tale there is a warmth of sentiment that is lacking in many of the stories, but even here there is the sting characteristic of Pirandello. The tragedy arises, as usual, from the meddling curiosity and gossip of people who are not concerned. It is the talkative landlady who lights the fatal fuse. The moral is the same as in countless modern plays where evil gossip breaks up the peace of families.

The same tender sadness appears in " La Camera in Attesa " (contained in the collection *E Domani Lunedì*). Three sisters and their widowed mother have been awaiting for some years the return of the brother and son, Cesarino, who went off to Tripoli on a military campaign. For fourteen months they have had no news of him, and as a result of repeated inquiry it has been ascertained that Cesarino has not been found among the dead or the wounded or the prisoners. Ever awaiting his return, the four women have kept his room ready for him. Every morning the water in the bottle is changed, the bed is remade, the nightshirt is unfolded, and once a week the old clock is wound up again. Everything is in order for his coming. Nothing shows the time that has elapsed except perhaps the candle, which in weary waiting has grown yellow, for the sisters do not change it as they do the water in the bottle. At first all the neighbours were greatly moved by this case, but little by little their pity cooled and changed to irritation, even in some a certain sense of indignation for what they called play-acting. But the neighbours forget that life only consists in the reality that we give to it. Thus the life that Cesarino continues to have for his mother and sisters may be sufficient for them, owing to the reality of the acts they perform for him here in the room which awaits him, just as it was when he left. The reality of Cesarino's existence remains unalterable in this room of his and in the heart and mind of his mother and sisters, who outside this reality have no other. Time is fixed immutable were it not for Claretta, the betrothed of Cesarino. The thought of her makes the four women note the passing time. In the first days she used to visit them daily, but gradually, as time dragged on, her visits became rarer.

The old mother, who counts the days that elapse between each visit, is surprised that whereas the departure of Cesarino seems only yesterday, so much time passes for Claretta. The culminating point of the tragedy arrives when the news is brought that Claretta is getting married. The mother lies dying ; the three daughters look at her with sad envy. She will soon be able to go and see if he is over there ; she will be relieved of the anxiety of that long wait : she will reach certainty, but she will not be able to return and tell them. The mother, though she knows for certain that she will find her Cesarino over there, feels a great pity for her daughters, who will remain alone and have such need to believe that he is still alive and will return soon. And thus with her last breath she whispers to them : " You will tell him that I have waited so long." And on that night in the silent house the room is left untouched, the water is not changed, the date on the calendar marks the previous day. " The illusion of life in that room has ceased for one day and it seems for ever." Only the clock continues to speak of time in that endless waiting.

Again and again the same theme recurs in the *novelle* in different forms. " What makes life is the reality which you give to it." Thus the life that Cesarino Mochi's mother and his three sisters live in that room of his is sufficient for them. If you have not seen your son for some years, he will seem different to you when he returns. Not so Cesarino ; his reality remains unchangeable there in his room that is set in expectation of his coming. In the concluding story of the ninth volume of *Novelle per un Anno*, entitled " I Pensionati della Memoria " (The Pensioners of Memory), Pirandello treats the same idea, but takes it up where the former story left off. Supposing even that the mother and sisters had been present at the death of Cesarino and had watched his coffin being lowered into the grave, would they not feel that he had departed for ever, never to return ? But no, gentlemen, Pirandello tells us that Cesarino's mother and sisters and many of us would find that the dead man comes back behind us to our homes after the funeral. He pretends to be dead within his coffin, but, as far as all of us are concerned, he is not dead. He is here with me just as much as you are, except that he is disillusioned. "His reality has vanished, but which one ? Was it the reality that he gave to himself ? What could I know of his reality—what do you know about it ? I know what I gave to him from my own point of view. His illusion is mine." And yet those people, though I know that they are dead, come back with me to my house. They have not got a reality of their own, mark you ; they cannot go where they please, for reality never exists by itself. Their reality now depends on me, and so they must perforce come with me : they are the poor pensioners of my memory. Most people, when friends or relations die, weep for them and remember this or that trait in their character which makes the feeling of bereavement seem greater. But all this feeling of bereavement, this sorrow, is for a reality which they believe to have vanished with the deceased. They have never reflected on the meaning of this reality. Everything for them consists in the existence or in the non-existence of a body. It would be quite enough consolation for these people if we made them believe that the deceased is here no more in bodily form, not because his body is buried in the earth, but because he has gone off on a journey and one day he will return from that journey. This will be their consolation. The real reason why we all weep over our dead friend is because he cannot make his presence a reality to us. His eyes are closed, his hands are stiff and cold : he does not hear or perceive us, and it is this insensibility that plunges us in sorrow. Owing to his death our one

The Little Fan

comfort has departed—the reciprocity of illusion. If he had only gone off on a journey, we could live on in hope like Cesarino's sisters, saying to ourselves : "He thinks of me over there and thus I live for him."

In the stories we have considered there are traces of a kindlier Pirandello. Sometimes he produces a deep emotional effect on his reader when he ceases to try to solve a problem or work out a knotted intrigue. In *Il Ventaglino* (The Little Fan)[1] we see a little scene in a public park in Rome on a hot and dusty afternoon in August. So subtle is the author's method of description in this story that we visualize the scene. The park is dusty and the yellow houses nearby are forlorn and desolate ; men are slumbering in the sultry atmosphere. On one seat a thin little old man with a yellow handkerchief on his head is reading a paper ; nearby a workman out of work sleeps with his head leaning on his arms. On the other side an old woman listens to the sad tale of a woman nearby, and then departs after giving her a piece of bread. Then there is a red-haired girl who walks up and down impatiently : she is evidently waiting for somebody. All these people Pirandello describes for us impressionistically. Amongst them appears poor Tuta with her baby in her arms. Tuta is alone in the world with her baby. She has but a penny in her pocket and the child is famished. "Not a single person would believe that she was in such hopeless want. She could hardly believe it herself. But it had come to that. She had entered that park to find a shady spot and had loitered there for the past two hours : she could remain on until evening, but then . . . where was she to spend the night with that child in arms ? And next day ? And the day after that ? . . . Ah, Nino, there is nothing for it but the river for both of us." Then Tuta watches mechanically the people

[1] *Novelle per un Anno*, Vol. I.

crowding into the park in the cool of the evening : children skipping, nurses carrying babies, governesses, soldiers in uniform. Something seemed to change her line of thought. She looked up at the people and smiled. She unbuttoned the neck of her coat and uncovered a little of her white neck. Just then an old man passed by selling paper fans. With her last penny she bought one. Then " opening still more of her blouse and starting to fan slowly her uncovered breast she laughed and began to look invitingly and provokingly at the soldiers who were passing by."

Such a story shows us Pirandello at his best, because in it he avoids any criticism of his characters. He limits himself to exposing objectively the results of his observations. In the majority of the stories the author tries to justify himself, and he insists on criticizing and interpreting his characters to us. In such exquisite stories as *Il Lume dell' Altra Casa, La Camera in Attesa* or *Il Ventaglino*, the characters and the atmosphere they create round themselves tell us all the inferences to be drawn. Pirandello tells us more about his characters than any preceding novelist : he allows them to blurt out all the thoughts that are passing through their minds. One of the reasons why nearly all his characters are abnormal is because he will not content himself with exposing their exterior, obvious personality, but tries to reach even their subconscious thoughts and actions. Pirandello never stops short at the objective observation of character : irresistibly he is driven on to interpret and comment critically upon the children of his imagination. And this critical and interpretative attitude of mind often chills the inspiration and kills the character. When Pirandello the critic and dilettante metaphysician appears on the scene, Poetry in fright takes to her heels and flees away. As we showed in the introductory chapter to this book, the whole basis of Futurism consists in pitiless

criticism of the past. The Futurists believe that
" Passéisme " (one of Marinetti's coined words) is
synonymous with all that is evil, because its devotees in
their thought and art are incapable of understanding
the essence of modern life. It is therefore not surprising
that Pirandello's works should be full of the close
reasoning and criticism of the modern mind, especially
as he himself is a vacillating Futurist—one who belongs
to the older generation and yet has found a place at the
table of the present-day youths.

Sometimes Pirandello's stories are feasts of dialectic
and there is no attempt at weaving a story. They are,
as it were, dialogues between the author and himself
about metaphysical problems, and no abnormality is
too exaggerated to illustrate his point. We find a woman
of forty years of age who allowed herself to be seduced
by a peasant youth of nineteen and became *enceinte*.
Then after marrying him to calm the scandal, she
commits suicide rather than allow him to possess her
again.[1] In another story a youth[2] who is in Holy Orders
loses his faith and goes back to his country village, to
become the butt for the ridicule of all. But he sees the
folly of everything and minds not their jeering insults.
His sensitive mind becomes pantheistic and turns to all
the manifestations of Nature, especially those plants and
flowers that bloom for but one short day. The more
fragile and humble those plants or insects, the more they
excited his compassion and moved him to tears. Sometimes it was an ant or a fly or even a blade of grass. All
these tiny things set off the enormous vacuity of the
universe, the unknown. For a month he had been
watching intently a blade of new grass growing between
two stones in a ruined chapel. Every day he went to
see it and protect it from marauding goats and sheep.

[1] *Novelle per un Anno,* Vol. I. Scialle Nero.
[2] *Nov. per un anno.* Vol. III. Canta L'Epistola.

One day he saw a young lady in the chapel, and distractedly she picked the blade of grass and put it in her mouth. Then the youth felt irresistibly impelled to hurl the epithet " stupid " at her. After hearing about this insult, her fiancé challenged the youth to a duel and wounded him fatally. When the priest was hearing the poor boy's confession at the point of death, he asked him why he had acted thus. He replied gently, " Father, for a blade of grass." And all thought that he was continuing still to rave. In other stories Pirandello draws on all his fund of grotesqueness in order to produce his " creepy " effect : peasants filled with insane hatred against rich neighbours who have lately arrived, or else a man who feels such loathing for his wife because of her infidelity that he locks her in the upper part of the house while below he brings in drunken prostitutes to sleep with him. In those stories life seems to be a hideous nightmare and everything is out of focus. Every character suffers from some fixation to the point of madness. The irony of Pirandello disappears, and all that we see is one of those grinning masks which frighten children. Such stories often produce a terrifying effect on readers, because these abnormal beings have a complete logic of their own—the logic of the madman. More than any writer of to-day Pirandello is able to convey to us the emotion of horror. Let us quote one story called " E Due " from the first volume of *Novelle per un Anno*. A young man one evening, while walking on the outskirts of the city near the bridge over the river, sees a man climb on to the parapet, lay down his hat there, and then cast himself into the river. Diego hears the terrible splash in the water beneath—then not a sound— absolute silence on all sides. And yet the man was drowning there beneath him. Why did he not move or shout for help ? It was too late. Pirandello in masterly manner suggests the surroundings as they appeared to the horror-struck youth. The houses opposite in darkness, in contrast to the lights of the city : in the silence not a sound except far off the chirrup of crickets, and beneath him he heard the gurgling of the dark waters of the river. And that hat—the hat which the unfortunate man had left on the parapet—it fascinates us as it fascinated Diego : he cannot drive it from his thoughts. Later on we find him on the parapet again. He took off his hat and placed it in the same place as the other had been : " He went to the far side of the lamp to see what his hat looked like on the parapet, under the light of the lamp like the other. He stood for a few moments, leaning over the parapet and looking at it, as if he himself was not there any more. Then suddenly he gave a grim laugh ; he saw himself stuck up there like a cat behind the lamp, and his hat was the mouse. . . . Away, away with all this tomfoolery ! He climbed over the parapet : he felt his hair stand on end—his hands quivered as they clung tightly on to the ledge. Then he loosened his grip and threw himself into the void." In such a story Pirandello shows qualities of subtle analysis and description which rival Maupassant ; it is only at the end, when the character watches itself act, that we see the cloven hoof of the Pirandellian. At other times our author touches the chord of Anatole France and leads us into a garden of Epicurus. The last *novella*, " All Uscita " (At the Gate), of the collection *E Domani, Lunedi* will be a fitting conclusion to our examination of Pirandello's short stories. We are at the gate leading from a cemetery, and we meet the phantoms of the Fat Man and the Philosopher who have recently died. The Philosopher, true to his vocation, starts immediately to weave his sophistries for the benefit of his grosser friend. He will continue for ever in the next world to reason and reason, just as the Fat Man will continue to wear his vesture of adipose tissue. The latter, however, will not be satisfied to be fat : he sees still the little garden of his house in the sunlight, the little pond in the shade with the goldfish swimming about ; he smells the fresh perfume of the new leaves and then the red and yellow roses, the geraniums and the carnations. All the philosophy in the world will not prevent the nightingale from singing or these roses from blooming. All these joys made this Fat Man accept the sorrows and the worries in his past life. They enabled him to accept with resignation the caprices of his wife, her infidelities that were legion. Life for him was possible because he had no illusions. He had even been relieved to hear that his wife had a lover, because he knew that all her hatred of him would be transferred to her lover. But that lover is not a fat man : he is jealous, and in one of his fits he will kill his mistress. And lo, she appears, a bloodstained phantom, running along as though pursued by her mad lover. All these phantoms relate their experiences, their desires which have never been satisfied. And death does not solve the riddle, because it is nothing but total disillusion. Thus the end is the same as in Anatole France's story " In the Elysian Fields "[1] when the shades, gathered together in a field of asphodel, converse about death as if they knew nothing of it and were as ignorant of human destinies as when they were still on earth. " It is no doubt," as the smiling cynic Menippus said, " because they still remain human and mortal in some degree. When they shall have entered into immortality, they will not speak or think any more. They will be like the gods." But the philosopher Pirandello will not become a god : he will be left behind at the gate to continue his reasoning for all eternity.

[1] A. France, *The Garden of Epicurus*, op. cit.

V

Pirandello: Dramatist

IT WAS THE WAR THAT REVEALED Pirandello's genius as
a dramatist. Most celebrated men of the theatre have
loitered round the stage-doors of their local play-house
at an early age : Goldoni related how as a child he
had constructed toy stages, and how later on he had
run away from school to join a company of strolling
players. How many moderns have not followed the
Venetian writer's example and felt themselves irresistibly drawn towards drama ? Pirandello in 1912 did
produce a small play in one act entitled *La Morsa*
(The Vise), a powerful study of a strong, pitiless man
who forces his wife to commit suicide when he discovers
her guilt. Another one of his one-act sketches, *Lumie
di Sicilia* (Limes of Sicily), came out in the year preceding the War. In a former chapter we have already
shown how the tortured family life of Pirandello reflected
itself in his novels and short stories. The Great War
added fuel to his pessimism, for it showed up the irrational
cruelty of life. His two sons, Stefano and Fausto, volun-
teered for military service, and the former was taken
prisoner by the Austrians. Lietta, his daughter, as a
result of the ceaseless, nagging persecution of her distraught mother, tried to commit suicide. In the midst
of all his troubles Pirandello sought relief in writing plays.
The celebrated Sicilian actor, Angelo Musco, eager to
discover comedies with which he could cheer up the

war-time audiences, persuaded Pirandello to write him a play. As a result, the latter began to dash off one play after another in rapid sequence. According to Nardelli, such was his proficiency that he actually wrote nine plays in one year. He was as rapid a worker as Goldoni, the author of fifteen plays in one year, for he wrote *Pensaci Giacomino* " in three and *Così È* (*se vi pare*) in six days.

Pirandello the seasoned novelist, at first found the theatre a place of many pitfalls. A modern novelist prefers in his work to adopt the slipshod, sprawling scheme *à la Cervantes* or *à la Sterne*, and so, when he writes for the stage, he is unable to raise a harmonious structure. As Lowell said in one of his lectures on the " Old English Dramatists " : " In a play the structure should be organic, with a necessary and harmonious connection and relation of parts, and not merely mechanical with an arbitrary or haphazard joining of one part to another." It is this constructive talent that so many novelists lack : they are able to create characters who reveal themselves in certain situations, and they can also plumb the depths of psychological analysis, but, as Brander Mathews would say : " They are devoid of the engineering draughtsmanship which plans the steel-frame, four square to all the winds that blow."

If we examine carefully the novels of Pirandello and his countless short stories, we reach the conviction that in him right from the outset there slumbered a dramatist. The style, the synthetic method of the short stories, is dramatic : the nervous, disjointed dialogue, reflecting not only a man's ideas, but also his reticences and reservations, is essentially dramatic in the modern sense. Pirandello's style, with its complexities, is highly suggestive, for he is never so much occupied with direct meaning as with inferences to be drawn. The reader is taken into his confidence and compelled to read between the lines if he would penetrate into the mystery of the drama.

It was not surprising that he should have turned his
thoughts to drama—the modern drama of suggestion
which Bracco had initiated so brilliantly in Italy with
Piccolo Santo (1908)—in order that his ideas might find
plastic representation.   For it was much easier to express
on the modern stage the fundamental antithesis of his
art between life which is ever in a state of flux and the
constructions by which men try to stop that ceaseless
ebb.   The new theatre of Pirandello, however, was a
different thing entirely to the old stage of which Anatole
France could use the following words : " The stage puts
everything before the eyes and dispenses with any help
from the imagination.   This is why it satisfies the great
majority, and likewise why it does not appeal very
strongly to pensive, meditative minds.   Such persons
appreciate a situation, a thought, only for the sake of
the amplifications it suggests to them, the melodious
echo it awakens in their own minds.   Their fancies are
unexercised in a theatre ; the play gives them only a
passive pleasure, to which they prefer the active one of
reading."[1]   This criticism of the theatre is entirely
incorrect with regard to Pirandello's stage, which is
eminently for the pensive and meditative, because the
plots are not so much mere *tranches de vie*, or tales of
blood and passion, as the plastic interpretation of some
profound thought.   The dramatist develops his often
banal outer plot in detail only so that the public may see
beyond it into its amplifications and awaken the echo
in their minds.   In addition, the plays of our author,
with their power of stimulating active reflection, are the
very antithesis to the passive art that Anatole France
talks about.   And Pirandello we might compare to
Socrates, the " Scurra Atticus," as he was called, who,
instead of writing out his lessons to pupils, preferred to

[1] A. France, *Garden of Epicurus,* Translated by A. Allinson,
p. 42.

give them dramatically according to dialogue. It was only in 1912-13 that he produced a drama. The reason, according to the eminent critic, G. A. Borgese, is to be found in Pirandello's timidity and reticence, characteristic of the scholar. He did not dare to present himself before the public with novelties which were bound to seem eccentric. It was repugnant to this sensitive, refined man to bring forth, even unconsciously, a dramatic technique so similar to the fantastic compositions of the futurist painters and sculptors.[1]

Already, in *Il Fu Mattia Pascal*, we can see that the true vocation of the author was drama. The style naturally expresses itself in abrupt, incisive dialogue ; the working up to the climaxes of the situations is done in accordance with dramatic notions. Pirandello, in *Il Fu Mattia Pascal*, showed that his main preoccupation was the expression of multiple personality—a preoccupation that has busied all the modern dramatists from G. B. Shaw to François de Curel.

I. TRIUMPH OF THE IRRATIONAL

Before we consider analytically the plots of the principal Pirandello plays, let us quote a remark of Henry James on the drama which exactly fits our author : " An acted play is a novel intensified ; it realizes what the novel suggests, and by paying a liberal tribute to the senses, anticipates your possible complaint that your entertainment is of the meagre sort styled intellectual." Pirandello often dramatizes his *novelle*, as, for instance, *Pensaci Giacomino* (Think of it, Giacomino), that most irrational story where old Professor Toti succeeds in making us admit that his most unconventional conduct was for the best. In the play Pirandello makes the

[1] G. A. Borgese, *Tempo di Edificare,* Essay on " Pirandello," p. 229. Milano, 1923.

old professor's triumph still more certain than in the *novelle*, for instead of ending with his persuasive speech to Giacomino, the author adds a scene showing the departure of the two with the child, while the village priest and the relations look on in dismay.

In comparing the play with the *novella* it is easy to see how naturally dramatic Pirandello is. In many places—notably the climaxes—the words of the short story remain practically unchanged in the play. The jerky, exclamatory style that sometimes seems singularly unattractive in the *novella* becomes an excellent medium for dramatic expression. In the play Pirandello has accentuated the Sicilian characteristics of the types, and whereas the *novella* plunges into *medias res* at once, the first act of the play gives an exceedingly subtle description of the surroundings of Professor Toti's school, and incidentally of his character. Cinquemani *bidello*, his wife Marianna, are observed with great sense of humour. In the second act the intriguing women and the priest show up admirably the petty gossip and scandal of a country town. The whole play is another example of Pirandello's satire against the gossip of bourgeois society. As in many of the stories which we have examined, the crisis arises owing to the ill-natured gossip of neighbours who do not understand the motives at work. And that gossip, which leaves Professor Toti imperturbable, tortures the heart and soul of the weak personalities Lillina and Giacomino. All those characters are the conventional members of the Sicilian upper and lower bourgeoisie, whom we have met so often in the works of Capuana, Verga, Martoglio, but they are mere puppets, all of whom move at the instance of a central figure who pulls their wires. Pirandello in nearly all his plays adopts this method of construction, a method which seems to be a derivation of the Naturalist " mouthpiece character " that we find so often in authors like Brieux. But

Pirandello goes further than any of his predecessors, because he is primarily interested in the multiple personality of man, and so he gives his central character a double personality—first of all a conventional personality due to his station in society ; then another, a real personality, due to his primitive nature, shorn of all conventions. From the perpetual contrast between the parts of this double personality, the author causes his sarcastic, but dramatic humour to rise. Thus Professor Toti has a double personality which is complex. First of all, he is an old secondary-school teacher who has taught in the same small town for years and years. He is as irremediably a member of the caste of schoolmasters as Doctor Graziano in the " 'Commedia dell' arte " with his mask was a member of the caste of pedants. But Professor Toti, beneath his outer personality has another far more vigorous personality that will not be kept in subjection. The ceaseless antithesis between these two personalities produces this play, which is a true grotesque in the way that it turns everything upside down. No more pungent example of the logic of the irrational could be found than this plot in which a husband forces the lover of his wife to return to her. It is characteristic of the *teatro grottesco*, which was initiated in the same year (1916) when Chiarelli produced his brilliant play *La Maschera e il Volto*. Chiarelli's play is based on a similar irrational idea.

In 1917 Pirandello produced another play dealing with Sicilian life and character, *Il Berretto a Sonagli* (Cap and Bells). The scene takes place at a little town in the interior of Sicily. The intrigue starts owing to the machinations of a dread woman called " La Saracena "—a modern " Celestina," who spends her days purveying evil rumours and breaking up well-ordered families. On this occasion her machinations are directed against the Fiorica household, which is composed of Beatrice Fiorica and her husband. Beatrice, who is possessed of an excitable, hysterical nature, believes La Saracena when the latter tells her that her husband is carrying on an intrigue with the wife of his clerk Ciampa, and has given her many jewels. In a fury of jealousy she determines to expose the two lovers, cost what it may, and with this purpose in view she resolves to send Ciampa on a pretext away to Palermo. Ciampa, before starting off on his journey, asks Beatrice to look after his wife while he is away. " With a wife, sardines and anchovies," he says, " it is better to keep the sardines and anchovies in oil and the wife under lock and key." Ciampa wants to be respected in the eyes of the world, and so, by giving the keys of his wife's rooms into Beatrice's keeping, he feels certain that her reputation will be protected.

In Act II Beatrice's revenge comes to fruition. Guessing that her husband on his return would call at Ciampa's house to see his mistress, she denounces him to the police and gives them the keys of the house which Ciampa had given her, in order that the two may be caught *in flagrante delicto*. But the result of her jealous vengeance recoils on herself. Cavalier Fiorica is arrested and the whole affair becomes the dainty morsel of the gossiping town. The chief one to suffer will be Beatrice herself, for, as her mother says, she will have to leave her husband's house and go home to her mother and remain shut up, as all eyes will be on her. " Free you call yourself—you have no status : you are neither a maiden, nor a widow, nor a wife." In the midst of all this commotion arrives Ciampa, back from the journey which he had undertaken for Beatrice. The arrival of Ciampa changes the play, which up to this had been farcical, into grim drama with very little of the laughing spirit about it. Ciampa, with his grotesque appearance, his long, tousled hair, his big spectacles, the clerk's pen in his ear, had been a comic Pulcinella, but now he becomes tragic. To Pirandello's mind these creatures of the world, with their mask which they wear unconsciously, are comic, but when their fellow-men brutally tear off that mask, the poor Pulcinella exhibits his naked soul to our sorrowful gaze. "Your sister," he says to Beatrice's brother, Fifi La Bella, "has taken my puppet and thrown it on the ground and then kicked it thus." (The throws his hat on the ground and tramples on it.) He goes on to say that he had been aware long since that his wife was unfaithful to him : how could it be otherwise, when he was a grotesquely ugly man, no longer young, and she was a beautiful and vigorous young woman ? But with great difficulty he had constructed his life as a puppet, and insisted on having that puppet respected. Then, unfortunately, the world, with its jealousies, its curiosities, had cast down that puppet. What course is left open to him ? Must he go back and kill his wife in revenge for her infidelity, and thus win the approbation of the world, like Savina's husband in *The Mask and the Face* of Chiarelli ? But there is another easier way of settling the whole business. Everyone agrees that Beatrice caused the trouble owing to her insane jealousy. The police magistrate tells them that the case will not be brought, owing to lack of evidence. Then Ciampa sees that the one solution for everyone is to make Beatrice out to be mad and to send her for three months to an asylum. In this way society will be satisfied and all will be well. Beatrice owes reparation to her husband in front of society, and if it is said that she was mad, there will be no more gossip, and Ciampa himself will have nothing more to vindicate. As for Beatrice herself, she will get off lightly with three months in a private asylum.

CIAMPA.

" It is for your good, lady. We all know here that you are mad. Now it is for the whole neighbourhood to know it. There is no need to get alarmed, for it is easy to act the madwoman : I shall teach you how it is done. It is enough for you to shout out openly the truth in front of all. Nobody will believe and all will take you for mad."

The bystanders, including Beatrice's mother, her brother and the magistrate, see the force of Ciampa's arguments—all except Beatrice herself, who becomes hysterical with impotent rage and is carried out shrieking while Ciampa remains alone on the stage, grinning grotesquely as the curtain descends on the play.

In Ciampa's words the whole point of the play is that we should stick firmly on our heads the madcap with its jingling bells, and go down into the public places and spit the truth at the faces of the people. Man would be able to live not a hundred but two hundred years were it not for the bitter morsels, the injustice, the infamy which ruin the stomach. If we could only open the safety-valve of madness, what relief we could get !

The character of Ciampa is a mouthpiece character like Professor Toti. In both cases society has torn the mask which had been constructed with great pains, and in both cases irrational logic saves the situation. As Ciampa says, " There is no madder man in the world than he who believes that he is right," and the author takes infinite delight in turning upside down all the accepted notions of right that have ruled society up to this. His extraordinary dramatic skill consists in the way in which he draws the sympathy of the audience for characters who are entirely devoid of moral principles as the world understands them. Professor Toti in real life would be ostracized by everyone just as he is in the play, and, however he tried, he would not succeed in making us accept his irrational logic ; but the stage with its fantasy puts us in a much more sensitive frame of mind and extracts sentimental tears from even the most unimaginative among us. Professor Toti enters our hearts and triumphs ; Ciampa, grotesque Pulcinella as he is, ends by touching a sensitive chord within us, when he tries to gather up the broken fragments of his mask. The procedure is just the same as in *Mattia Pascal* ; the author starts by playing a satiric tune, then he sentimentalizes, and when we begin to drop soft tears, the cloven hoof suddenly appears again and the play turns out to be a grotesque comedy. In some points *Il Berretto a Sonagli*, with its central figure Ciampa, recalls *Los Intereses Creados* (The Bonds of Interest) by Benavente (1907), a play that deserves to be called one of the forerunners of the Italian *teatro grottesco*. In that play Crispîn the knave from Picardy makes a fortune for his master and himself by weaving bonds of interest with the chief men of the city, so that it will be to their profit not to ruin, but to exalt them both. The final scene resembles this play, for Crispîn is faced by society just as Ciampa is, and he succeeds in proving logically to the satisfaction of all that the only solution is to accept the irrational. Benavente brings on the stage the ancient puppets of the " Commedia dell' Arte," but he makes them appear human, and at times there descends a fine thread woven of sun- and moon-light, which makes human beings, just as those puppets, seem divine. Pirandello makes those characters from Sicilian everyday life seem puppets. Ciampa in the earlier part of the play is true to life, and with his grotesque appearance he lives. Afterwards, when he becomes a mouthpiece for the author's logic, he loses his flesh and blood.

In the plays we have considered Pirandello has drawn

all the characters from the life of his own island, and in spite of his tendencies towards solving problems by reason, they remain Sicilians, whose native character-istics have been slightly exaggerated by the author for the purpose of his *rire macabre*. We notice the gradual evolution in the author from the sad romantic little play, *Lumîe di Sicilia*, with which he initiated his dramatic career, to the profoundly satirical play *Il Berretto di Sonagli*, where we see the Sicilian in Pirandello gradu-ally begin to fade away before the European dramatist who is mainly occupied in presenting intellectual paradoxes.

Pirandello, in spite of his bitter pessimism, in spite of that little demon of humour within him, could express the poetry of Sicily and also its realism. But whereas Verga had been able to express the soul of the peasant attached to the soil, Pirandello as time went on preferred to take for his theme the lives of the bourgeoisie in towns like Girgenti or Catania ; the characters are not rooted in Sicily, but are true to any region of Italy. The author in abandoning his Sicilian types tries more and more to evolve drama that will satisfy his desire for feasts of dialectic ; the tendency towards abstract theories tested by experiment on puppets becomes more apparent. The heroes and heroines of Pirandello's plays are all exactly alike in that they worship iron logic. They are puppets who accept no compromise with their way of thinking and are ready to face any obstacles in their path. As an Italian critic has pointed out, there is a close similarity between their attitude towards life and that of the Ibsen heroes.[1] Brand, Rosmer, Rebecca West, Nora Stockmann are symbols of man's struggles towards the complete expression of his individual person-ality. True to their own logic, they thrust aside the

[1] *Nuova Antologia*, 1st Fenruary, 1921, article on " Pirandello," by S. A. Chimeng.

conventions of the world and attempt to scale the mountain snows where Brand has set his church. But Ibsen, as Farinelli has pointed out, produced the tragedy of his heroes by this very struggle.[1] Brand and his fellows cannot shut their eyes to humanity around them. They feel that man must struggle on to achieve the triumph of his own individuality, but this triumph is a defeat ; they know that they are vowed to destruction, not only in themselves, but also in their ideals. With that consciousness of death and extinction in their souls, they struggle on against hopeless odds, and their position is like that of a little boat tossed on the furious billows of the ocean which sooner or later must engulf it. The image of a strong man caught in the meshes of a net from which he tries vainly to extricate himself, which has been applied to Shakespeare's tragedies, is also true of Ibsen's dramas. With profound feelings of sadness we watch those buskined heroes struggle manfully, only to be broken on the wheel of Destiny, and this struggle produces the feeling of waste which Bradley says is the essence of tragedy. Pirandello, like Ibsen, is passionately attracted by personality and its manifestations, but whereas Ibsen makes the individuality of his characters triumph, Pirandello makes his characters represent the triumph of his own pessimism. They are rarely hurled on to the stage and allowed to struggle there towards individual expression, but are forced to remain for ever as symbols of the author's theories. The attitude of Pirandello the sarcastic humorist does not resemble that of the titanic Northern master, whose stormy nature did not prevent him from weeping for his valkyries ; rather does it resembles lightly the Ibsen of *Wild Duck*, who pessimistically recants his former views.

Pirandello, like Ibsen, would pour contumely on Gregers Werle, for all his modern, individualistic notions,

[1] A. Farinelli, *Ibsen*, Torino, 1922.

and would say : " Let us live on in our illusion ; let
anyone beware of waking us from our dream." Like
Unamuno, he would envy the power possessed by the
child to create a world of fantasy and consider life as a
game, and the lesson which the Spanish philosopher
draws from the life of Don Quixote and Sancho, that
what matters is not what we are, but what we wish to
be, is also preached by the Sicilian. From *Il Fu Mattia
Pascal* to the latest drama of Pirandello the heroes try to
create their own world apart from that of their fellow-
men, and the dramatic conflict arises from the attempt
made by society to destroy their dream castles. And
Pirandello, above the dust of the battle, looks on at the
struggle with his features set in a sarcastic grin. At times
he approaches that serenity which Duhamel says does
not mean indifference to the great happenings of contemporary times, but a lofty way of judging men and
their deeds.

The most complete expression of Pirandello's sceptical
serenity is to be found in *Così E* (*se vi pare*), " Right You
Are (If you think so)," which was presented in 1916.
It is a dramatization of a short story which is contained
in *E Domani, Lunedi*.

II. " WHAT IS TRUTH ? "

The central idea of the play may be summed up in
the words of a critic : " What is truth ?   Truth does not
exist : truth we have in ourselves, we are truth : truth is
the representation that each of us makes of it." This is
the moral which Pirandello has upheld in his parables.
Few plays of our author show more completely the
qualities and defects of the Pirandellian dramatic technique. As critics have shown, Pirandello resembles one
of those amazing acrobats who perform, prodigies of
balancing on the tight-rope and keeps his public in

open-mouthed wonder at his eccentricities. Nobody in the world has the exclusive possession of truth, because there exist so many truths as there are thinking brains to conceive them. Which of the two protagonists is mad ? At one moment we are convinced adherents to the truth as explained by the weak-eyed Signora Frola, but then Signor Ponza, fierce and wild-looking, bounces into the room and drives away our former notions in favour of his version. With wonderful skill Pirandello draws us chasing after him excitedly. It is all like reading some astonishing detective story that spurs our excitement right to the end. For three acts our interest never flags, and yet when we analyse the play we find that there is practically no plot at all, as we can see if we compare the play with the *novella* from which it was derived. The *novella* is a simple little story, lacking all the brilliance of the play. Pirandello exposes the curious case of Signora Frola and Signor Ponza and lays stress on the curiosity of the little town of Valdana—" unlucky town, a magnet for eccentric strangers." But he stops half-way in the story without developing the idea. Signor Ponza never appears to make a climax to the tale, and there is no Laudisi to act as interpreter of the author. In the case of *Pensaci Giacomino*, Pirandello did not have to add much to the general structure of the story in order to make it a play—beyond creating some brilliant secondary dramatic characters. In *Così E* he has had to create nearly everything from the merest sketch, and his method is a model to dramatists. The first act contains all the exposition that we find in the *novella* and concludes with Laudisi's sarcastic words—" So you are looking at one another in blank amazement, eh ? The truth ? Ah ! Ah ! Ah ! " In the second act there is another climax by the introduction of Signora Frola and Signor Ponza, not one after the other, as in act one, but together. Pirandello produces a masterly *coup de scène* by making

Signor Ponza arrive just at the moment when Signora Frola in another room is playing on the piano some music of her daughter. He hears her speak to the ladies round her :—

SIGNORA FROLA.

" Ah ! my poor Lina ! . . . if you only could hear my daughter Lina . . . . how well she plays it ! "

PONZA (nervously).

" Her Lina ! Her Lina ! "

AGAZZI.

" Her daughter, I suppose ? "

PONZA.

" Do you hear what she says ? ' How my Lina plays ! '
(*Again from within.*)

SIGNORA FROLA.

" Oh, no, not now. She doesn't play any more since that happened. That is perhaps what she feels most, poor girl."

One of the most striking points about the construction of this play is the masterly way in which Pirandello shows the gradual crescendo through the three acts of the town gossip. So clever is he at showing this that he communicates the feeling of curiosity to the audience, and it would be difficult to find a Laudisi in the stalls or in the balcony. His method is to create plenty of secondary characters and show objectively their silly little vanities. Tall, stiff officials like Centuri, puffed-up, self-important, suburban women like Amalia Agazzi, conceited, stuck-up modern girls like Dina Agazzi, old and wizened lumps of concentrated curiosity like Signora Cini—all of them contribute to make this one of Pirandello's most attractive plays. And for richness of type and varied psychology Pirandello's characters in this play resemble the grotesque Pulcinellas and Harlequins of Callot engraved in the heyday of the ancient " Commedia dell' Arte."

As in the other plays of Pirandello we have considered, we find the most conflicting notions expressed with perfect logic. Both Ponza and Signora Frola are reason itself in their utterances, for they are convinced of the truth. Pirandello, like Cervantes, constructs his world of illusion to exact proportions, and everything can be explained. Over and above this idea concerning the individual reality, Pirandello had the desire of satirizing fiercely gross, idle curiosity, and this gross curiosity appears in most of his short stories and plays as a central theme. If it were not for the meddling Prefect and citizens, nothing would have disturbed the harmony of these three people's lives, but the curiosity will not die away, and the author's great skill is shown in the way he makes it grow in intensity like a fever.

He develops the pathos of the situation by contrasting the suffering of those poor, defenceless people with the cruel behaviour of society. There is a note of genuine pathos in Signora Frola's words to the Prefect : " Yes, Prefect ! If we are forced to live thus—it does not matter, because we are happy and my daughter is happy, and that is enough for me. Do think of it, for if not, there is nothing left for me except to go away and never see her again even from afar. For pity's sake let them leave us in peace."

The character of Laudisi is the most conspicuous

example in Pirandello's theatre of the mouthpiece character. In other plays such as *Pensaci Giacomino* or *Il Berretto a Sonagli* we noticed such a personage, but in each case it was the hero who was selected and there was a true dramatic reason for his philosophizing. In *Così E* Laudisi is not necessary to the action at all, for we do not meet him in the *novella*. His function resembles that of Jaques in *As You Like It*—a prop for the author's philosophy. Laudisi, in fact, undertakes the duty of the ancient chorus and interprets the play for us. He resembles the Punch and Judy man working Punch and his wife, for Ponza and Signora Frola never seem to be real human beings. But Laudisi does not become a flesh-and-blood character, he arouses no real feeling of interest in us at all, no sympathy, and much of his philosophizing seems extraneous to the play. To the modern epigrammatic dramatist such characters are useful as purveyors of aphorisms : Jacinto Benavente in many of his works makes use of such a character to express his own conceits concerning life in general. As various critics have pointed out, we should not imagine that Pirandello has meant in this play to prove seriously the philosophical principle *esse est percipi*. Nothing could be further removed from his humorous spirit : the play is a satirical joke against those people who consider truth a ready-made object, fixed and immutable. Pirandello, like all the modern philosophers from Kant to Bergson, looked on life as something shifting from second to second in spite of all the efforts of men to arrest the tide and enclose it. This conflict between the victorious forces of life and the form which men construct as a refuge is the subject of many plays of Pirandello, but more especially of *Il Piacere dell' Onestà, Il Giuoco delle Parti, Non è Una Cosa Seria* and *L'Uomo, La Bestia e La Virtù*.

III. " THE MASK AND THE FACE "[1]

In *Il Piacere dell' Onestà* (The Pleasure of Respectability),
Fabio Colli, a dissolute young marquis, has seduced
Agata Renni, a young girl, and made her *enceinte*.
There is no possible means for Fabio to render adequate
justice to the girl, as he is married. He, however, thinks
of a good plan. He has a friend, Angelo Baldovino,
also dissolute and in addition bankrupt, whom he
persuades to marry Agata. Angelo, he feels sure, will
be a *mari complaisant*, and he will be able with greater
security to continue his intrigue with Agata. Angelo
shows himself perfectly willing to agree to his friend's
proposals, for he is in dire distress and wants to break
away from his life of vice and become an honest member
of society. Like so many characters of Sicilian and
Neapolitan drama, Baldovino is a portentous rhetorician
and possessed of an inexhaustible power of splitting logic.
His long sentences and tortuous reasoning recall *Don
Pietro Caruso* of Bracco. The following example gives a
good idea of his character : " You, at any rate, might
ask me why I am doing this for you ? Why ? Well,
mostly owing to my own fault, but also owing to the faults
of others. Besides, owing to the difficulties I am in at
present, I cannot do otherwise. It is easily done,
Marquis, to wish oneself one thing or another ; the rub
is whether we can be what we wish ourselves to be. We
are not alone, for with us is the beast—the beast which
carries us. It is no use beating it, for it never comes to
reason. Go and persuade the ass not to munch grass
near precipices—it will put up with thrashings, cudgel-
lings and floggings, but it will continue to go there,
because it cannot do otherwise. And when you have

[1] It is significant that Pirandello has entitled every volume
of his plays " Maschere Nude " (Naked Masks).

beaten and kicked it, and gazed into its sorrowful eyes, well, excuse me, do you not feel pity for it ? I say pity, but you must not make excuses for it : the intelligence that makes excuses for the beast ends by becoming a beast itself also."

Angelo Baldovino, with his tortuous reasoning, has a very obstinate and mulish personality, and one which the Marquis Fabio had not bargained for. He marries Agata and saves appearances, but he insists that they should continue to be respected after the marriage.

" Appearances," he says, " must not only be kept up in front of society, but also in front of me. In that way, if there is any evil action done, it will be done by them, not by me." Angelo lives altogether for the others : " I have not," he says, " any existence save for appearances. I am up to my ears in figures and speculations, but they are for others ; there is not a single halfpenny that belongs to me. Here I am in this beautiful house, yet I hardly see or touch anything. Sometimes I'm astonished to hear the sound of my own voice or the noise of my footsteps, or again to find that I need to drink a glass of water or rest myself. . . . My life is a delightful one—purely abstract." Angelo, contrary to the majority of the characters of Pirandello, has assumed his mask consciously, and this has the effect of crystallizing his actions still more completely. His rigid code of honour for himself ultimately imposes a rigid honour on Agata also. Despite herself she refuses to meet her former lover, in order not to be unfaithful to her husband. In her house Angelo is absolute master and commands her as he likes. She tells Fabio that she cannot continue to be his mistress unless she leaves the house. Fabio then determines to weave a plot against Angelo. He lays a trap for him which will render it necessary for him to steal money, and then after the theft has been committed it will be possible to get him cast out as a thief. But Angelo, who has been scrupulously accurate in his dealings, sees the trap laid and confronts Fabio. He, however, agrees to pass as a thief and go away out of the country on condition that Fabio should steal the money. Angelo's reason for wanting to go away, even at the cost of appearing as a thief, is that he finds himself becoming more and more attracted towards Agata. We have now reached the point in the play where the mask begins to fall off and the true man appears. Angelo had worn the mask of husband and had seen only the mask of wife which Agata had been wearing. Now, however, the masks fall off, and he finds that he is a man desperately in love with Agata the woman. It is for this reason that he determines to go away in spite of the attempt of Agata and her mother to prevent him.

BALDOVINO.

" For pity's sake, lady, do not make me lose my head ; do not let me lose the power which I still possess, of seeing the consequences of actions which others blindly perform —blindly, mind you, not through any lack of intellect, but because when a man lives, *he lives and does not see himself live.* I see because I came into this house *not to live.* Do you wish to make me live ? "

Angelo Baldovino, like Mattia Pascal, now hears the call of his flesh and finds it impossible to continue being a mere abstraction. The development of the situation is exactly the same as in the early novel : the characters, after throwing off the mask, begin to affect us emotionally. To them all he says : " What about me ? Do you think that I can remain here always as a light only, for you ? I too have my poor flesh that cries out ! I too have blood, black blood that is full of the bitter poison of my memories." The play ends with the triumph of Angelo, now a man of flesh and bones, no longer an abstraction, to whom Agata gives her love   Agata's change of character is explained by Angelo.   She had loved Fabio as a mistress, but then the marriage with Angelo and the rigidly virtuous attitude adopted changed her from a mistress into a married woman.   Thus both of them had assumed the mask of marriage merely as an artificial form ; but life, ever in flux and reflux, deceived them and washed away their former mask and created another new one which they will have to wear in future. From the dramatic point of view there are many defects in this intensely intellectual play.   The long tortuous speeches of Angelo end by wearying the audience.   His change from an abstract character into a real man at the end of the play is too sudden, and there does not seem to be enough motive shown.   Agata, Maddalena, Fabio have no real dramatic personality, but flit about uncertainly.   The play is interesting on account of its subtle arguments, but it needs the most consummate actor's craft to save it on the stage.

The hero of *Giuoco delle Parti* (The Game as He Played It), 1918 Leone Galla, is no less of a cool logician than Angelo Baldovino, though he adopts a different procedure.   Whereas Angelo insists on his wife respecting the code of society, Leone Galla, like the heroes of the modern plays of Romain Coolus or Crommelynck, accepts with resignation the rôle of betrayed husband. He realizes that this is his destiny, for he is married to a capricious, sensual woman called Silia.   And so he allows her to carry on her intrigues in his own luxurious house with her lover Guido.   But Leone Galla, being a characteristic Pirandellian hero, must justify this serenely cynical attitude with all the weapons of the tortuous logician.   " We must," he says to his friend Guido, " no longer derive satisfaction from living for ourselves, but

we must watch others live and even watch ourselves
from without." Leone, in adopting the mask of the
betrayed husband, has released himself from all prejudices, all beliefs : he has no faith in anything except
what is grossly material, like Ulrico Nargutta in Bracco's
play *I Pazzi* (1922). His one great satisfaction in life
is to be a *gourmet*, and hence he spends all his time with
his cook, whom he calls Socrates. The serene indifference of Leone cannot fail to irritate the sensual and
hysterical Silia : her faculties are not attuned to modern
logic, and she feels ever more and more oppressed by the
intolerable presence of her husband. " Can't you kill
him for me ? " she exclaims laughingly to her lover.
Then, according to the usual Pirandellian method, a
small unforeseen event happens which sets the intrigue
in motion. As Leone Galla leaves, Silia, as a joke,
throws an empty eggshell at him, but unfortunately it
misses its mark and falls into the midst of a party of four
drunken young men who were walking near the house.
These four Don Juans imagine that Silia's innocent jest
is an advance to them, and so they storm the door and
make for her room. Silia, who happens at that moment
to be closeted with Guido, has a Machiavellian notion :
she first of all locks Guido up into an adjoining room ;
then she makes herself charming to the drunken revellers,
with the object of leading them on to greater insolence
in their behaviour towards her. Secretly, however, she
tells her servant Clara to run and call in the neighbours.
When they arrive she tells them that she has been
insulted.

All this scene she has provoked for the purpose of
inducing her husband to expose his life for her in a duel.
She obtains the name of one of the four drunkards—the
Marquis Miglioriti, a renowned swordsman, and determines to make Leone, her official husband, demand
satisfaction. The act concludes with a love scene

between Silia and Guido : she now imagines that a way has been found of touching her phlegmatic husband to the quick. When in the next act she tells him that he has to fight a duel for her, Leone, who is dressed as a cook and entirely engrossed in his culinary experiments with his servant Socrates, does not shrink at the news. With the gravest imperturbability he agrees to fight and perform to the end his duty as official husband. But he insists that Guido, who had been present when Silia had been insulted and had been unable, by reason of his delicate position, to render help, should be his second. Between the two men the conditions of the duel are drawn up. Guido persuades Leone that if the duel takes place, it must be carried out to the death, for, knowing that the Marquis is an expert swordsman and that Leone has never held a foil in his life, he hopes that thus his rival will lose his life. In the third act the morning of the duel has arrived, and Guido, accompanied by the other second, Doctor Spiga, goes to Leone's apartment. They are in great excitement, as the time appointed approaches and Leone is not yet out of bed. At last he appears, sleepily rubbing his eyes, clad in pyjamas. To the hurried exclamations he replies that he does not intend to fight the duel. " It is not my business," he says, " to fight this duel : it is Guido's business : I challenged, because he could not under the circumstances, owing to my wife."

With the calmest assurance he exposes his logical reasons to the company. He has acted entirely in accordance with the " giuoco delle parti " : he has performed his part of the bargain ; Guido must perform his :—

" Ah ! you and my wife thought you could play see-saw and use me as a prop : you thought, I suppose, that you could deprive me of my life by a trick ? You have missed your aim, my dear friends, I have outplayed you." And in spite of all the protests of the gentlemen present, who threaten to publish abroad his dishonour, he holds firm to his resolve. He has played up to the end his part as decorative husband. Now the time has come to fight in reality, and this duty belongs to Guido, who is the real husband. By the laws of duelling, when one of the parties is absent, his second must take his place, and Guido thus sees himself constrained to act as substitute for Leone. While the duel takes place in the garden below, Leone is left alone with Silia, who is in an agonized state of mind. She tries to empty the vials of her hatred on Leone, but he treats her with the utmost disdain.

LEONE.

" I have punished you."

SILIA.

" Yes, but at the cost of dishonouring yourself."

LEONE.

" But it is you that are my dishonour."

Soon afterwards Doctor Spiga arrives with the news that Guido has been killed. Leone remains deep in thought. As the curtain descends, Socrates the servant comes in to announce that breakfast is served.

In many respects *Il Giuoco delle Parti* resembles *Il Piacere dell' Onestà*, but it is much more brilliant. Leone Galla recalls closely Angelo Baldovino. He has the same desire for developing sententious reasoning, but less moral priggishness. The two characters assume a certain line of conduct in life as a mask, and act up to that mask with rigid consistency. Angelo, however, is less inhuman than Leone, for he gradually falls under the spell of the wife he has married under bribery : Leone is an extreme Pirandellian and ironically inhuman. When played by a subtle actor like Ruggeri, his part makes a profound impression on the stage. There is a great dramatic moment at the end of the play where Leone bursts forth into violent vendetta and exhales his hatred against his rival. A critic, however, has pointed out that there is nothing in the play to prepare our minds for this change in his character. There was nothing to warn us of the secret contrast between the appearance and the fundamental reality which is the essence of the *teatro grottesco*.[1] The transformation in the character of the central figure only seems to occur at the end of the play in order to produce a climax, a *stonatura* that will send the public home well content with their evening's amusement. In spite of this criticism, *Il Giuoco delle Parti* remains one of the most brilliant and characteristic plays of Pirandello. The number of aphorisms and the paradoxical nature of the plot should make it a great success on the English stage.

It is easy to see that these paradoxical plays of Pirandello are true to a dramatic tradition that has existed in Italy ever since the days of Flaminio Scala and Loccatelli and the " Commedia dell' Arte," when the purpose of the dramatists was to develop the most surprising intrigues and add to the *lazzi* that could be performed by Pulcinella or Arlecchino. Many of the characters of Pirandello resemble the quick-witted servants of the improvized play weaving their subtle plots. In the first act Silia, the coquettish, capricious, sensual heroine, trying to hoodwink her husband, resembles the frivolous heroines of the Bracco farce comedies, like Clara Sangiorgi in *L'Infedele* (1894), but Pirandello does not look on the world with the frivolous glance of the Neapolitan dramatist :

[1] S. D' Amico, *Teatro dei Fantocci*, p. 100. Firenze, 1920.

rather does he grimace sarcastically and give wing to his disdainful satire. In plays like *L'Infedele* or *La Fine dell' Amore* there is nothing to take away the heartiness of our good-natured laugh, nothing to destroy our optimistic belief in the joy of life. In plays like *Il Giuoco delle Parti* the scenes of farce always mingle with tragedy. It is as if the author wanted us to look beyond his stage of comedy towards the true moral of his play, which is a tragic one. Such plays impose a severe tax on the mentality of the ordinary theatre-going public. If they look on the play as a comedy, they are dismayed by the brutal sarcasm of the author and by the death of one of the characters. If they look on the play as a tragedy, they find it difficult to reconcile their view with the air of comic " persiflage " that pervades the majority of the scenes. Marco Praga in his account of the play describes the mixed feelings of the audience when the play was first performed in Milan in 1919. " One comedy was acted on the stage," he says, " and another in the auditorium of the theatre."[1]

Every fresh play of Pirandello came as a surprise to the Italian public, who for so long a period had confined their dramatic sense within the narrow conventions of bourgeois, sentimental drama. As Marco Praga says again : " The first representation of every new Pirandellian play reminds one of the burlesque introductory words which the clown in a circus prefixes to each of his astounding feats—' something still more difficult.' "[2] The difficulty always arose owing to the quicksilver, inconsistent mind of the author. In the intervals of the play impassioned discussions began between the Pirandellians and their enemies. Most people only listened to the problem propounded in the play, and shut their ears and eyes to its execution. The attitude taken up

[1] M. Praga, *Cronache teatrali*, 1919, p. 104. Milano, 1920.
[2] *Idem, ibid.*, 1922. Milano, 1923.

by many resembled that of the English towards the earlier Shaw plays. It took some time for people to appreciate that hard, crystalline quality of Pirandello, that faculty for examining the world behind all its masks and conceits. He has often been compared with Bernard Shaw, but the comparison is not apt. Shaw, G. K. Chesterton says, is one of the ten per cent of humanity gifted with normal sight ; Pirandello surpasses the other ninety per cent in looking on the world through abnormal eyes. The world that takes on beautiful colours for the greater part of humanity, to Pirandello seems grotesquely horrible, peopled by the " Jabber-wocks " of his imagination. His humour is the most baffling imp that ever sailed into the spectacled critic's ken. The plays are nearly all entitled comedies ; the laugh, however, is never kindly and rose-coloured, but harsh and metallic. Like so many modern plays, there is an outer and an inner plot. The outer, objective plot is comic, but the inner, subjective plot is tragic. It is ever the story of Canio the clown putting on his motley to laugh, whilst at his heart gnaws passionate sorrow. Over and above that comedy with its undercurrent of tragedy we see the author snarling his contempt for human society.

In the next play we shall consider, *L'Uomo, La Bestia e La Virtù*, we see the most exaggerated expression of this harsh humour of our author, and it is perhaps that peculiar harshness which makes it one of the least attractive of all his plays. If we consider the title " apology " which he has given to it, we can see his aim. It is called apology, as Praga says, because beneath the outer farce Pirandello meant the public to see a tragic satire. The public, however, on its representation refused to see the tragedy, and became irritated by the harsh comic that seemed so epileptic owing to his jerky style.

The protagonist of *L'Uomo, La Bestia e La Virtù* is Paolino, one of the petty schoolmaster tribe to which Professor Toti belonged. Paolino, like Toti, bears a grudge against society for having to din knowledge into the heads of idle boys, and for having to preserve immutably that mask of drudgery. But Paolino has not been able to escape the temptations of the life-force. He falls in love with Signora Perrella, the mother of one of his pupils. Signora Perrella has the misfortune to be married to a sea captain who spends nearly all his time away on voyages. When he does return to his home after four or five months' navigation, he uses any pretext in order to get into a rage with his wife and leave the house in high dudgeon. Thus the unfortunate woman has no enjoyment of the society of her husband. The real reason for this treatment is explained in the play as being due to Captain Perrella's fear of having another child. Signora Perrella, treated harshly by her brutal husband, takes the only natural course : she seeks consolation elsewhere, and this soft duty falls to Paolino. But their happiness is short-lived, for Signora Perrella finds that she is *enceinte*. What are they to do ? The Captain is expected home soon, and he will surely find out his dishonour. Paolino is at his wits' end, trying to discover a solution to the terrible difficulty. All would be well if the Captain during his twenty-four hours on shore would consort with his wife, but this is impossible owing to his fixed determination. At last Paolino, with the aid of his apothecary friend Pulejo, bethinks himself of a trick. He obtains certain drugged pastries, which are to be placed before the Captain at dinner in the hope that they will act as a potent aphrodisiac. In addition, he insists on Signora Perrella (whose decorous modesty the author is at great pains to prove) wearing a flaring dress, very much *décolletée*, and rouging and powdering her cheeks. The savage humour of the situation arises from Paolino's nature. He is supposed to be a straight, open-minded fellow who could never do any unworthy action. Yet owing to his having yielded to temptation, he has to act another part that is entirely uncongenial to him. He is passionately in love with Signora Perrella, but for the sake of society he cannot declare his love ; nay, he must even force her into the arms of her recalcitrant husband by means of all the trickery he can think of.

Pirandello means the figure of Paolino to be tragicomic, and thus we see him struggle despairingly with himself, curse himself and rail against fortune. But in spite of his epileptic behaviour, he does not interest us or draw more than a smile from us. He resembles rather one of those grotesque little Æthiopain marionettes from the " Teatro dei Piccoli " that jumps on its wires madly. As many critics have pointed out, the interest of the play dies down after the first act. In the first act where Paolino struggles with himself, there may be a faint interest, which is altogether lacking in the other two acts, for after the arrival of Perrella we are only interested in whether he will eat the pastries or not. In the last act the incident of the five flower-pots would have made any audience in Renaissance Florence or Parma rock with laughter. No other play of Pirandello is so full of the *lazzi* that we associate with the " Commedia dell' Arte," the *gros sel* that comes traditionally from the ancient *novella*. To a public reared on the notions of the sentimental bourgeois comedy of the nineteenth century, these gross jests must have seemed in doubtful taste, but they are characteristic of Pirandello in his attack on accepted dramatic conventions. It is the one play of our author where the comic spirit is combative and might be represented, as George Meredith would say, " by the sculptured group of Laughter holding both his sides, while Comedy pummels by way of tickling him."

In most of the plays of Pirandello which we have considered, sentiment and romance are relegated to an obscure
corner, while the author, with his acrid humour, pulls
to pieces playfully the vices and follies of humanity.   In
the four plays we shall now consider there is a decided
contrast to the former plays of Pirandello which we
criticized.   It is as if the author felt sudden alarm at the
trend his dramatic mind was taking and determined to
turn back and write plays in the idiom of his forerunners.
In each of the plays, *L'Innesto, La Ragione degli Altri*, and
Ma non è una Cosa Seria, Pirandello has constructed pieces
according to the rules laid down by William Archer or
Brander Matthews—plays wherein passion is allowed to
run its course impetuously, instead of being diverted into
little canals by an overmastering intellectual process.
Adherence to the accepted rules of theatre-craft by the
author in these plays does not prevent him from arguing
in his characteristic manner and from darting his nimble
spirit of humour, so that we end by saying that these
plays are variations by Pirandello on the old refrain.
We must not think they are plays of passion like *Tragedie
dell' Anima* or *Piccolo Santo* of Bracco ; Pirandello constructs his scenes in a totally different manner to Bracco,
owing to his passion for reasoning and arguing.

The characters of *L'Innesto* or *La Ragione degli Altri*, like
Signor and Signora Ponza, have the same desire to
reason out their troubles.   But everything is relative :
the characters we shall now consider forget occasionally
that they are puppets, and cry out their pain in human
fashion.

In *L'Innesto* (Grafting), which was produced in 1917,
the protagonists Giorgio and Laura have lived seven
years of uninterrupted, happy married life, though no

children have come to grace their union. One day Laura goes to sketch in the gardens near her apartment in Rome. While she is at work she is attacked by some scoundrel and raped brutally. A few hours later she is found in a fainting condition by some passers-by. Giorgio is half crazed when he finds his unfortunate wife. The terrible news has the effect of stirring in him a fierce sexual jealousy that resembles hatred. Instead of feeling pity for Laura's overwhelming suffering, he becomes obsessed incessantly by the thought that another man has possessed her body :

" Can't you understand that what torments me cruelly is that the most brutal injury has been inflicted without any sin on her part ? It is all the more cruel for me ! If she had been guilty, my honour would have been betrayed, but then I could exact full toll of vengeance. Now it is my love for her that is betrayed : can't you understand that there is nothing crueller for my love than this necessity imposed on it, of showing pity ? "

Giorgio has the personality of the primitive savage man —all instinct. " I ought," he says, " to be generous, while within me my feelings roar out like a wild beast." Such hatred does he feel towards Laura that he is ready to go away from her for ever, but when the decisive scene takes place between them, he falters in his resolve owing to sexual attraction. Again, however, their peace is disturbed by a fresh trouble : Laura is *enceinte*, and she feels certain it is as a result of her misfortune. She is living in the country in a house surrounded by a beautiful garden. An old gardener explains to her the principles of grafting plants. If the plant that is grafted is to bear fruit, the grafting must have taken place while the plant is in sap : if it is not in sap, the graft can never bind. Laura, who feels within her the blossoming of a new life, welcomes the old gardener's botanical theories as a symbol of her own case. According to the time-honoured stage convention of the past, Pirandello aids the exposition of Laura's case by the parallel episode of Zena, the country-woman, who had been seduced by the son of her master. Laura has no fears for the future Her child will be Giorgio's because it was only Giorgio that she loved. What matter if Giorgio is not physiologically the father : her thoughts, her love had only been for him. But Giorgio, when he hears the irrational ideas of Laura, does not take her point of view. Arguing logically, he insists on the destruction of the creature she bears within her, and admits no other course. But in Laura, as in Bracco's heroines Caterina Nemi and the Marchioness Claudia di Montefranco, there rises up the feeling of maternal love.

The vision of this well-worn theme of maternal love, that has occupied the stages so long owing to writers like Bracco or Brieux, shows how much of a throw-back for Pirandello this drama is. But there is a great difference in the treatment Pirandello gives to the subject. In plays like *Maternità* (1903) and *Tragedie dell' Anima* (1899) of Bracco, the wife ceases to be wife and asserts her supreme function of motherhood. In this play of Pirandello Laura does not voice the claims of her maternal instinct, but of her love for Giorgio. She makes her maternal instinct serve the purpose of proving how overmastering was her passion for him. Ibsen had shown in the case of Agnes, the wife of Brand, that the mother must yield before the wife, for woman's greatest duty is to follow her husband even at the cost of her child.

Bracco, Ada Negri, Brieux and other modern writers set maternity as the ideal, the goal for woman. Pirandello, with greater logic, seems to combine both ideas ; woman's maternal love is the expression of her complete love towards her husband. In her illusion she longs that he should feel the same emotion as she does.

LAURA.

" I have never argued : I have loved : I could die with love of you, and I have been yours in a way that no woman in the world has ever been, and you know it. . . . It is madness, I know, but I so wished to carry you away with me here amidst these plants that understand my madness."

At first Giorgio remains fixed in his immutable position, and Laura resigns herself to go away from him for ever, but Giorgio, like the majority of male characters in modern feminist drama, is a weak man : he desires passionately the love of Laura ; it is necessary for his life, and so he gives way and accepts her illusions.

In *La Ragione degli Altri* (The Rights of Others), which was produced in 1915 under the title " Se Non Cosi," we find perhaps a more striking instance of Pirandello's logical method. The heroine, Livia Arciana, as the author admits in the preface, is an ineffective character for drama ; but her function is not to awaken emotion so much as to interpret the logic of the author's mind. In this case, as in *L'Innesto*, Pirandello has taken a conventional plot and worked it out in his own way. To explain matters he has written as a preface to the play a letter to the heroine, in which he asks her forgiveness for giving her such an ineffective part to play ; but she should remember that all the originality in the play only takes place on account of her particular way of thinking and feeling.

Livia Arciani has the misfortune to be married to a husband who is unfaithful to her. Though she realises that all is finished between them, she tries to keep up an appearance of harmony for the sake of the world, and endures her anguish in silence. But owing to her father's inquiries, the truth comes to light. Livia's union has been a childless one, but her husband Leonardo has a daughter by his mistress Elena.

To Livia's logical mind the issues seem clear : Leonardo should go where his child is. " Where the children are," she says, " there is the home, and in my house there are no children." The plot resembles that of *Alma Triunfante* (1902) of Benavente, where the heroine tries to sacrifice herself in favour of her husband's mistress, by whom he has a child. If it had not been for her father, Livia would have gone on enduring in silence and pretending to pay no heed to Leonardo's conduct. But now that the mask has been torn away, the whole affair must come to light. Leonardo, however, is not really in love with Elena. Now that his momentary passion has died away, he realises that he loves his own wife far more, and it is only on account of the child that he is attracted to Elena. In the climax scene of the second act with Livia, where he falls again under her spell, we realise what the end of the play will be. In the third act the scene changes from Livia's luxurious apartment to the drab lodgings of Elena. Elena is no less wearied of Leonardo than he is of her ; she is worn out by privations, and when Livia comes to see her, she willingly renounces any intention of continuing her relations with Leonardo. But Livia then exposes her remorseless logic. She is willing to take back Leonardo, but on one condition, that Elena should also renounce the child and let her bring it up as her daughter. It is of no use for Elena merely to renounce Leonardo, for, as Livia says : " He does not belong to me as long as he belongs to the daughter here which you have unlawfully had by him, and which I have not been able to give him." Livia, in coming to see Elena, has renounced all her rights as wife, and recognized that above those rights is the duty imposed on Leonardo by

Elena's child. Elena, though she agrees to renounce Leonardo, will not renounce the child. Against Livia's reasoning she retorts : " I am the mother."

" What do you want from me ? Nothing, then : the matter is as it was. The child remains here. If he wishes, let him come and see her, but the child is to stay here with me."

But Elena, although she is armed with all the rights which maternity confers upon a woman, is powerless before the onslaught of Livia's cold logic, who replies that it is no use for her to pretend that things can go on as though nothing had happened.

" You," she says, " have committed the sin both of taking away from a woman her husband, and of giving to that husband a daughter. You now wish to give me back my husband, but you cannot do so any more, for he is now not only my husband : he is father here."

To this Elena replies : " You are raving, lady ! I have given the child life, my blood, my milk. Does that not count with you ? She is born from my flesh : she is mine ! What cruel torments you inflict upon me by asking from me such a sacrifice in the name of my daughter."

But Livia, in speaking of the future of the child, has touched Elena on a tender spot. If the child goes to the rich house of Livia, she will be cared for and her future will be assured : if she stays in these poverty-stricken surroundings there will be nothing but misery ahead for her. These thoughts run through Elena's mind after the departure of Livia, whose parting words had been that Leonardo was to stay with his child. With great dramatic skill Pirandello unfolds a scene wherein we see the struggle in the mind of this poor mother.

If she sacrifices her love for her child, Dina will have everything she wants : " You would not have to play with those ugly moo-cows, Dina, with that old shepherd without legs . . . for you would have gold toys, but you would not have your mother any more."

The scene rises in a gradual crescendo to the climax, when Elena tells Leonardo to go away and take the child with him.

The curtain descends on the stage, where sits Elena alone, with the little hat in her hand and gazing through tears at the toys belonging to the child that has gone from her for ever.

In this play Pirandello has allowed himself to appeal to the emotions of his audience as in *L'Innesto*, and in the last scene he has again touched the note of pathos of dramatists like Roberto Bracco.   It is a most curious play, owing to the absence of the heroine at the climax at the end.   The sympathy of the public inevitably turns completely round to Elena, the mother whose child has been snatched from her ; but we can imagine Pirandello laughing sarcastically at those of the public who consider this play of his a tragedy of Elena.   If we look at the title-page, we find that he has entitled the play a comedy, according to the favourite device of the modern writers of grotesque plays who like to laugh at the old-fashioned stage.

To allow our minds to dwell altogether on the last sentimental scene of the play is to misunderstand : the real point of the work is the scene between Livia and Elena, where the former exposes her logic.

Livia, as a critic has said, moves on a higher plane than any of the other characters, for she analyses the rights of the others and makes them all sink before the rights of the child, which are the highest.   She is the only one who has managed to set her logic above passion and sentiment. Leonardo is torn between his freshly aroused passion for his wife and his devotion to the child whom he will not renounce. Elena defends her rights as a mother : she wishes to send away Leonardo while keeping the child for herself. Livia alone looks beyond her own good to that of the child. From a dramatic point of view the play is a success, though with regard to Livia it cannot be said that her character avoids the dangers that lie in wait for the mouthpiece puppet. For the stage she argues too much, and at times she very nearly suffers from priggishness, so imbued is she with logic. The play, however, is so complete that it pleases both sections, the Pirandellians and the Philistines. The Pirandellians can take interest in the scenes of discussion on the knotty problem, the rest can let their hearts be touched by the said story of Elena.

If *La Ragione degli Altri* is the triumph of logic, *Ma non è una Cosa Seria,* which appeared in 1918, may be said to be its defeat. In the former play the author worked on gradually to the triumph of reason, gathering together every thread. In the latter the characters start off by working according to Livia's method, but life deceives them in their logic, and they have to tear off their assumed mask. The play, like *L'Innesto* and *La Ragione degli Altri,* is not characteristic of Pirandello in its general plot. In writing it he did not think of his favourite problems, but of the stage, and Marco Praga has pointed out that the play was written for the great actress Emma Gramatica.[1]

The heroine, Gasparina Torretta, is a character from the bourgeois drama of our days, a worn-out, shabbily-dressed girl of twenty-seven, who acts as drudge in a boarding-house. As the author says in the stage directions, she would be a nice-looking, vivacious girl but for

[1] M. Praga, *Cronache teatrali.* Milano, 1921.

the life of privations that she has had to endure and which earn her the nickname " Scarparotta " (" Down-at heels ") from the inmates of the boarding-house. Everybody treats her badly and casts on her shoulders the burdens of the establishment. The first scenes of the play are devoted to a most animated satire of the guests at the boarding-house, and with savage glee Pirandello makes those ridiculous puppets dance through their follies for us. Few of the modern dramatists know better than he does how to put on the stage such comic scenes. Professor Virgadamo is a fat, placid old school teacher who stutters ; Grizzoffi peppery and always ready for a quarrel ; Barranco a prosperous man from the country whose prosperity has not prevented his nose from growing to an awkward size ; Miss Terrasi a timid schoolmistress ; Magnasco a very fat, bald-headed man of fifty who tries to dress like a young dandy, and brings his prostitute friends to the house—all these different types are described for us with the skill of a novelist who has Dickens's power of caricature. Poor Gasparina has a very difficult time mediating between her guests, who spend their time in quarrelling. Nobody ever speaks a kind word to her except old Signor Barranco. She is alone and friendless in the world.

To the boarding-house comes young Memmo Speranza with his friend Vico Lamanna. Memmo is a young dandy of the town who has spent most of his patrimony and health in the pursuit of the attractions of vice in every form. One of his recent escapades with women has drawn him into a duel, from which he only just escaped with his life at the cost of a serious wound. Memmo is the gay, young frivolous Don Juan, recalling Aldo Rigliardi of Butti's play *La Corsa al Piacere* (1900), a character that is very popular in Italian and Spanish drama. " I am," he says, " like straw. I go on fire suddenly ; a fine blaze and then I end in smoke." Every action he does is for fun, and suddenly, when seated with his friends in the hotel, he thinks of a joke that will surprise even his sceptical companion Vico Lamanna : he will marry Gasparina. His one worry in life has been the fear that he might one day shackle his independence by entering on the bond of matrimony. By marrying Gasparina, the poor, unkempt boarding-house drudge, he will satisfy his passion for joking and strengthen his own position. Neither Gasparina nor anybody else would take the marriage seriously, and so he would be free to continue his bachelor life of pleasure with the comfortable feeling that it would be impossible for any designing woman to set her cap at him. To Gasparina he states his plans, and after a great deal of persuasion, amid the laughter and jests of the assembled guests, who applaud Memmo's latest mad prank, the girl blushingly agrees to the bargain.

Thus Memmo and Gasparina assign each other a part to play, and they put on masks accordingly, but life with its ceaseless ebb and flow has but scanty respect for those who imagine that they can play a fixed part. The development of the play rises from the impossibility of keeping on the mask which they had assumed. In this respect the play is but a variation of *Il Piacere dell' Onestà*, in which Angelo Baldovino undertakes for a bet to marry the girl whom the libertine marquis had seduced. Angelo Baldovino bears a close resemblance in character to Memmo Speranza, and the crisis in both plays happens in the same way. Two months after the arrangement we see what a change has come over Gasparina : she has become much younger-looking owing to her tranquil, serene life in the country. Her clothes are well made and give her an attractive air. Both she and Memmo have kept to their bargain and have lived separate. While Gasparina has rested quietly in the country, Memmo has been getting into still greater difficulties with his various love intrigues. But old Signor Barranco, who had always kept a soft corner in his heart for the poor boarding-house drudge, follows her to her country retreat and presses her to release Memmo and marry him. Meanwhile, Memmo, who has only seen Gasparina at rare intervals, begins to be attracted by her good looks and rejuvenated appearance. The news that Barranco wants to marry her if only he will release her from the bond, decides him, and he falls in love in dead earnest. The play ends in broad farce with a scene between the three characters. Barranco in his stuttering voice timidly tries to explain to Memmo that he is in love with Gasparina ; Memmo tries to convey to the old man that he is not disposed to release her, for he has fallen truly in love with her, and the Professor must leave them alone, as he is *de trop*. Gasparina, in reality, is in love with Memmo, but owing to a sense of her own dignity she tries to persuade him to annul the marriage, which had never been consummated. In the end Barranco departs and the two lovers are left together : the marriage for a joke has become a marriage in earnest, and life has triumphed over logic and reason.

Few plays of Pirandello are more effective on the stage than *Ma non è una Cosa Seria*, on account of the splendid opportunities which the author gives to the heroine and the hero. In the first act Gasparina is untidy and dirty— one of the wearied herds of " generals " who direct the domestic operations of modern lower middle-class life. In the second act there is a great change in her appearance : she has regained health and colour, but her clothes, though the opposite extreme to those she had worn in the first act, are not smart owing to their lack of taste and their awkwardness. It is only in the third act that the transformation is complete, and Gasparina evolves into a dainty little woman, fit to attract the jaded taste of a *viveur* like Memmo. At her first appearance in this

act the author shows her flushed with summer heat,
wearing a straw hat and carrying roses and carnations
in her hands.   In Memmo Spernaza we see a character
eminently suited to the subtle modern school of Italian
acting.   In the first act he is all devoted to *lazzi* and
elegant " persiflage," but in the second and third acts
we see the Pulcinella gradually fade away and become
a human being.

Ma non è una Cosa Seria, like the three other plays we
have been considering, is an admirable exposition of the
struggle between the logic that men's minds set up and
crystallize and life's vital force which rushes heedlessly
on and sweeps away this logic.   Magnasco in the play
admirably sums up Pirandello's idea in his conversation
with the frivolous Loletta, one of the *demi-mondaine* visitors
to the boarding-house.   Magnasco sees in Memmo's
marriage with Gasparina the triumph of logic.

MAGNASCO.

" Look here, Loletta, his marriage has been the
triumph of logic—a model of abstract reasoning which
ran its course wonderfully well.   Ah ! you don't understand, my dear Loletta !   Do you know what logic is ?
Well, imagine a kind of filter-pump.   The pump is here
(he points to his head).   It stretches down to the heart.
Suppose you have a sentiment in your heart.   The mechanism which is called logic will then pump it for you and
filter it ; then that feeling at once loses its heat, its muddiness ;   it cools and becomes purified—in a word, it
becomes idealized and flows wonderfully well, because,
I tell you, we are outside life, in abstraction.   Life
exists where there is muddiness and heat and where
there is no logic, do you understand ?   Does it seem
logical that you should weep now ?   It is human ! "

" I should like to know, then, why logic was given to us."

MAGNASCO.

" Because Nature, that is so kind to us, has not willed that we should suffer only on account of our sentiments and our passions, but that we should also become poisoned with the corrosive sublimate of logical deduction."

These words Pirandello seems to have taken practically word for word from Pirandello's essay on " Humour," published in 1908, wherein, among other things, he discusses what he calls that infernal little mechanism called logic. Every man puts on an exterior mask as best he can—an exterior mask, for the one which he wears within him does not agree with the outer one. Thus man is for ever masked, without wishing it or even knowing it, with that which he imagines in good faith he represents, whether it be good, beautiful, generous, unhappy. This makes us laugh if we think of it, for a dog, when the first fever of life has passed, does nothing but eat and sleep—it lives as it should live, with its eyes shut, patiently waiting for time to pass. What does man do ? Even as an old man he is always in fever ; he raves, but without seeing himself do so ; he cannot help striking an attitude even in front of himself, and he acts so many parts that he wishes to believe true and worthy to be taken seriously. He is helped in this play-acting by that mechanism of logic which all men should have allowed to rust away without ever touching it. But no, some of them have shown themselves so proud and happy in the possession of it that they started to try to perfect it with all their zeal. Aristotle went so far as to write a book about it, which is used still in the schools in order that youths may learn quickly the art of bamboozling themselves. Many poor people think that by means of this logic they will save themselves from all the ills of which the world is full, and they pump and filter away, until their heart remains as dry as a piece of cork and their brain becomes like a chemist's shop, full of those jars which have on their black labels a skull between two cross-bones with the inscription " poison."[1] Memmo Speranza had schooled himself in this logic that Pirandello speaks of—he had reduced his life mathematically to a series of egotistical enjoyments. He tries to wear permanently the mask of a nonchalant Don Juan who skips lightly from conquest to conquest. Life, however, plays the trick on him as it does on Gasparina, who imagined that she could carry out to the end the marriage joke without ever falling in love herself with her mock husband.

The notion of Pirandello with regard to man's logical reasoning is interesting as a criticism, not only of his characters, but also of his own personality. In many of his works we find that he plays about so long with the poisonous contents of that chemist's shop which he calls the brain, that he forgets to leave any shred of emotion for his audience.

In other plays he seems to divide the play into two sections : first of all there is the outer plot of emotion, which runs its course, and touches our sentiment ; then there is the secondary plot, which is generally centred in one character who argues *à la* Pirandello.

The complete drama arises, then, from the shock and antithesis between the central Pirandellian mouthpiece character and the other conventional puppets who seem to move on a different plane.

---

[1] Pirandello, *Umorismo*, pp. 217–218. Roma, 1911.

V. A PIRANDELLO MIRROR PLAY

Very often the dramatic conflict in Pirandello arises from the transformation which takes place in the mind of a man when the situation, wherein he has for years lived unconsciously, is suddenly revealed to him in all its terrible nakedness, and he at last appears to himself as he has up to this appeared to others. Such recent plays of Pirandello, Professor Tilgher has grouped together under the title *Teatro dello Specchio*, and he quotes Pirandello's words of definition as to these works :

" When a man lives, he lives and does not see himself. Well, put a mirror before him and make him see himself in the act of living, under the sway of his passions : either he remains astonished and dumbfounded at his own appearance, or else he turns away his eyes so as not to see himself, or else in disgust he spits at his image, or again clenches his fist to break it ; and if he had been weeping, he can weep no more ; if he had been laughing, he can laugh no more, and so on. In a word, there arises a crisis and that crisis is my theatre."[1]

In *Tutto Per Bene* (All for the Best), which appeared in 1920, the hero at a point in the drama sees as in a mirror his own image as others have seen it, and straight-way every illusion of his life falls to the ground. Martino Lori, a worthy civil servant of many years' standing, has for sixteen years been a widower. Though his wife has died so long ago, he still venerates her memory with the utmost constancy, and finds his only consolation in life in his daughter Palma. Great interest is taken in her by Senator Manfroni, a famous scientist, and it is chiefly owing to him that she is educated and introduced to

[1] A. Tilgher, *Voci del Tempo*. Roma, 1923. Essay on Pirandello.

the man who marries her—the Marquis Flavio Gualdi. Manfroni goes so far in his kindness as to give her a big dowry. Martino Lori, being a poor man weighed down by the cares of life, does not question the bounties of his benefactor : he, however, sometimes feels a pang of sorrow when he notices that his daughter reserves the major part of her affection for the Senator.

In the first act the scene is laid in Lori's house, where a wedding party is being held for Palma and the Marquis Flavio Gualdi. Our surprise at the treatment of the poor old father ·Martino grows every moment : he does not seem to count in his own house and nobody pays any attention to him. All his attempts at showing affection to his only daughter who is leaving him are treated with scant respect. He thinks the reason for his neglect is that Palma, owing to the help of Manfroni, is leaving his modest home for the great world, where she will be welcomed as the wife of a Marquis. In the scene of farewell between father and daughter, the latter barely conceals her impatience at his sad reproof for her manner of treating him. In the second act the secret deepens and our curiosity increases to know why everyone looks with strange eyes on Martino. By a *coup de scène* of the old Scribe drama, the mystery is revealed. The scene takes place in the luxurious drawing-room of the Marquis's house during an evening party at which Manfroni and all his friends are present. Martino Lori is alone in the drawing-room, sitting on a sofa. The servants put out most of the lights and leave the room in semi-darkness. Palma suddenly enters the room at the back, and seeing somebody sitting on the sofa, imagines that it is the Senator, and says " Father." Lori then rises up in joy, thinking that she has come to him to say good night affectionately. What is his amazement to find that Palma, when she approaches him, shrinks away from him in alarm.

Lori in dismay wants to remonstrate with her ; then Palma gives vent to her temper and lets out the secret.

LORI.

(certain that the word " Father " had not been addressed to him).

" Then have you reached the point of calling Manfroni father ? "

PALMA.

" Oh ! let us put a stop to this : I call him thus because I should do so."

LORI.

" Is it because he has acted as father to you ? "

PALMA.

" No. Look here : let us put a stop once and for all to this play-acting. I am sick of it."

LORI.

" Play-acting ? What do you mean ? "

PALMA.

" Play-acting, play-acting—I tell you I am sick of it. You know very well that he is my father and that I should call him father."

What a terrible shock for poor Martino Lori ! He discovers all in a flash that his beloved wife, whose memory he had worshipped as a saint, had been unfaithful to him with the Senator. And all people know it and had known it for years—except he, the one most concerned, who for years and years had been weeping

172

over her grave. And he had continued ever since to accept gift after gift from his enemy, while everybody, including his own daughter, believed that he knew the facts, but preferred to pretend ignorance in order to advance himself in his career. It is for this reason that his anxious solicitude at the marriage of Palma had occasioned such irritability in Manfroni and Palma. No scene in any of the plays of Pirandello we have examined up to this reaches the tragic intensity of this scene between Lori and Palma. Lori is face to face with the tragic revelation which destroys his only hope in life, and his last illusions.

Now that he sees himself as others see him, in the magic mirror, he becomes a truly human character, and his sufferings awaken emotion in us. With extraordinary clearness he sees his life's inexorable destiny. There are certain moments of internal silence when our soul divests itself of all the customary figments and our eyes become sharper and more penetrating : we see ourselves in life, and life itself, as though we were stark naked : we feel a strange impression creep over us, as if in a flash a fresh reality was lit up for us, different to that one which we normally see—a living reality that transcends human vision and human reason. With a supreme effort we attempt then to regain normal consciousness of things, reconnect our ideas, and feel ourselves alive again in the usual way. But unfortunately we can no longer give faith to that normal consciousness, to those connected ideas, to that customary view of life, because we know henceforth that they are only an illusion created by us in order to live, and that beneath there is something else which man may not face except at the cost of death or madness.[1]

This momentary flash of reality has struck Lori and made him reel with giddiness. His whole life is turned

[1] L. Pirandello, *Umorismo*, p. 215.

upside down, and he now sees what it was in reality
during those sixteen years. He understands now things
whose existence he never suspected before, and on this
day he really can say that his wife has died. The situation resembles slightly that story of Guy de Maupassant
entitled *Bijoux*, where a husband mourns many years for
his wife who had died. He looks upon her always as a
model spouse, until one day, when, being short of money,
he pawns some of the cheap glass imitation jewels with
which his wife used to adorn herself. To his amazement
the glass jewels are in reality precious stones, and it turns
out that the model wife had received them as guerdons
for the amorous favours she had distributed during her
married life. The husband, after weeping over the
destruction of his illusion, makes a fortune out of the
sale of his wife's jewels and marries a woman *qui le fit
beaucoup souffrir*. Martino Lori has not even such conso-
lations. He finds that Palma, his one joy in life, is not
his daughter, and that he is alone in the world. What
is he to do in revenge? He determines to rush off to
find Manfroni and inflict punishment upon him. He
will kill him. But on reflection Martino realizes that
he cannot bring himself to do this. Twenty years have
elapsed, and all the world believes that he has acquiesced
willingly in his dishonour. How could he, then, perform
the deed? In presence of Manfroni and Palma he would
make the former assert to the latter that the calculations
were wrong and that she is his own daughter. Palma,
who now feels affection for Martino, is disposed to believe
his story. She begins to regard him as her true father ;
but Martino then suddenly declares his inability to act
this fresh play, having within him the consciousness
that he is acting.

Another means of revenge comes to his mind : he
possesses secret information against Manfroni which
would be enough to dishonour his name in the world of

science. Manfroni owes his fame to a clever plagiarism of the unpublished notes of a former colleague. If he publishes these notes which he has in his possession, he can destroy the outer, worldly personality of his hated enemy. Up to this day he had never yielded to the temptation of exposing Manfroni, owing to Palma, who had received many benefits. Even this vengeance is impossible ; who would believe Martino's story—Martino, the poor dishonoured husband—against the name of a famous scientist ? There is therefore no use in doing anything : " All my weapons of revenge," he says, " have fallen from my hand—I have none left, not even a pin." Only one way out of the difficulty remains : Palma, her husband and Manfroni are the only people who knew the true state of Martino Lori's mind, and that he had never known of his dishonour. Thus the solution is to continue in public the same old mask play, only this time he will play consciously the part that formerly he played unwittingly. One great positive benefit has come out of the whole imbroglio : Palma, whom he had believed to be his daughter, had never esteemed him before ; now, when there is the certitude that she is not his daughter, she begins to feel true affection and esteem for him.

Assisted by Palma's affection, Martino Lori can bear up against the world, and the play ends with the words of Pangloss, the philosopher : " Everything for the best." It is not only in the last words of the play that we can see the similarity in tone to Voltaire's immortal *Candide*. Voltaire wrote his spirited tale in order to deal a resounding blow at the optimistic philosophy of Leibniz, whose theories he symbolizes in the form of Pangloss.

Pirandello, with the added cruelty which our own sceptical age has added to Voltaire's eighteenth-century incisiveness, pulls to pieces all the illusions of life to see how they are made. He separates the real from the ideal in a manner contrary to his predecessors, who held that the function of the artist was to combine them in an artistic synthesis. He nails illusions to a coarse, brutal reality, and then laughs bitterly at them. Pirandello's mirror theatre, to which *Tutto Per Bene* belongs, marks the convulsed exasperation of the Pirandellian humour. The drama arises entirely from the violent antithesis between the real and the ideal, and so cleverly are the effects managed that the conflict seems to arise logically out of the characters themselves, not out of the brain of the author and his preconceived ideas. The play is derived from the *novella* of the same name contained in the volume entitled *La Vita Nuda* (Naked Life), and it would be instructive to make a close comparison between the two texts. The first section of the *novella* is retrospective, and describes the marriage of Lori with the daughter of the Professor whose notes Manfroni stole. The second section describes their unhappy married life, and it is only in the third that the wife dies. In the fourth section Lori suddenly begins to suspect the reason for Manfroni's interest in Palma, and the story ends with his visit to the tomb of his wife : "That evening he had something new to say to the dead woman." It will be noticed that Pirandello, in writing the play, has used his great command of dramatic technique to create a central *coup de scène* in order to reveal the truth to Lori. The revelation in the *novella*, which occurs in the last few pages, is not so convincing. It is interesting to note also that the play finishes with a phrase of hope instead of despair, as in the *novella*.

Tutto Per Bene is a good example to show Pirandello's power of making puppets that have jerked about the stage, moved by the thick threads of the showman during the greater part of the play, suddenly become creatures of flesh and blood. Martino Lori in the first act and most of the second is a marionette without any real existence of his own beyond that which the author gives him as mouthpiece character ; but suddenly, when the magic mirror is put in front of him, this marionette becomes human, just as the chessmen of Alice's dream grew to human semblance. When the shock in the play takes place, the wooden puppet becomes a human being and stirs our emotions by his sorrow. The aim of the author in this play, as in the majority of the other plays, is to show how individual every man's life is, and how limited the world that surrounds him is by his own individual consciousness. Then, by means of some exterior event, generally of trifling importance, that man is suddenly brought face to face with himself as he has appeared to other people. He looks in the mirror, and the mirror does not reflect back the familiar image to which he has been long accustomed, but a deformed image like those shown in those mirrors at fairs, which distort grotesquely the human semblance.

VI. PIRANDELLO AND TRAGEDY. HENRY IV.

All famous writers have a symbol which sums up their genius. Some, like Victor Hugo, chose the eagle ; others preferred the swan with its death-song. Above Pirandello's theatre we should set a huge question mark. His drama is the drama of interrogation. In order to try to answer these questions on the stage, a complete change of dramatic technique was necessary, and for that reason many of the plays of the *Teatro Grottesco* were fantastic extravaganzas and the exact antithesis to the sentimental bourgeois comedy or the naturalist drama with its *tranches de vie*. Nearly all the Pirandello plays seem to move in a sphere far removed from our real life. If we examine the many volumes of *novelle* which he has written, we find that the greater number deal with abnormal beings and madmen, whose vagaries he treats with as much seriousness as Ariosto or Cervantes. But the spirit of Pirandello has not the kindly charity of Cervantes : in his acrid, biting disdain of human society he resembles rather Dean Swift. Just as Cervantes created his greatest character in order to show the antithesis between illusion and reality, so Pirandello has followed suit in making the hero of his play *Henry IV* a madman.

When we call *Henry IV* a tragedy ,we must bear in mind the new idea of tragedy as it presents itself to the modern dramatists. *Henry IV* is not a tragedy in the sense that *Piccola Fonte* of Bracco or *Strife* of Galsworthy are tragedies : nor is it a tragedy in the mediæval sense. In Pirandello's mind the distinction between tragedy and comedy is very slight, and many plays that he has labelled comedies are far from having the slim, feasting smile that we associate with the comic spirit.

Plays such as *La Ragione degli Altri* are marked comedies, and yet they end in a cry of despair. *Henry IV*, however, is on a more lofty plane than the rest of Pirandello's plays : it is an intensification of the author's spirit of humour, a summing up of that disdainful attitude which he uses against human society. It is the sort of play *L'homme aux rubans verts* would have written, determined as he was *à rompre en visière à tout le genre humain.* The hero of the play is drawn on a larger scale than any of the characters we have considered, and becomes the complete expression of the play. In this sense, perhaps, the title tragedy, referring as it does to the tragedy of Henry IV's soul, might tally with Aristotle, who has defined tragedy as " an imitation of an action that is serious, complete, and of a certain magnitude."

In most of the plays which we have considered the author has taken a well-worn dramatic theme and worked it out in surprisingly original variations. Thus very often we look on the play as a paradoxical burlesque of the conventional drama : we feel that the author is pulling strings for the puppets and grinning grotesquely behind the stage. The public for this reason often adopted the hilarious attitude towards Pirandello that the English public in the early years of the century adopted towards Bernard Shaw : they fixed him immutably in their minds as a humorist and refused to be led into believing that he meant to be serious. But with Pirandello the grotesque comic arises from his serious spirit of adventure as he investigates the realms of reason. Like Bernard Shaw, he does not consider his characters farcical, for they symbolize his philosophy of life, and their extravagant conduct appears completely logical to his mind. The majority of the public who go to witness a Pirandello play listen to it with their ears attuned to the bourgeois sentimental play which preaches the triumph of society and the biggest herd. Pirandello, who stands on the shoulders of Ibsen the individualist, always sets the individual at variance with this stupid law of the majority, and gives him all his care and sympathy, however mad his pranks may be. Henry IV, as well as exposing the fundamental ideas of Pirandello with regard to reality and illusion, voices the aspirations of the individual to create his own world in this storm-tossed universe.

The action of the play centres in a rich young Roman gentleman of contemporary days who one day took part in a historical pageant. As he was interested in historical matters, he dressed himself up to represent Henry IV, the Emperor of Germany who lived in the eleventh century. In the pageant he rode beside a lady with whom he was very much in love, called Matilde Spina, and she had dressed herself up as Matilde di Toscana, the celebrated enemy of the Emperor. Matilde Spina, however, does not welcome Henry's suit, and prefers a man called Belcredi, who also takes part in the procession and rides behind Henry. During the procession the horse of Henry IV suddenly rears up and throws its rider to the ground head foremost. The result of the fall is that Henry becomes insane. At first nobody thinks that the fall has been serious, for Henry picks himself up and it seems as if he had got off with a slight stunning. When, however, two hours afterwards, all the guests had assembled in the drawing-room of Henry's villa and everyone was jokingly acting his part, it became apparent that Henry was playing in earnest. He was no longer a mask, but madness itself.

Henry's madness is of a curious kind : it consists entirely in making him believe that he is Henry IV, and as he is a man of wealth, his friends do not shut him up in an asylum, but let him live on in his sumptuous house and keep up his illusion. He is surrounded by many servants, who are specially coached in their parts, so as to represent different historical personages who were vassals of the Emperor. For the curious feature of Henry's madness is that he is painfully accurate on the history of his character, and often he causes dismay among the members of his retinue who do not know how to act their part.

For twelve years this madness endures, and then suddenly he becomes cured and awakens from his lethargy. But entering on his right senses is no pleasure to him, for he realizes, like Mattia Pascal, that his place has been taken in the world : Matilde Spina has gone away with Belcredi, his hated rival. How can he take up the thread of his former life again ? All will refuse to accept him as he was, and will treat him as a madman still. There is nothing left for him but to continue acting his kingly part and enjoy the spectacle of watching humanity from outside. So well does he carry out his scheme that none of his friends or servants notices any change in him, and so for eight years he continues his conscious madness. All this story which we have related has taken place before the curtain rises on the first act. The first act thus consists of a very clever exposition by dialogue of the past events. The first scene shows us the servants of Henry who are acting the part of the Emperor's four secret counsellors—Arialdo, Landolfo, Ordulfo and Bertoldo. Arialdo, Landolfo and Ordulfo are occupied in trying to explain the duties to Bertoldo, who is a new servant just arrived. Bertoldo finds himself in a great difficulty, because he has made up the history for his job, thinking that Henry IV of France was the character in question. Pirandello scores a good point in this first scene by his mixture of the mediæval and the blatantly modern. The hall and throne are in the severe style of the dark ages, the servants are dressed in the traditional costumes. Then we get the Pirandellian humorous contrast when we hear the modern slang terms and when one of the young men nonchalantly lights a cigarette. Two vulgar modern pictures that hang near one another complete the incongruity of the scene. In one of the pictures we see a representation of Henry IV as he was on that fatal evening when he fell off the horse. Twenty years have elapsed since that evening, and Henry, instead of being twenty-six, is forty-six, but that picture, as Landolfo says, is like a mirror wherein he may see an eternally youthful image of himself.

One day at the end of the twenty years his former fair mistress, Matilde Spina, arrives at the castle, accompanied by her lover, Belcredi, her daughter Frida and Frida's fiancé. With them also comes a mental doctor who is to make a last attempt to solve the riddle of Henry's mental complaint. By means of the picture which hangs on the wall, the author suggests to us how beautiful Matilde was twenty years before, and the contrast between her present and her past image is striking. She is now a fine-looking woman of forty-five, who makes up for her rapidly disappearing charms by a violent use of rouge and other cosmetics. In addition, her hair in the picture is black, whereas now she wears a yellow wig.

In Belcredi we are supposed to see the villain of the piece, the hated rival of Henry IV. It appears afterwards from the play that Belcredi, who was riding behind Henry and Matilde, inspired by hatred towards his rival, pricked with his sword Henry's horse and thus caused the fatal fall. Nobody, however, except the victim himself, saw the rascality, and all believe it an accident. Belcredi is a familiar type that has appeared often in the plays : he is a character who not only says humorous things, but is the cause of the humour of others at his expense. Nobody takes him seriously : his bird-like head and nasal drawl make him the Pulcinella of the play. The entrance of these people in modern clothes produces an amusing antithesis. However, in order to meet Henry IV, they must disguise themselves as characters of the eleventh century. Matilde Spina becomes again Matilde of Tuscany, Belcredi disguises himself as a monk, Pietro Damiani, one of Pope Gregory VII's envoys. At last the Emperor appears. Pirandello with great skill has worked up the excitement and expectation of the public by withholding the entrance of the protagonist until late on in the first act.

Henry is extraordinary in appearance. He is close on fifty years of age, very pale in complexion, and his hair at the back of his head is grey, but on his brow it has been dyed in a very crude fashion. On his cheeks, showing up against the tragic pallor, are bright spots of rouge, which give him the impression of being a wax doll. As robes he wears the garb of penitent, just as the real Henry IV did at Canossa. After him come three servitors bearing the Imperial crown, the Eagle sceptre and the globe with the cross on it. Henry takes the keenest delight in making his visitors feel the incongruity of their position : he runs through the whole gamut of madness, and laughs at the antics they have to perform in order to second him. With savage glee he shows Matilde that he is aware of the ravages that Time has wrought in her appearance.

" We all continue to cling desperately to our opinions of ourselves, just as the man who grows old dyes his hair. What matter that this dyed hair of mine cannot be a reality for you, since it is to some degree one for me ? You, my lady, do not dye your locks in order to deceive others, nor even yourself—but only to cheat your own image a little in front of the mirror. I do it for a joke : you do it in dead earnest. But I know that even you, my lady, are in a masquerade, however earnest you may be."

In the second act Donna Matilde, Belcredi and the doctor are in serious consultation concerning Henry. The doctor, who is a grotesquely pompous character, filled with ridiculous notions of his own importance, has been studying Henry's madness carefully, and advocates the necessity of an attempt at image cure. He says that Henry's peculiar sardonic humour and jesting against himself belong to a particular kind of madness which makes its victims diffident of themselves before strangers. Matilde, however, is uneasy : she feels that her ancient lover has recognized her, especially as he had remarked at once that her hair had been dark, whereas now it was dyed golden. She also comments on the fact that Henry right from the outset showed a strong dislike to Belcredi in his disguise as Pietro Damiani the monk. Henry, she hints, felt a strong dislike, because, being gifted with that subtle intuition that some maniacs have, he guessed that Belcredi was her lover. The doctor, however, evolves a plan :

DOCTOR.

" If we can manage to arouse him, and sever at one blow the already slackened threads which bind him still to his fiction, and thus give him back what he asks for (he himself said : ' One cannot, my lady, always be twenty-six years old ')—if we can free him from that torment which is a real one even to him—if, in a word, we so arrange it that he may be able at one moment to recover the sensation of distance and time—we may then hope to set him going again like a watch which has stopped at a certain hour."

The doctor's plan is to confront Henry with Matilde and her daughter Frida, both dressed as Matilde of Tuscany. The sudden shock of seeing the daughter and the mother as the one person will restore to him the conception of time.

Like a theme ever recurring through the mazes of orchestration of a symphony, the idea of distance and time is repeated again and again in this play. Pirandello by this constant repetition conveys to the audience the tragedy of Henry IV, whose life has been immobilized in the mask which he had assumed voluntarily that fatal day. While he is fixed immutably as Henry IV, the Emperor, twenty-six years old, just as if he was a watch that had stopped ; and while he has remained motionless, out of life, the others have all lived and grown old. Now Matilde Spina and Belcredi, aided by the doctor, wish to tear off Henry the mask which he has worn so long and bring him again into their life, which can no longer be his, for life has left him behind.

It is the same idea as we noticed in *Berretto a Sonagli*, where the mask which Ciampa has patiently constructed is rudely torn off his face and he is forced to take revenge.

Meanwhile a revolution has been taking place in the mind of Henry, and he tells his story to his henchmen. Up to this point in the play he has been strong enough in his hatred and cynicism to carry on his play-acting and cast dust in the eyes of the world. At last the climax comes—he cannot go on playing—the sight of his enemy Belcredi, who has gone all these years unpunished, maddens him. " Can't you understand," he says to his four henchmen, " how I trim and dress them and make them appear before me as frightened clowns ? And you are amazed that it is only now that I tear the clownish mask off them and reveal them in all their make-up : as if it was not I who constrained them to mask themselves just to satisfy this whim of mine to play the madman." Henry is closeted in the dark hall with his four body-servants. The scene recalls the last scene of *Castello del Sogno* (Dream Castle) of Butti (1912), where Fantasio sits drinking with his two followers, Metiste the drunkard and Logo the philosopher, whilst all the rest of his retinue have rushed off to join the armies of progress. With subtle dramatic sense Pirandello has constructed this final scene of Act II—the darkened stage, that symbolizes the confused uncertainty of the four young men, the sinister figure of the Emperor in his mediæval garments, holding the solitary lamp that lights up his queer wild features. Thus Henry explains the trick he has played on them all ; he is not mad, but sane, and he may now give vent to the bitterness against the world which wellnigh overwhelms him—bitterness even against his servants who acted parts in the mad masquerade. To the four followers there comes a feeling of sadness that now their pageant is ended : " What a pity," says Landolph, " to think that, dressed up like this and with so many beautiful robes in the wardrobe, this comedy was only done in jest." But Henry reminds him that they are the fools, for they ought to have known how to create a fantasy for themselves instead of acting it for him. They ought to have acted just for themselves, feeling themselves live in the history of the eleventh century at the court of the Emperor. Every day they could clothe themselves in that dream which would end by not being a dream any more, for they would have become part of it and absorbed it with the air they breathed. " To think that eight centuries in advance of this remote age of ours, so high-coloured and yet so sepulchral, the men of the twentieth century live in ceaseless stress and anxiety to know how their fate will turn out, while you, on the contrary, have already your place in history with me." These words of Henry again recall Butti's play where Prince Fantasio addresses the young stranger who has come to the castle of dreams to win away the Prince's sister Ebe. Fantasio, like Henry IV, tries to make his guest give up the life of the modern world and live with him, deep in everlasting dreaming of the past. " Would you reach," he says, " that state of mind when the Past may only seem a puff of smoke of recollections, the Present a sudden glow, which kindles and is quenched, the Future a mist which the eyes of Desire and Expectation in vain try to pierce . . . you will have power over everything, for the phantoms of your mind will assume shape and your idea become reality ! " In living this life of the past Henry was able to cheat inexorable Life which changes incessantly. But now the spell is broken, and he is unable to put on the mask again. In Act III the *coup* prepared by the guests takes place : Frida takes up her position, in the niche formerly occupied by the pictures of Matilde, and when Henry enters the hall she calls to him. Pirandello here produces the greatest effect in the play, for he communicates to us in the audience the terror of Henry, who for a few seconds is uncertain whether he he is not mad in reality. At first he leaps back, trembling in every limb, in terror, but when the others enter the hall, he sees, with rage, that all has been a trick. The news has been spread abroad that he has only been playing the madman, and he sees that it is now time for him to have his revenge. Belcredi and Donna Matilde try to persuade him to go away with them and start life again. But Henry tells them that his turn in life had passed away. " I understood," he says, " at once that not only had my hair gone grey, but that I was grey all over, and that everything in me had crumbled and fallen to pieces. I understood that I should arrive like a hungry wolf at a banquet which already had been cleared away." After telling them all of the treachery which had caused his terrible fall, and emptying the vials of his vitriolic sarcasm, he turns to Frida. She is the Marchioness as he knew her, and so she must be his in this new life which is to compensate for the many years of insensibility that have been his fate. He seizes her in his arms to carry her off. Belcredi rushes at him, but Henry in a flash draws his sword and drives it into him. The unfortunate Count is borne off dying ; his last words to Henry are : " You are not mad." The curtain descends on Henry, who is now in an agony of terror at the result of his masquerade which has driven him to murder. Calling his valets round him, he shivers for their protection, saying : " Now, of necessity . . . here together for ever."

In many of the plays that we have considered there are faults due to intellectuality ; the characters all seem to have come from the same mould and, as a critic has said, rather than various characters, they appear to be parts of the same character which is placed in situations that for ever vary and yet are for ever identical. So obsessed is the author by the problems of multiple personality, that he never takes the trouble to create many characters, but uses the same character in all its extensions. We can, however, point to an undoubted development in Pirandello's works starting from the early attempts like Liolà, an evolution which culminates with Henry IV. Every successive play is a further attempt made by this philosopher-dramatist to give full expression to his vision of the world. In each case he has presented a banal story and given puppets rather than human beings the task of exposing the theme. But beneath all the marionette framework we can hear the ever-mounting tide of life which is to sweep away all these temporary dykes constructed by man. Henry IV is a complete realization of Pirandello's dramatic sense, for he has created a character from a greater store of emotion. In spite of the tortuous reasoning in the play and the fireworks of dialectic, there is an atmosphere of dignity and sadness which approaches the ancient conception of tragedy. There is also a sense of fate dominating the whole drama, and this gives it a universality that we do not find in other plays of Pirandello. The style is striking, owing to its extreme simplicity ; the dialogue, though characteristically Pirandellian, owing to its disjointed, suggestive nature, becomes an admirable instrument for the author's philosophy. Even the most minor character is drawn vigorously. One of the most interesting figures in the play is Belcredi, the sceptic and humorist, who seems to play the part of a modern Touchstone, for the author gives him the crumbs from his philosophical banquet. Belcredi bears a certain resemblance to Laudisi of *Così È*, owing to his detached view of life. Only at the end of the play do we realize that his grotesque humour conceals his remorse for having been a villain. Matilde Spina is not so well drawn by the author : it is difficult to know whether she is just simply a ridiculous character or a modern and more unconventional Mrs. Alving who regrets the life she has led in the past. The doctor, who personifies the new mental doctors of to-day, recalls

Floriani, the hero of Bracco's play *I Pazzi* (1922). Pirandello no less than Bracco satirizes the self-sufficiency
of the scientist who claims to understand completely
even the most recondite nervous disorders. The play,
however, completely turns on Henry IV, and Pirandello,
in common with the modern dramatists of Expressionism
like Andreev, develops the action chiefly by the hero's
monologues. He is not a mere stage-struck hero who only
awaits the inspiring interpretation of an actor like Ruggeri
in order that the message of the play may reach the
public ; every speech he utters contains words of profound wisdom, and there are some critics who call him
the Hamlet of the twentieth century. Well might
Pirandello apply to himself the words which Shaw used
with reference to Shakespeare : " I am greater than
Shakespeare, because I stand on his shoulders." He has
given his hero the same tendency towards introspection
and melancholy as the Prince of Denmark. But whereas
the wickedness of the world and his own misfortunes
have the effect of making Hamlet rise from dejection to
Olympian rage, in Pirandello's hero all turns to that
strident humour which is the very antithesis to the spirit
of the gentle Shakespeare. There is no doubt, however,
that Henry IV, like Hamlet, is a tragedy of reflection,
for the striking parts of the play are those impassioned
quasi-monologues where the hero shows to excess his
speculative habit of mind. Pirandello has followed
Shakespeare's example by developing in this way the
character of his hero. The disgust of Henry IV
against the human race recalls Hamlet's disgust at the
shallow superficiality of his mother's mind, or else
Timon's rage at the destruction of his ideals. Henry IV
also, like Hamlet, is a humorist—a humorist whose
humour has a bitter tone about it. All the world is out
of tune, and he sees with merciless clearness its faults
and failings. Fate in depriving him of his wits had taken

away all *joie de vivre* from him, and when he awakens again to consciousness he sees the world inhabited by the foul spectres of his own imagination. Playing the external maskplay of Henry IV does not absorb his mind, nay, it gives it full scope for brooding reflection, and thus it happens that in those fevered monologues he pours forth his bitterness against the entire world. Like Timon he could cry :—

> " All is oblique ;
> there's nothing level in our cursed nature
> but direct villany."

With extraordinary skill the author in his development of the play keeps up the puzzle in the minds of the audience as to whether Henry is mad or sane. It is only at the end of the second act that Henry tells his followers that he is not mad at all, but has been playing his part all through. This comes as a surprise to those who expected that the play would contrast Henry IV as a true madman with Henry IV who acts the madman. A dramatist of olden days would have tried to get all the story within the framework of the play, and would have started off with the accident and Henry's fall. This would probably have required five acts and a complete disregard for the unities of Time. Pirandello, however, follows Ibsen's more modern method of narrowing down the limits of the play and leaving the general story to be worked out by retrospective exposition. It is the same method that was so successfully employed in *Ghosts*, a play which consists, as William Archer says, in withdrawing one by one the veils from the past. Then, in order to work off a characteristic Pirandellian surprise trick, Henry blurts out that he has not been mad at all during the play, but only pretending. From a dramatic point of view there does not seem to be any need for him to tell his servants just at that particular point of the play : he might have told them at the end of the first act. The episode seems to be dragged in to provide a fine climax to the second act—an effective obligatory scene which would conciliate the many-headed. Pirandello in the play did not concentrate his attention on the madness or sanity of his character, but on the episode of Matilde and Belcredi. Henry had been living eight years in blissful content amid his fantastic surroundings, without anyone suspecting that he was only acting a play. Then Matilde and her lover arrive with the doctor for the purpose of making a final attempt at curing Henry. The arrival of Matilde and the sight of her declining beauty make a terrible impression on Henry, for then he sees the extent of time that had passed. Wrapped in his fantastic robes, and gazing always at his portrait which reflected his image when he was twenty-six, he had lost all notion of the fleeting foot of Time. The discovery of this new reality drives him into a paroxysm of anger against his fatality. He feels then a fierce desire for vendetta and a momentary disgust with his present masked life. To his bodyguard he vents his spleen : " Get up, you sheep. Have you obeyed me ? You could have put the strait-waistcoat on me ! . . . crush one with the weight of a word—that is nothing !—a fly !—All our life is crushed thus by the weight of words—the weight of the dead. Here I am. Can you seriously believe that Henry IV still lives ? And yet I live and keep you living men at my beck and call. Those are my wishes. Does it seem a joke to you that the dead should continue to endure life ? Yes, here it is a joke : but get out of this place into the living world. The day dawns ; time lies before you—dawn. This day which lies before us—you say, We shall enjoy it. Yes, go and salute for me all those old traditions and all those conventions ! Go on speaking. You will repeat all the words which have been already said ! You think that you are alive, whereas you are only following in the steps of the dead."

How disjointed and irregular the style of Pirandello is when we compare it with the sensitive, imaginative style of other dramatists, and yet how admirably suited this jerkiness is to the moments of crisis in his dramas. Not only do we see the dramatic conflict of Henry IV, but we also catch a glimpse of the struggles in our own minds —struggles that we can rarely manage to express, but which Pirandello with his great artistry represents plastically for us. The true moral of the tragedy of Henry IV is the antagonism between Life and Form. It is the tragedy of Life that is choked by a form only meant to be ephemeral, but which swallowed Life altogether. This is the central idea, not only of this play, but also of every Pirandello play. Life with its forces is in antithesis to the form which the individual adopts or else the form which society imposes on the individual. Henry IV is thus really a repetition in nobler harmonies of *Tutto Per Bene*, where the individual suddenly finds himself face to face with the mirror which reflects back an image of himself, not as he sees, but as others see him. In both cases there is nothing for the poor victims to do but to put on the mask again and act their part, concealing as best they can their torment.

The perpetual antithesis between reality and fantasy which runs through Pirandello's play recalls, as we showed, Butti's allegorical attempt to treat the same subject in *Castello del Sogno*. Butti, however, only looked at the subject from his nebulous, poetical mind, and aimed primarily at producing a symbolic poem, whereas Pirandello has brought his work into the clear light of day. The comparison between the two works shows how different was the spirit which inspired the Milanese writer and the Sicilian. Butti treats his subject in a

mystical way without a spark of humour, and in the end
he shows the defeat of Fantasio, the champion of the
dream world. Through the medium of Fantasio, the
poet tried to express the contrast that existed in his mind
between fantasy and the inexorable reality of life.
Pirandello, on whom the spirit of impish humour ever
attends, has not limited his play entirely to the fantastic,
but with wonderful skill has fused the fantastic with the
realistic in a most dramatic way. *Il Castello del Sogno*
is not a dramatic play, because only one side is shown
and there is no real conflict. *Henry IV* is full of dramatic
contrasts which produce drama. And Henry IV,
pseudo-madman, does not express in the drama his
thoughts and mental reservations, but our nebulous,
unexpressed fancies.

VII.   THE IMAGINATION OF WOMEN

In *La Signora Morli una e due*, which appeared the
same year as *Henry IV*, we get the clearest example in
Pirandello of the drama of double personality. In an
essay on the author, G. A. Borgese states the problem
of personality thus : " We pronounce," he says, " the
little word ' I ' with a slight emission of voice, and we
regulate ourselves, or believe that we regulate ourselves,
as if each of us were a monad. But when we consider
the question carefully, how many discordant elements
do we find making up this apparent unity ! How many
definite aspects does a man present to himself and to
others ! What deep gulfs separate our lyrical and intimate self from our social and practical self, our self of
to-day from ourself of to-morrow ! "[1]   Pirandello was
not the only writer to be obsessed by this problem of
double or multiple personality : we find traces of it in
the great majority of the modern works included under

[1] G. A. Borgese, *Tempo di Edificare*, p. 224.   Milano, 1923.

the title of "grotesques." The problem arises ever more frequently in these contemporary days, when the antithesis between society and the individual, the mask and the face, becomes more pronounced.

Signora Evelina Morli, a young married woman with a child, Aldo, has the misfortune to be abandoned by her scapegrace of a husband, Ferrante Morli. After many hardships, Evelina becomes acquainted with a lawyer, Lello Carpani, who falls violently in love with her and makes her come to live with him. Under the influence of the meticulous and worthy man, Evelina leads a life of exemplary devotion which effaces the recollection of the wild days she had spent with Morli. By Lello she has a daughter Titti, whom she brings up together with Aldo. When the play opens the scene is laid in Lello's house : a visitor calls to see the lawyer. This is no other than Morli, who has returned after many years' wandering in America, where he has managed to make another fortune. Lello does not know who his strange visitor is, but Evelina recognizes him immediately. Morli says that he has not come back with any intention of trying to exercise an influence over his true wife, but only to see once more his son Aldo. Then the conflict breaks out. Evelina, with a mother's quick intuition, guesses that Morli wants to take away her son. While the dispute waxes hotly, Aldo comes in and demands to know the reason of the quarrel ; he has the right to know who the stranger is. In this scene it is Aldo, the son, who becomes the mouthpiece of the author's logical reasoning. Evelina wants to keep him with her as well as Titti, but he shows her that this is unjust. It is right that she should remain with Lello and Titti, but his duty is to follow his father, Morli. Aldo thus departs with his father. In the second act the scene changes to Morli's house at Rome. Feeling that with subtle care he would be able to make Evelina return to him he dispatches a telegram to her saying that Aldo is seriously ill and in danger. Evelina in hot haste rushes to Rome, only to find that it was all a trick in order to make her stay with Ferrante. Irresistibly she feels herself drawn within the circle of attraction of her former husband. Artfully Ferrante recalls their days of mad passion and extravagance many years ago—those days when she had been very different in character. After her union with Lello she had put on the mask of virtuous, humdrum housewife and put away the frivolous pranks of her youth. When she comes again to Ferrante, her personality reverts to its former state: even Aldo, with his quick intuitions, notices the change: she seems no longer to be his true mother, whom he had considered as the wife of Lello. Evelina feels herself strangely attracted towards Ferrante, and she hearkens to his tempting words that she should stay on with him for ever. But then to her mind there comes with pressing insistence the thought that with Lello there is her daughter Titti, and again her maternal instinct tortures her. An insoluble dilemma confronts her: should she stay with Ferrante and Aldo, living a life of gay folly that appeals to one side of her character, or should she return to Lello and Titti to take up again the threads of her steady life of duties? The dilemma resembles that of Ellida in *The Lady from the Sea*, when she is tempted to follow the mysterious stranger. With all the ecstasy of her mystic temperament Ellida aspires towards Romance, which is embodied in the stranger, but then, when her lofty-souled husband lets her choose, she chooses the life of duty and devotion. So it is with Evelina; she feels a strong affection towards the man who helped her when she was friendless and gave her his protection. "Here," she says, "life has neither head nor tail: over there with Lello there is tranquillity I have never thought whether I was happy or not:

there was so much to do and to look after. Here it is you who give all. Over there it is I who give, and I have the satisfaction of knowing that I give life to others." This is the same motive as in *Candida* of Shaw, where the heroine rejects her romantic poet lover Marchbanks and decides to remain with the prosperous, placid clergyman Morell, because she feels that he is the weaker of the two and so all the more deserving of help and compassion. The same moral appears in Benavente's play *Más Fuerte Que El Amor* (1906), where he says that " compassion is stronger than love, for if it did not exist, life would become a struggle between wild beasts." It is compassion which makes Evelina, in spite of Ferrante's entreaties, stand firm to her union with Lello. When she returns to him, he at first will not pardon her, for he suspects that she has given herself to Ferrante. Lello is a highly moral man and cannot bear up against the gossip which assails Evelina on all sides. After a big struggle he had managed to have her respected in spite of the disaster which had ruined her early life, and now all his efforts had been in vain owing to her fatal attraction towards Ferrante. It is only with the greatest difficulty that Evelina can explain to him that she, in common with so many heroines of the New Theatre, has a double personality. She had been attracted as in a dream towards the evocation of her past life with Ferrante but this dream did not prevent her from realizing that her true life was with him.

Signora Morli is an interesting play for the thesis it upholds—a thesis in some ways opposed to the moral of plays like *Il Piacere dell' Onestà* and *Ma non è una Cosa Seria*. In those two plays the protagonists voluntarily embarked on a certain part. Angelo Baldovino and Memmo Speranza undertook the part with the certainty that they will be able to carry it out until the end. But the life force which actually controls caused them to throw aside their mask and reveal their true selves. In *Signora Morli*, as in *Henry IV*, we see the triumph of the opposite point of view. Both protagonists in these two later plays undertake a certain line of conduct, and as in the case of the former two plays, the forces of Life cause them to falter. But then clear reasoning comes to their aid, and Henry IV decides that the best course for him is to reassume his mask of fantasy, and Evelina Morli realizes that it is better for her to forget the mysterious attraction of the man she loves by instinct and give herself up entirely to the life of duty which she had raised up for herself with infinite trouble. *Signora Morli* is like *The Lady from the Sea* modernized and bereft of all its romantic colouring and emotion. The practical, bourgeois modern world is not propitious to Ellida, who for ever hears the echo of the ocean's monotony. And Pirandello has complicated the issue by the two children.

In *Henry IV* Pirandello shows how a world of fantasy is imposed by Fate on an individual and he is forced to act his part. Afterwards, as a result of a tragedy, he is forced to reassume this mask of unreality. In *Vestire Gli Ignudi* (Naked), which appeared in 1922, there is the exposition of an analogous problem. The heroine of the play, in order to give interest and romance to her life of humdrum drudgery, creates a fiction. But alas ! the fictional character which she has given herself is torn from her by the world and she is left naked. Thus the play works the opposite way to *Henry IV*, as if it were the converse to a Euclid proposition. Ersilila Drei, the heroine of *Vestire Gli Ignudi*, is a poor little governess who has been employed by the Consul at Smyrna for his child. Owing to the pressing attentions of a young naval officer, Laspiga, who was *de passage* at Smyrna, she falls a victim under promise of marriage and becomes his mistress. Laspiga, like the proverbial Pinkerton, abandons her and goes away on his ship. Ersilia, whose weak nature is morally enfeebled by her misfortune, falls a prey to the wiles of the Consul, who is attracted by her charm. She thus neglects her duty, and one day the child, who has no one to mind her, falls over a parapet and is killed. As a result, Ersilia is driven away on account of her culpable negligence and arrives at Rome, where she drifts from bad to worse, until finally she determines to commit suicide. The cause of her final determination is that she hears the announcement of marriage of Laspiga, her former lover. Ersilia, the poor downtrodden governess, meets with the fate of the weak who are vanquished by life. Her attempt to poison herself fails—owing to the prompt attentions of the doctor. In the hospital, as she lies in a precarious condition, a bright idea strikes her mind : she determines that she will end her life romantically. As her days are counted, she determines to inspire pity in the world by a sad story of her sufferings, and so to a journalist she gives a highly coloured account, not omitting any detail that would show up her innocence. The journalist publishes a full account of the interview, giving the names of the Consul and the naval officer. Contrary to expectations, Ersilia gets better and goes to stay in the house of Ludovico Nota, an old novelist who has been attracted by her sad story as related in the papers, and offered her charity. As in the case of *Henry IV*, Pirandello has used the retrospective method of exposition, and by skilful means little by little through the play he unveils the story of Ersilia's past.

The first act is one of the characteristic Pirandello scenes : the rooms of the novelist are dingy in style ; and the landlady, Onoria, who is a hard, bony woman recalling her counterparts in Dickens, looks with great disapproval on Ersilia's presence in a bachelor's rooms. No writer excels Pirandello in drawing a scene of modern bourgeois tawdriness. The bare room looks out on the street, and every now and then there can be heard the shouts of the newsvendors, the noise of cars passing, the hubbub of hurried life. At one moment during the act an accident takes place under the windows of the house— an old man is run over by a car and killed. The varied shouts and confusion are a striking contrast to the subdued scene within, where the wan Ersilia relates her woes. Pirandello, following the external symbolism that we find in Ibsen's plays, means the antithesis between the street and the room scene to indicate the struggle in Ersilia's mind. After her dismissal and consequent arrival in Rome, she had sunk to such depths of poverty that she had to sell her body to passers-by, and now it is only by the good graces of Ludovico Nota that she can avoid going on the streets again. Her peace of mind is destined to be of short duration, for the story published in the newspapers attracts great public notoriety and comes to the ears of the Consul and Laspiga. The former sees his name compromised by this tissue of falsehoods related by Ersilia. The latter, as a result, meets with a blank refusal of marriage from the girl to whom he was engaged. Realizing how cruel he had been to a girl whose love was so strong that she tried to poison herself for him, he rushes to Ersilia's lodgings to try to make tardy amends and marry her. But when he is there he meets the Consul, who has arrived in a state of fury to expose the lies of Ersilia. Ersilia is browbeaten by all. She realizes that she should not have failed to kill herself : naked and exposed to the horrors of the world, she had made a valiant attempt to cover her nakedness by creating a great illusion around her suicide. But owing to her unexpected return to life all her plans have been shattered.

Ersilia by her fate proves the truth of a favourite maxim of Pirandello that no one is what he seems to be. She had tried to create for herself, even in death, a beautiful mask to cover up her sad reality, but Life has tricked her and has destroyed the mask. In masterful scenes the author exposes her tortured mind, first with Laspiga, who in vain tries to placate her by promising marriage, then with the Consul, who vents his fury on her and accuses her of totally ruining his life, but ends by begging her to yield to him : " Let us," he cries, " unite together our despair." But Ersilia feels in the position of " Fu Mattia Pascal " when he tries to get back to life again : nobody will accept her point of view and there is nothing to do but to make a second attempt to kill herself. As long as she remains in life she will be pursued mercilessly by the world.

In the last act the climax comes with Ersilia's second attempt at suicide, and this time the poison works quickly and the play ends with the old-fashioned death scene that recalls *Morte Civile* of Giacometti. Ersilia, surrounded by her friends, has time before she dies to make a long speech explaining the point of the play, in case any one in the audience might not have understood it, for Pirandello in spite of his obscure complexities followed that maxim for the dramatist which is enunciated by Benavente :—

" Everything that is of importance to the proper understanding of a play must be repeated at least three times during the course of the action. The first time half the audience will understand it ; the second time the other half will understand it. Only at the third repetition may we be sure that everybody understands it, except, of course, deaf persons and some critics." And Ersilia has got to be precise with her audience, for the plot is difficult to grasp, as it nearly all takes place before the play begins. It may be said that this is the extremest case of the retrospective method in Pirandello's plays, and there is no doubt that on account of so much having happened before the curtain rises, we are only slightly interested in the development of the play. From the first act it is evident that Ersilia is a poor weak creature who is hopelessly defeated in the battle of life, and we have no interest in her because she does not react against her fate. The skill of the dramatist is altogether devoted in the play to the task of gradually unfolding for us the history of her past life, and no dramatist is more skilful in this. The crowded streets and the hopeless cruelty of modern life engulf such lost waifs as Ersilia, and in each succeeding act the dramatist lays stress on this idea. However pathetic a figure Ersilia is, we cannot help feeling that she, like all the other Pirandellian heroines, is a victim to her creator's logic. She ceases to be the poor, downtrodden woman who could never do anything right, and becomes a thinking machine. In the scene with Ludovico and with Laspiga and Grotti the Consul, she argues like a Professor of Psychology. When Laspiga offers to marry her, she does not accept his offer with alacrity, as all girls of real life in her position would have done, but prefers to unravel her own tortuous psychology. As a result of her rather nebulous, uncertain personality, the other characters who act as satellites to her fade away into abstractions. Ludovico the old novelist, who thinks that he has found copy for a new book in Ersilia's adventures, leaves her to her fate when he finds that her imaginative story is a fake. We cannot help feeling that in real life he would have been all the more interested when he was told the truth, for Ersilia would then become an interesting subject for a novel like *Il Fu Mattia Pascal*. Laspiga and the Consul do not seem to be characters of flesh and bones ; both only seem to exist in order to give Ersilia a chance of pouring out her woes. It is a cold play, and one that does not convince us like *Henry IV* or *Così È*.

In *La Vita che ti diedi* (1923) Pirandello develops the

same thesis as in *Vestire Gli Ignudi*. Anna, the heroine, who has been for years separated from her son, has managed to evoke a mental image of him which becomes a reality to her. This image satisfies her until the return of the son, but then a conflict begins in her mind. The newly-arrived son, she finds, is utterly unlike the image in which she had seen him embodied. Death, however, descends suddenly and kills him off, and so the poor mother is left again to the morbid presence of the phantom she had created. Death has no power over this phantom son, whom she for ever sees in her imagination, and so the onward course of life is arrested. It is the same idea as the short story *La Camera in attesa*, where the mother and the sisters ceaselessly tend the empty bedroom of their brother with the feeling that he is sure to arrive back. Time stops for them. The same unforeseen event, however, awakens Anna from her dream as awoke the mother and the sisters in the former story. Lucia, who had been Anna's sons's mistress, comes in search of him. She had been unable to continue her life of hypocrisy with her husband and children, and she cannot live without her lover. She confesses to Anna that she is *enceinte* by him and that she is determined to remain for ever at his side. Anna, whose whole life and thoughts are entirely centred on the recollection of her son, does not tell Lucia that he is dead. The whole scene is a most successful piece of tragic irony, for the audience know that he is dead, and Anna's words to Lucia have a double sense as she tries to calm the suspicions of the latter, who wonders why he is not there to receive her.

LUCIA.

" Can't you tell me where he is ? Don't you know ? How can we let him know ? "

DONN' ANNA.

" Wait, wait ; we shall make him know, yes——— "

LUCIA.

" But how can you, if you don't know where he is ?
I hope he hasn't gone off on a long journey without
letting me know ! "

DONN' ANNA.

" No, no—he can't be far away—he can't be far
away. . . ."

LUCIA.

" He was afraid probably to tell you where he was
going—perhaps it was you who advised him to go ? "

DONN' ANNA.

" I didn't know."

Donn' Anna's hopes rise high because of the arrival
of Lucia. Her son exists still, because he lives in Lucia's
heart also. But the arrival of Lucia is destined to awake
her from her dream, just as in the *Camera in attesa* it was
the arrival of the fiancée who awoke the mother and
the sisters from their weary waiting. It is Lucia by her
tears, when she finds out the truth, who makes Donn'
Anna understand that her son is really dead. Before,
she had not believed her own senses, even though she
laid him out in his coffin with her own hands. He was
so different to the son she had known years before that
she did not recognize him. Then she turns to Lucia,
because she bears within her the life that springs from
her son. Lucia must stay with her always and forget all
her ties, her husband, her other children. But then she
sees that this too is impossible : " As soon as the child

you bear within you is born, as soon as you give my son life again—you will then be the mother and I shall not. He will never more return to me here. It is all over. You will have my son again with you over there—tiny as he used to be—with his golden locks and his laughing eyes—just as he was. But he will be yours, not mine any more. You, you are the mother : I begin to die really now."

Such a play reveals to us the passionately sad spirit of Pirandello in a more striking way than either of the two preceding plays. Donn' Anna is a truly tragic figure on the stage, and Pirandello has created her with emotion. More even than *Henry IV*, it is an expressionist play like Andreev's " soul theatre." It is the tragedy of one personage : the rest do not count—they are only minor satellites deriving their light from the central figure. And Pirandello uses them as supers to construct the surroundings of this exalted woman. There are many tricks by which he makes our flesh creep—the darkened, empty stage, the ghostly light from the wings. The stage directions sometimes help his purpose considerably, as, for example, in the second act, where he describes the room : " The stage remains empty and darkened ; with just the reflection of that one ghostly light outside the door on the right. After a long pause, without the slightest noise, the chair which is in front of the writing-table stirs gently as if some invisible hand was moving it. After another shorter pause, the light curtain in front of the window is lifted on one side, as though by the same hand, and then falls. (Who knows what things may happen unseen by anybody, in the darkened and deserted rooms where somebody has died ?) "

This example is a characteristic stage direction of Pirandello and shows how many tricks he has at his disposition for producing his theatrical effect on the audience.

VIII. THE THEATRE FROM WITHIN

Six Characters in Search of an Author

The majority of the plays of Pirandello which we have considered deal with the problem of reality and unreality, and, as many critics have shown, this master of irony with his band of marionettes has transported on to the stage the anti-logical and anti-rational ideas of contemporary philosophy. He is an idealist in the sense that he allows the mentality of man complete supremacy and makes thought the leaven which sets Life in fermentation.[1] Reality becomes a matter to be judged by the individual who feels the emotion intensely, not a matter to be judged by the cold opinion of the majority. The only test for the reality of any experience is the emotion which engenders that reality : Laura, the heroine of *L'Innesto*, has a child by the man who ravished her, but her love only exists for her husband Giorgio, and so she feels as a reality that the child is his. In *Tutto Per Bene* Martino Lori persuades Palma to accept the reality that he is her father, though both know that she is the daughter of another. Pirandello sees deep down into human character beneath all the manifold constructions which society has raised as a protection of the majority. If we take a comprehensive view of the plays, we shall find that the whole collection resembles a set of symphonic variations on the same theme, reality and illusion which, like the fundamental motif of *Tristan and Isolde*, rises by contrast.

The next play we shall consider—*Sei Personaggi in cerca d'Autore*—acts as a kind of coda to the symphonic variations of Pirandello's previous works. It sums up Pirandello's philosophy and also exposes his theories with

[1] A. Tilgher, *op. cit.*, p. 205.

regard to the art of drama. If in the other plays the author turns his searching rays on the life of the world, in the *Six Characters* the process is reversed, and we gaze into the world of the actor, behind the brilliantly lighted stage, into the dingy dark spaces where work the wire-pullers for the puppets. No more striking attempt has ever been made to show the successive steps in the evolution of a character from the moment it leaves the author's brain until it expresses itself on the stage for the public in the crowded auditorium. The majority of people imagine that the characters which fret and strut their hour upon the stage are all dependent on the author's will, as new-born children are attached to their mother. Pirandello in this play shows that such an idea is erroneous. When a character is born, he says, it acquires such individuality, such independence that it can release itself entirely from subservience to its author and appear in situations and conflicts for which it was never intended. The idea of setting the character in conflict with the author seems to have occurred to Pirandello, first of all, in " La Tragedia d'un Personaggio " (The Tragedy of a Character), a *novella* contained in the collection *La Trappola* (1913). In that *novella* the author described how he used to give the characters of his future stories an audience every Sunday morning from eight until one o'clock, when they were allowed to ask questions and argue to their heart's content. This privilege was not limited to the children of the author's fantasy, for other characters from books which he had read used to force their way into the reception-room and insist on exposing their arguments and complaints.

" Nature," he says, " uses the instrument of human fantasy in order to follow her high creative purpose. A character in a play comes to life just as a tree, as a stone, as water, as a butterfly, as a woman. And he who has the fortune to be born a character can afford to jeer even at death, for he will never die. And to live for ever, he has no need of amazing gifts or miracle working. Who was Sancho Panza ? Who was Don Abbondio ? And yet they live on eternally as live germs—just because they had the good luck to find a fertilizing womb, an imagination which knew how to bring them up and nourish them so that they might live for ever."

With delightful fantasy Pirandello makes his six phantom characters arrive at a theatre while a rehearsal is in progress. The stage is bare except for the prompter's box, a small table for the manager and various chairs scattered about. The company are rehearsing one of Pirandello's plays, *Il Giuoco delle Parti*—a play which is giving great trouble to the actors and the plethoric manager, who exclaims : " Ridiculous, do you call it ? What can I do if no good plays come from France and we are reduced to put on the stage plays by Pirandello, which require a ' highbrow ' to understand them, and never satisfy either the actors, the critics or the public ? " Then, to the great amazement of all, the six characters advance up the stage to the manager. As the author says in a stage direction, " a tenuous light surrounds them, as if radiating from them—it is the faint breath of their fantastic reality."[1] They are characters that the author had sketched out temporarily in a play that he was writing, but was unable to finish. Feeling that their nature has only been half realized, they have come to propose to the manager that they should be allowed to act the drama which seethes within them.

[1] These words are from the stage directions in the original edition. In the revised edition, published in 1925, the author states that the best way to prevent the Six Characters from being confused with the actors of the company is to make them wear light masks cut in such a way that eyes, nostrils and mouth are left free. " The six characters," he says, " must not appear as phantoms, but as ' created realities,' immutable creatures of fantasy. They are more real and consistent than the voluble actors."

The Six Characters are as follows :—

The character called the father is about fifty, hair reddish in colour, thin on the temples, but not bald. His thick moustaches curl round his still fresh mouth, which opens often into a queer, uncertain smile. He is rather fat and pale, with a large, expansive forehead. His blue, oval-shaped eyes are clear and piercing ; he wears light-coloured trousers and a dark coat. In manner he is gentleness itself, though at times he has violent outbursts. The mother seems to be terrified and crushed under an intolerable weight of shame and humiliation. She is dressed in widow's weeds, and when she lifts her veil she reveals a face of wax-like pallor. Her eyes she keeps continually lowered. The stepdaughter is a girl of eighteen, most self-assured and impudent. Her elegant, showy black frock reveals her beauty. She shows the utmost contempt for the timid frightened manner of her young, gawkish brother of fourteen, who is also dressed in black. She shows a great tenderness towards her little sister, a child of about four years, who is dressed in white with a sash of black silk round her waist. The son is twenty-two years old, tall, and, as it were, encased in an attitude of disdain towards the father and of supercilious indifference towards his mother. He gives us the impression that he has come on the stage against his will.

From this description it will be seen that not all these characters have the same degree of dramatic vitality. The father and the stepdaughter were evidently those that struck the author's mind with the first flush of inspiration, and so they are very nearly completely realized. The others are on different planes. The mother and the gawkish boy are nebulous characters whose personality did not appear clear and defined to the dramatist's mentality. The former, as the author says, is not a woman ; but she is a mother, and her drama

lies in her children. The son, with his haughty super-
ciliousness, had only occurred *en passant*. As these Six
Characters owe their existence to dramatic creation,
they cannot prevent themselves from rushing to express
themselves : they must get the opportunity of reaching
their completion as parts of the drama. With the help
of the manager and his company, they hope to be able
to draft their play. The manager, like all managers, is
of a crusty disposition, and objects strongly to this un-
warranted interruption of his rehearsal : " What do you
want here ? " he cries. " We want to live," answers the
father excitedly. " Where is the text of the play ? "
continues the manager. But the father then replies :
" The drama is in us : we are the drama, and we are
impatient to represent it : our inner passion drives us to
this." Then, to prove their words, they start off spon-
taneously acting the play and gradually fitting into their
place in the dramatic scheme. The actors and actresses
at first are inclined to laugh and jeer at their strange
visitors, but gradually they become interested in the
scene. The play, developing as it does in a queer, jerky,
explosive manner, is entirely characteristic of Pirandello.
It is not like the *Spanish Armada* play in *The Critic*, where
high-sounding, ridiculous bombast is parodied with keen
thrusts, nor is it a play for the author to air his satiric
" persiflage " like *Fanny's First Play*, by Bernard Shaw.
Pirandello, as in all his other plays, is looking past the
stage and its actors to the abstract problems of life. He
has made another great attempt to express dramatically
the various phases that man's mind goes through.

The plot centres in the unhappy father who is married
to the character known as the mother. They have one
child, the haughty-looking son. The father had a clerk
in his business who frequented his house as a friend.
Seeing that this man was in love with his wife, he made
her go away with him rather than have her moping at

home. The son he kept by him as his solace. The mother when she went to live with the clerk had three illegitimate children by him—the stepdaughter, the boy of fourteen and the baby. Meanwhile, the father has found life still more wearisome without his wife. " After she went away," he says, " my house seemed suddenly empty. She was my incubus, but still she filled it—I wandered about through the rooms aimlessly." The son, through lack of his mother's influence, grew up taciturn and austere in manners. Then the father became curious to find out the whereabouts of the other children of his wife. He felt tortured by remorse for the way he had treated her. " I really wanted," he says, " to believe that she was living in peace and plenty, devoting herself to the simple cares of life, fortunate because she was far away from my inner complex struggles." He longed to see the three illegitimate children who had grown up around her. One day he went to visit the school at which the eldest stepdaughter attended as pupil. Then soon afterwards he plucked up courage and gave her a present of a straw hat ornamented with a garland of roses. " It was first of all," he says, " curiosity and then a feeling of tenderness that attracted me gradually towards my wife's family." But the wife looked with dismay on his increasing intimacy with the daughter, and in order to break off the relationship, she disappeared to another city with the clerk and the three children. The father then lost all traces of them for some years. In the interval the mother sank into poverty owing to the death of her companion, and in dire straits she returned to her native city and started working for a living. The stepdaughter was now a grown girl of eighteen, and she acted as intermediary between her mother and the fashionable Madame Pace, for whom the former did sewing. The " modiste " establishment of Madame Pace had many other attractions in addition to dressmaking. It was a convenient " rendezvous " for clandestine lovers, and private rooms were provided for the purpose. The stepdaughter, being beautiful and of an easy disposition, was easily led astray by the astute " celestina " Madame Pace, and led a life of vice. At this point the drama broke out in all its violence. The father, though a most respectable member of society, was a frequenter of Madame Pace's establishment. To the stage-manager he excuses himself thus : " Each of us, sir, in society before the others is clothed in dignity. But each one knows within himself what unconfessable things take place there. We give way to temptation only to rise up again soon afterwards, and with great anxiety re-establish in all its pristine solidarity our dignity, as if it were a tombstone which conceals from our eyes any sign and any recollection of our shame." On one of his visits to the shop he meets the stepdaughter, and as he does not recognize her, he accompanies her upstairs in order to satisfy his lust. The sordid deed is about to be consummated, when, by one of those wonderful and characteristic stage coincidences, the mother suddenly enters the room and shrieks in terror when she sees the guilty pair. The father then, after the narrow escape he has had, welcomes his wife. He will bring her back with her children to his home and at last there will be peace for all. But as the saying goes, " l'homme propose, et Dieu dispose " ; the house, instead of reflecting a new life of harmony, becomes a veritable Bedlam. The stepdaughter knows the true history of this grey-haired old satyr who had exposed so clearly his vicious propensities, and feels fierce hatred as well as disgust when she finds that he was her mother's husband. No less does she loathe the haughty, supercilious son who looks on all the newcomers as intruders. The mother, between the blatant bad temper of the stepdaughter, the silent contempt of the son, and the horrible incident of Madame

Pace's parlour, is completely broken in spirit. Her greatest torments arise from the fact that she cannot approach her eldest, legitimate son and explain all the tragedy. His silent disdain and indifference are more wounding to her than the acute sensation that shame is impressed indelibly on her family. Her troubles do not even end at this stage ; one day the youngest child, who was playing in the garden near a pond, falls in and is drowned. The brother of fourteen, seeing his sister drown, draws a revolver from his pocket and shoots himself.

Such is the plot of this nebulous nightmare play which Pirandello sketches out for us by means of the Six Characters, with their jerky, excitable utterance, punctuated by the interruptions of the manager and the actors. Indeed, it may be said that this play in the making, with its complexities, is only a slight exaggeration of the author's usual method. With its fantastic personages it gradually thrusts the original play into the wings, and all the actors and actresses listen in breathless interest when the stepdaughter begins to describe the scene in Madame Pace's parlour. The manager, who sees the possibility of a striking play, casts the parts for his company : they must watch the performance of the characters so as to make their own performance afterwards as lifelike as possible. One character is wanting to the scene—Madame Pace herself.

The characters, however, by arranging the stage in a manner that suggests the modiste's shop, evoke Madame Pace herself. She appears at the back of the stage, to the amazement of the actors and actresses. Her hair wears the artificial hue of peroxide ; rouge and powder conceal the wrinkles of her fifty years. At her arrival amidst the Six Characters the obligatory scene starts, irresistibly impelled by their violent desire to achieve complete self-expression. When the scene is finished, the manager's company then repeat the scene after their own fashion. The scene performed by them seems altogether a different thing : the leading actor who is taking the part of the Father enters with the breezy manner of an old *beau* ; the leading lady playing the Stepdaughter becomes the conventional stage barmaid type. The Father and the Stepdaughter naturally cannot recognize themselves in the stage-struck poses of their interpreters, and break out into impatient gestures of disapproval and laugh satirically.

FATHER.

(At once, unable to restrain himself.)

" No ! "

(The Stepdaughter, seeing the leading actor make his entry thus, bursts out laughing.)

MANAGER.

(Turning round, furious.)

" Silence ! Stop that laughing at once ! We can't go on like this ! "

STEPDAUGHTER.

" Excuse me, sir, it is most natural that we should laugh. The lady there (pointing to the leading lady) stands there still ; but if she is meant to be me, I can assure her that if I heard anyone say ' Good evening ' to me in that way, I should burst out laughing as I did."

FATHER.

" Yes, it was the manner, the tone ! "

MANAGER.

" What are you talking about—manner and tone ? You stand aside at once and let me see the show ! "

LEADING ACTOR.

" If I have to represent an old man entering a house of doubtful reputation——! "

MANAGER.

" Don't mind them, for goodness' sake ! continue : the show is going splendidly."

With wonderful subtlety Pirandello has analysed the contrast between the reality that exists in the mind of the author and the conventional art of the stage. The characters of the author, with the bloom of his sensitiveness still upon them, cry out for their own individuality, but the manager answers that they only achieve personality through the actors.

" Your personality is only raw material here, and the actors give body and shape, voice and gesture to it. And those actors—according to their lights—have known how to give expression to far nobler material ; while your play is so small that if it holds its own on the stage, the merit, believe me, will be entirely due to my actors."

FATHER.

" I shouldn't dare to contradict you, sir. But consider that it is inhuman suffering for us who are constituted thus, with these bodies, these features—— "

MANAGER.
(Interrupting impatiently.)

" As to your face, my dear sir, make-up will remedy that ! "

FATHER.

" Yes. But what about the voice, the gestures ? "

MANAGER.

" Oh ! well—here you cannot be yourself ! Here it is the actor who represents you, and that is all I have to say."

FATHER.

" I understand, sir. But now I think that I can guess why our author who saw us live thus did not wish to bring us on the stage. I do not want to offend your actors—Heaven forbid. But I think that . . . however the actor strives with will-power and art to assume my personality, his performance can hardly be a representation of me as I really am. It will be, with the exception of the make-up—an interpretation of me as he sees me— not as I feel myself in my inner consciousness to be."

In this passage we again perceive the " teatro dello speechio "—the mirror showing the individual a reflection of his own image which he cannot recognize. The mirror, in the case of these phantom embryonic characters, is dramatic art itself, which distorts and deforms Life. Tilgher points out in his criticism of the play that Pirandello unconsciously transforms those phantom, half-realized characters from the plane of fantasy on to the plane of life as it is lived.[1] This dualism adds to the ever-increasing confusion of the play, which ends in chaos. The chaos arises chiefly because each of the characters, obsessed by his own reality which has to be respected, tries to capture the centre of the stage, the place in the limelight, to the detriment of the others—all except the Son, who keeps on announcing in a surly voice that he did not want to be brought into the play at all. The manager in vain tries to enclose them within the hard-and-fast rules of the stage that are tempered by long tradition, and rebukes the Stepdaughter for monopolizing the attention.

[1] A. Tilgher, *op. cit.*, p. 186.

" I will not stop ! I see that you and he have arranged what is possible on the stage. . . . I understand. He wishes to arrive at once at the scene of his mental processes ; but I want to represent my own personal drama."

MANAGER.
(Annoyed, shrugging his shoulders.)

" Oh ! Just your part ! Excuse me, but there are other parts as well as yours ! There is his part (points to the Father) and the Mother's part ! On the stage it is not right for a character to come too much into prominence and put the others in the shade. The right course is to keep them all within a neat scheme and only show what is capable of representation. I know full well that each of us has an inner life which he longs to reveal. But the difficulty consists in setting out just what is necessary with regard to the others, and at the same time in that slight revelation hint at the life which lies within, undiscovered."

These words of the manager are characteristic of the psychological dramas of Butti, Bracco and Pirandello. They recall the critical preface which Bracco wrote to *Piccolo Santo*, where he said that a comprehensive synthesis of significant signs can confer to the stage the necessary clearness for rendering even what is not truly expressed. The dialogue and outer action in *Piccolo Santo* are merely outer symbols which are to put the audience into the intuitive state of mind when it can understand the hidden play.

In the last part of the play a fierce argument starts between the manager and the Father as to the meaning of the word reality. The manager disputes the latter's contention that the Six Characters are more real than human beings. But the Father sustains his point : " Human beings," he says, " are ever-changeable, and their reality changes from to-day to to-morrow, and on they pass and die away, but the character created by the artist's imagination has its life fixed within immutable bounds."

The tragedy of all these characters comes from this rigidity ; they are fixed in the one disastrous reality of their lives. The Mother is fixed in the moment of horror when she found her guilty husband with the Stepdaughter; the Stepdaughter is fatally attached to that sordid room of the modiste where she must play her scene of climax. The Father, too, is for ever fixed to that scene which shows up only one side of his reality. It is thus that he states the drama arising from this : " The drama, sir, in my opinion, lies in the conscience that I have, and that each of us has. We believe ourselves one person, but it is true to say that we are many persons, many according to the possibilities of being which exist within us. We are one for this and another for that person—always diverse and yet filled with the illusion that our personality is always the same for all. . . . Now you understand the treachery of that girl : she surprised me in a place where she should not have known me, and in a way that I could not exist for her. She then insists on attaching to me a reality which I could never have expected to assume for her in a fleeting, shameful moment of my life." To that fleeting moment of his life, when his unsuspected cave-man personality came to the surface, the Father is indissolubly linked, and to the end of time he will have to go on playing his part. It is the same idea as we find in *Henry IV* and other plays of Pirandello. Henry IV assumes the mask of Emperor for one evening's enjoyment, but by the irony of Fate he is crystallised in that mask by madness. When he recovers, he finds that there is no possibility of throwing off the mask, for it has attached itself to him inextricably. The world will not accept his existence except as the Emperor, and so he returns to play the part.

The Father came to life in the author's mind as the protagonist of the scene in the dressmaker's shop, and however he strives, he must remain fixed in the situation. He cannot, like real human beings, change from one personality to another, for he has been crystallized as one personality.

With great art Pirandello shows by means of those half-evolved characters, in contrast to the actors of real life, the antithesis between Life and Art. The Six Characters, with their violent striving towards self-expression, are driven on by their Life impulse : they have no discipline, no power of synthesis, and so their play can never reach any conclusion. If art is to be produced, there must be harmony and the characters must all work towards that end. But the Son, who is only a very faintly sketched character, and one that seems to have appeared only as an afterthought to the author, refuses to work in with the others towards a conclusion. Then the morose boy character to whom nobody had paid any attention draws a revolver and kills himself and the play, and the characters rush off the stage carrying his body. He, too, had acted, driven on by blind impulse. The play thus fails to emerge, because these characters, with their raw vital impulses, will not co-ordinate and accept the dictates of the manager. The manager on his side is not characteristic of the brilliant producers that contemporary dramatic technique has evolved ; he makes a very poor attempt to cope with the difficulties raised by this complex play. Instead of realizing that such a play must pass through the complicated process of evolution before it can take shape, he greedily tries to improvise it, perhaps led astray by the example of his ancestors of the " Commedia dell' arte " with their *zibaldoni*. In the figure of this bloated manager, Pirandello satirized the usual stage-struck producer whose few thoughts are centred on the box office and on the "long run." Thus the play, which starts by being a profound study of art and life, a contrast between reality and fantasy, ends as a grotesque of the Cavacchioli or Antonelli type, showing up by flashlight the seams and fissures in modern stage illusion.

In the last act of the play the author seems to say over and over again to us by means of his fantastic characters : " How difficult the art of evolving plays is ! Not only must the dramatist catch his idea and imprison it within his mind, he must also observe Life minutely and draw general conclusions from his observations. But even then his task is not nearly over. The phantom children of his imaginations, like the Six Characters, are self-willed : they will not co-ordinate in harmony, but prefer to think of themselves as the nucleus of the whole play. They are the products of the author's fantasy—that quicksilver fantasy which darts hither and thither with utter lack of discipline. Even when the author has succeeded in marshalling his characters together, how is he going to enclose them within the traditional stage ? how is he going to transfuse their chaotic impulses into the human actor, who has the task of transmitting their message to the world ? " All these questions Pirandello seems to ask himself, and it is a tribute to his sincerity that he has not tried to answer them *ex cathedrâ*. It is for this reason that the play which begins seriously ends as a grotesque farce. Pirandello was fundamentally a humorist, and in writing this play he was not exclusively occupied with thoughts of proving any universal truth about Life and Art. Up to a certain point he allowed his brilliant fantasy to work its way, aided by logic, and raise a construction, but then there appeared his humour—

that malign imp which delights in pulling the construction down about his ears. In the first part the author was intent on his subject, but as soon as the characters began to function symmetrically the humour started to wither them, and when we recall the savagely grotesque, farcical satire of *L'Uomo, la Bestia e la Virtù*, we shall agree that the finale of the tragedy of the Six Characters, which the critic Tilgher called absolutely absurd, is logically true to Pirandello's quaint humour. Many qualities in the play are characteristic of the humorist, especially the brilliant aphorisms. No dramatist of our times in Europe, with the exception of Jacinto Benavente, had a greater wealth of those gems of lightning thinking that spring from the brain of the humorist. These sudden flashes light up his dialogue and allow his thought to transfix our minds. Examples could be multiplied like the following : " A fact is like a sack which will not stand up when it is empty. In order to make it stand up we must put into it the reason and sentiment which caused it to exist."

" Every one of us has his own reality which must be respected before God even when it is harmful to oneself."

" Please do not mention illusion : for us that word is particularly unpleasant."

In *The Six Characters* Pirandello analysed the whole essence of dramatic illusion. From the days when Aristophanes in *The Frogs* held a trial of the respective representatives of drama and weighed Æschylus and Euripides in the scales, down to modern times, the subject of dramatic criticism has been treated frequently on the stage. Writers mostly devoted their attention to contrasting, as Moratin did in *La Comedia Nueva*, the man of common sense with the pedantic, bombastic dramatists or else they preferred to parody dramatically, as Echegaray did in *El Critico Incipiente*, or Shaw in

Fanny's First Play, the idiosyncrasies of critics and their contradictions.

At first sight it would seem that Pirandello's play is a twentieth-century prolongation of Sheridan's *Critic*. Sheridan places the burlesque tragedy of the Armada and Don Ferolo Whiskerandos within his comedy, and satirizes the dramatic ideals of his day through the medium of Puff and Sir Fretful Plagiary. The burlesque tragedy enclosed within Pirandello's play is a grotesquely deformed modern tragedy, and one which would be intolerably depressing if the author had not written it in a satiric mood. But Pirandello has not really followed Sheridan's mood and written an exaggerated tragedy in order to satirize the drama of his time : the tragedy of the Six Characters becomes an instrument in his hands for interpreting the fundamental problems of the theatre. He is not criticizing exclusively the stage-manager or the actors or the critics, but the fundamental essence of dramatic art ; and no one up to this has probed its mysteries with more acumen than he has in this play. Mr. Ashley Dukes, in his brilliant apology of Expressionism in modern drama, includes Pirandello among the expressionists. " One of the aims of the expressionists," he says, "is to present character subjectively. We are asked to regard the persons on the stage, not only with our own eyes, but through their own emotional nature."[1] On the objective stage it is a difficult task to present subjective drama, yet Shakespeare accomplished the task in *Hamlet*, and Ibsen in *The Master Builder* and *The Lady from the Sea*—those noble symphonies of the inner and outer life. Pirandello, who is an heir of Ibsen, has followed his example, and in *The Six Characters* he pushes the subjective portrayal of character to its logical conclusion. Ashley Dukes says that characters subjectively presented are like sleep-

[1] A. Dukes, *The Youngest Drama*, p. 133. London, 1923.

walkers functioning in response to a hidden motive.
They go through the play wrapped in a mantle of
sublime egoism.   Their part is not to listen, but to
speak.   This criticism applies to the Father and the
Stepdaughter, each of whom pays no heed to the other,
so convinced are they of being the nucleus of the drama.
Their attitude resembles that of Zero and Daisy, the
two machine-made clerks in *The Adding Machine*, by
Elmer Rice, who express aloud their subjective uncon-
nected thoughts as they tot up the interminable figures.
But Pirandello has not followed Rice to the extreme
limits of Expressionism ; he still clings on to the clear,
well-knit dialogue of his predecessors.   And it is this
clear, unexaggerated, well-balanced spirit which gives
Pirandello that great ascendancy over the dramatists of
the Modern Movement in Italy who lose themselves
amid the maze of the grotesque and the fantastic.

Now that we have considered Pirandello's chief play
dealing with the evolution of dramatic character, we
should give our attention to *Ciascuno a Suo Modo* (Each
in his Own Way), 1924, which treats the same subject,
only from a different angle.   In this play the author
presents a grotesque Pirandellian play on the stage.
Then after each act he has what he calls an " intermezzo," wherein we are transported to the other side of
the footlights and listen to the excited commentaries
made by a bewildered public.   Some are haughty
Pirandellians, and gaze with serene imperturbability on
the excited philistines ; others are dramatic critics who
are afraid of compromising their reputations by showing
enthusiasm or disdain ; others, again, are honest folk
who are frankly entirely befogged by this new author,
so much at variance with the old romantic drama.
Then we suddenly meet two excited people—an old man
and a young woman.   They create a disturbance in
the theatre and rush on to the stage.   We then learn

that the play represented on the stage is a key play, and
the infuriated pair have recognised their own sad life
story as related by the actors. Thus there are in
Ciascuno a Suo Modo three planes of reality. The play in
the first act appeared on the foreground as a representation of incidents from real life. Then in the first
" intermezzo," when the scene shows the *foyer* of the
theatre with its gesticulating public, the scene of the
first act is driven into the background and appears as a
fiction created by art. At the end even the *foyer* of the
theatre and the spectators are driven into the background when it is known that the play represented on
the stage is a key play constructed by the author from a
cas célèbre recently discussed in the newspapers—the story
of the actress " La Moreno," the Baron Nuti and the
sculptor Giacomo La Vela, who committed suicide on
account of them. The presence in the theatre amidst the
spectators of " La Moreno " and the Baron Nuti establishes a degree of reality still closer to life than that of the
spectators, who are only discussing a piece of fiction. In
the final choral " intermezzo " Pirandello shows all the
conflict between these three planes of reality wherein the
real personages of the drama attack those who are on
the stage and the spectators who try to interfere. Thus
the play cannot go on any more. *Ciascuno a Suo Modo* is
a variation on a theme in *The Six Characters in Search of
an Author*. In that play one of the central ideas is the
contrast between the fixed reality of the literary character
and the ever changing reality of human beings. The
tragedy of the Six Characters is that they are fixed in the
one disastrous reality of their lives. The Stepdaughter is
fixed to the sordid scene in Madam Pace's parlour ; the
Stepfather, too, is fixed eternally to that shameful reality
which was only a fleeting moment, only one side of his
character. In the second play " La Moreno " becomes
infuriated because she sees herself fixed on the stage in

an instinctive action which is unworthy. It is interesting also to compare the two plays in other points. The Six Characters can scarcely contain their merriment when they see the attempt made by the actors to represent them—the Father and the Stepdaughter cannot recognise themselves in the stage-struck poses of their interpreters.

In *Ciascuno a Suo Modo* Pirandello seems to contradict his former thesis. Baron Nuti and " La Moreno," so far from laughing at the actors' attempt to represent their personality, become passionately serious, as if they recognised their innermost thoughts. And to make his meaning more explicit, Pirandello at the end makes them copy the actors on the stage. In the acted play the old man insists on carrying away the young woman with him in spite of her repulsion from him. So too does the Baron Nuti prevail on " La Moreno," and the astonished spectators watch the stage scene repeated in real life before their eyes.

Now that we have examined these two plays, we cannot but agree that they mark a date in the history of the Italian theatre which it will not be possible for the old drama to ignore. They have turned the theatre as we know it inside out. No other dramatist of modern times has analysed with such logical clearness the whole essence of theatrical illusion. Not only is Pirandello a dramatist gifted with a talent for vivid epigrams, but he is also a metaphysician, and though that is sometimes a danger to him, his clearness of reasoning admirably balances his sensitive temperament. As to the fundamental ideas contained in *The Six Characters* and *Each in his Own Way*, we must not think that they have sprung straight from Pirandello's brain. Other authors have thought of similar ideas, but have not developed them in the same way. In no less a work than *Don Quixote* of Cervantes do we find a precedent to *The Six Characters*. As Spanish critics have shown, Cervantes was the first great writer in modern literature to establish definitely the conflict between the reality and fantasy. In that work for the first time we find the character claiming the right to live independently. In the second part of *Don Quixote* the principal characters of the work begin to show us a double personality ; they are real beings who live their own life independently and yet they are also literary figures. Bartolomé Carrasco, the student from Salamanca, comes and tells Sancho that Don Quixote and his squire are already the subject of books and that many things were related about them by the historian.[1]

As Professor Castro shows, we have there the theatre within the theatre, and Sancho and his master henceforth always feel that their life is material for a future historian who will take them as models. Don Quixote was disconsolate, thinking that the historian might not write of his noble adventures with all the dignity they deserved. We thus find the same fear on the part of the character lest he may be misunderstood by the interpreter as we noticed in Pirandello's plays. Of course there are many differences between Cervantes and Pirandello ; in the former the characters are conscious that they have a full life of their own, for they have been realized by the author ; in the latter the dramatic conflict really arises because the author has never completed the evolution of the Six Characters. But the despair of Don Quixote and his squire is nearly as great as that of " La Moreno " and Baron Nuti when they find that they have been put into the book of so doltish a writer as Alonso Fernández de Avellaneda, who would be utterly incapable of understanding their complex personality. In later days Spanish writers have treated the theme of the character *versus* the author. Miguel de Unamuno

[1] Americo Castro has discussed the problem of Cervantes and Pirandello in an interesting article published in *La Nación* Buenos Aires, April 16th, 1924.

in his novel *Niebla* (1908), also anticipates the method of Luigi Pirandello. The plot is a vain unvarnished story of love and jealousy. But Augusto, the wronged party, does not end the story in the conventional manner. He goes off to find the author. When he meets him at Salamanca, he informs him of his intention to commit suicide. The author, however, tells him that he cannot die, as no such person exists in reality as Augusto. He must go on living in the fantasy of his author. Unamuno, thus, does not drive the idea so far as Pirandello, who says that when a character is born it obtains such independence even of the author that it can acquire a meaning which the author never thought of giving it.

PIRANDELLO'S ART THEATRE

In 1925 Pirandello founded an Art Theatre in Rome. He established it in the Teatro Odescalchi, where Guido Podrecca had shown his famous marionettes. Pirandello's intention was to build up a school of drama which would cause a Renaissance of the theatre in Italy. The play chosen for the opening night was a short one, entitled *La Sagra del Signore della Nave* (Sanctuary of Our Lord of the Ship). It was a significant play to choose, because in it the author experimented with new scenic effects. It describes a tumultuous festival in a port of southern Italy, where the people pay homage to a famous image of Christ which has saved many of them from shipwreck. It is more of a pageant than a play : we hear the babel of excited voices, and in the distance the rat-tat-tat of drums. Old fishermen wearing huge, conical hats and worn-out velvet clothes, prostitutes in gaudy colours surge round excited youths revelling in drunken intoxication. There are long tables laden with platters of roast pork and mammoth flasks of red wine. In order to enable the audience to join with the actors in this kermesse the author set up a low bridge linking auditorium and stage. The bridge was fitted with machinery which made it stand erect in the centre of the stalls or sink flat on the ground when it was not required. Along that bridge the various people wending their way to the sanctuary at the back of the stage passed from behind the backs of the audience. Men, women and children kept up a chattering din ; pedlars, vagabond fiddlers, and mandolinists ; rugged sailors who have been miraculously saved by Our Lord of the Ship. They are dressed in white with red sashes and blue shirts and they carry votive tablets on which are painted stormy seas and the apparition of Our Lord. Pirandello in the play with subtle art mixes the religious with the profane. He takes a young tutor, a poetic idealist, and contrasts his sensitive nature with the coarse brutality of the rest of the people. The poet cannot understand the relation between gluttonous sensuality and the religious festival. He is disgusted to see the men catch hold of a huge pig and slaughter it in the most brutal manner possible ; he trembles and grows pale when he hears the beast squeal in pain as the blood gushes forth in torrents.

That huge pig is the darling of Signor Lavaccara, the father of his young pupil. Signor Lavaccara had been unwilling to hand the pig over to the slaughterers : he felt a bond of sympathy, for was he not himself fatter than the pig ? The pig had been one of the family, and used to eat out of his hand. He had given him the name Nicholas. And so he rushes after the crowd, shouting out : " Tell him not to slaughter it. I'll give him back his money ! " The end of the play resolves itself into a discussion between the tutor poet and Signor Lavaccara. The poet refuses to believe that Nicholas the pig was intelligent. " What is a pig and its intelligence compared to the divine intelligence of

man ? " Signor Lavaccara will have none of the
poet's arguments. He contrasts the humanity of his
wonderful pig with the idiocy of mankind, and he tells
the poet to gaze around and note the bestial behaviour
of the crowd, who by now are stupefied by gluttony,
lust and drunkenness. "There is your humanity—
there it is," he shouts, "do you recognize it now ? "

All of a sudden a booming church bell is heard. The
red sun sinks behind the horizon, the howling mob are
hushed in terrified silence as the bell tolls. The door
of the church opens, and a very tall priest appears,
holding up on high the macabre, blood-stained crucifix.
The bell tolls, the organ sounds from within the church,
and amidst the clouds of incense we see the crowd
sink upon their knees murmuring "mea culpa".
The procession following the crucifix slowly descends
from the stage and passes along the bridge through
the midst of the audience.

In such a play Pirandello endeavoured to show new
methods of production. He was eager to link up the
various arts, always bearing in mind the notion that
the theatre should be a meeting-place of the Arts.
He wished, also, to reform acting in Italy, and create a
school capable of giving the subtle nuances required
by modern drama. He made experiments with the
technique of the traditional "commedia del'arte" and
encouraged his actors to improvise. It was after many
experiments that he produced in 1930 the play *Questa
Sera Si Recita a Soggetto* (To-night We Improvise).
Here as in *The Six Characters in Search of an Author*, he
shows a play being made, and he marks the antithesis
between the passion of the characters in their own
drama with the artificiality of the stage-producer.
Pirandello is even more scathing against directors and
producers in this play than in the former. The theme
is based upon the story " Leonora Addio " from the

collection " Terzetti "—a study of fierce Sicilian jealousy.
Pirandello takes the theme of jealousy and watches
how the producer, Dr. Hinkfuss, will treat it. Dr.
Hinkfuss is full of his own importance, and exclaims
that as producer and stage director he is supreme in
the theatre. " I have," says he, " a greater rôle than
the playwright, for I bring to life what is enclosed in
the playwright's written work." Dr. Hinkfuss therefore will not allow the drama to develop itself, but
insists on breaking it up into various tableaux. He
dictates to the actors how they are to play their parts
so as to fit in to his preconceived plan. But the actors
refuse to be puppets, and insist on playing their parts
independently. As the play deals with Sicily, Dr.
Hinkfuss wishes to drag in local colour, something
which will symbolize traditional Sicily, and so he
arranges at the beginning a religious procession, with
choir boys in black, and girls in white veils, followed
by a representation of the Holy Family. But the events
of the drama of jealousy are in themselves so violent
that they crowd out the picturesque procession, which
has nothing to do with the play. Dr. Hinkfuss tries
to plan effective entrances and exits for the characters,
but the swift-moving drama breaks down all his schemes :
the characters are in agony, and refuse to fit into any
scheme. They end by driving him off the stage.

As in *Ciascuno a Suo Modo* the play ends in chaos and
recrimination. Above it all we find the author nodding
his head sadly, and saying : " Life obeys two forces
which are opposed to one other ; and those two forces
do not allow it to assume definite form or to be for ever
fluid. If Life moved eternally it could never acquire
consistency ; if it acquired consistency it would never
move. And yet Life must have both consistency and
motion."

In considering the later theatre of Pirandello we should

give full credit to the great actress Marta Abba, who became the Muse of his work. Many of the plays are dedicated to her, and one feels that they were specially written for her. There is a passionate quality in her acting which gives new beauty to Pirandello's tragic plays and her success was assured right from the time when she created the part of Ersilia Drei in *Naked*. Take for instance the play *Diana e la Tuda* (1927), where the author actually describes the heroine in terms of Marta Abba : " She is very young, and marvellously beautiful ; her curly auburn hair is arranged in the Greek fashion ; her green eyes, long, large and luminous, gaze limpidly and sweetly like the dawn. At times, when she is sad, they have the grieving character of a turquoise. Her lips have a sorrowful expression, as if Life awakened feelings of disdain and bitterness in her. But when she laughs, she is all of a sudden enveloped in a luminous grace that lights up everything.

Marta Abba is Italy's most versatile actress. We have seen her excite the critical Roman audience to enthusiasm in D'Annunzio's *La Figlia di Iorio*. But she adopts a different technique in the Pirandello plays. Instead of the slow-moving, tragic heroine of D'Annunzio trailing clouds of poetry, we find the tormented, modern woman caught in the snare of life. As Giuncano says to Tuda : " When you were a child you moved more easily—you darted here and there—then a little less—always less and less until . . . do you think that you have lived ? You have finished dying."

Another play that showed the excellence of Marta Abba's acting was *Come tu mi Vuoi* (As You Desire Me), 1930. The heroine Cia, the beautiful wife of Bruno Pieri, was the centre of a happy family, all who knew her loved her, and then came the tragic day when she disappeared. During the War, when northern Italy was invaded, Pieri's villa was plundered, Cia was raped and carried away by the brutal invaders. Everyone believes that she is dead. Ten years have elapsed, Pieri's villa is rebuilt, and life continues as before. Then, all of a sudden, we hear that Cia has been found in Berlin. Under the name Elma, she is a dancer in a cabaret, and is the mistress of Karl Salter, a coarse, sensual German writer. Do not think, however, that Elma has any affection for Karl : she hates him like poison, and loses no opportunity of pouring scorn upon him, and mocking his poor talents as a writer. And so she continues her career of drunkenness and debauchery. But Elma, like so many modern romantics is a tormented soul. She exclaims against modern life, and calls human beings beasts, with the difference that beasts at least are endowed with the wisdom of instinct, and are natural, whereas when man tries to be natural he becomes a destructive fool. Woe to us if we had not reason as a strait-jacket. It is in this state that Boffi, a friend of Pieri, finds her and he ends by persuading her to flee away from Salter and go back to her husband in Italy. She thus ceases to be Elma, and becomes again Cia. One day in the villa she finds a diary, written by Cia during her early years of marriage. After reading it she tries her best to transform herself into the noble soul of Cia, as she lived in that diary. But she finds that it is impossible to persuade the world to recognize her full identity as Cia. Difficulties of every kind arise. Finally, Salter arrives from Vienna, bringing with him one who is said to be the actual Cia, a poor, mad woman. The family crowd round calling her by name, but she remains passive, smiling idiotically. Cia the heroine in a temper revolts against their misbelief, for she realizes that her attempts to start a new life were futile. She had wanted a true love and faith, but she had not found it in Bruno Pieri's house. And so she leaves him and returns to her old life in Berlin with Karl Salter.

The plot of *As You Desire Me* might be criticized by many as far-fetched, but actually it is closely similar to the famous Bruneri-Canella case of mistaken identity which aroused such interest in the Italian Press in 1929.

THE MYTHS OF PIRANDELLO

In spite of the official sanction given by the Italian Government, and in spite of its brilliant artistic success Pirandello's Art Theatre ended as a financial failure. It was a noble example for the idealists to follow and it linked Pirandello's name with the great artists of modern Italian drama, such as Bragaglia, Guido Salvini and others, but its failure must have deepened the maestro's pessimism. If the Teatro Odescalchi (or the " Theatre of the Twelve " as it was called at first) had fulfilled its expectations, Rome would have become a great experimental centre for modern drama and Pirandello would have spent all the remaining years of his life there. But circumstances forced him to become a nomad and wander from one country to another, supervising performances of his plays. In Italy he had received the highest distinctions, including membership of the Italian Academy, and in 1934 world recognition came to him after he had been awarded the Nobel Prize for Literature. His name blazed in electric lights over the cinemas of the world when Greta Garbo, Hollywood's heroine of mystery, played in *As You Desire Me*. It was Fame that turned Pirandello into a nomad. " Henceforth," he said one day, " I live in the vast world : the hotel is my home and all my worldly possessions consist of a typewriter. My life does not change whether I am in Milan, Berlin, Paris or New York. My beautiful dream of a patriarchal existence in the bosom of my family has faded away into thin air. What good is my house to me? It would have to be a caravan on wheels to be of any use to me." People who saw Pirandello in those later years used to call him a Chinese Buddha immersed in his own meditations. He had released himself from the miseries of the world and, like the most fervent devotee of Schopenhauer, had killed in himself the will to live. He had got rid of his worldly possessions by dividing all his royalties in equal parts among his children. "All that I have left," he said, "is a great pity for humanity compelled to live the allotted span upon this cruel earth."

When we consider the plays written in the last eleven years of Pirandello's life, we find that they resemble modern Platonic dialogues in which the master plays the part of a melancholy Socrates. Each drama contains, in addition to the argumentative dialogue, an element of myth. The author uses the imaginative story or myth to illuminate his arguments and he prophesies to his audience. Let us take, for example, the play *L'Amica delle Mogli* (The Wives' Friend) 1927, which, in common with many of these later plays, is dedicated to his friend and pupil Marta Abba. The heroine, like Marta, has auburn hair and is nobility personified. Her virtue is in contrast to the rest of society with its petty meanness and corruption. Marta by her noble nature dominates those wretched creatures of instinct. She arranges their marriages, prepares their homes, settles their quarrels and unites them when they have broken away. It is Marta who gives every one of them life, for it is her goodness which illuminates their existence. The curious part of it all is that none of those men had asked Marta in marriage. Her reserve had made them timid and tongue-tied. Consequently they marry inferior wives and regret for ever their memories of Marta. As for Marta, she lives for the others but not for herself. She symbolizes mythical purity surrounded by the forces of evil. In the end the evil machinations of Venzi, the Iago of the play, triumph, and Marta concludes the play by saying to her friends : " Leave me ; I wish to remain alone." That is the destiny of noble women like Marta, who are Valkyries far above the corrupt world of man.

In *Trovarsi* (Find Oneself), 1932, Pirandello takes up the myth of the last play and treats it in a different way. In this case the author studies the effect the profession of actress has upon her personality. The play is a parallel to D'Annunzio's novel *Il Fuoco* (The Flame of Life), wherein he describes the queen of all actresses Eleanora Duse—*quella donna solitaria e nomade che pareva portare per lui nelle pieghe delle sue vesti la frenesia delle moltitudini* (that lonely wanderer who seemed to carry in the folds of her robes the frenzy of the multitude). According to Pirandello a great actress like Marta Abba (he calls her Donata Genzi in this play) must forswear real life and live entirely within the mask of the fictitious character she creates upon the stage. It is said that Marta Abba absorbs herself so entirely in her characters that she is like one who has been hypnotized. Pirandello, in the play, describes her as pale and distraught, with great tragic eyes. Marta Abba in those later plays banishes his malicious imp of humour and inspires him to write tragedy. No longer do we live among the grovelling mass of humanity : we are transported into palaces where aristocrats talk in a style that at times resembles D'Annunzio's.

Donata-Marta's tragedy is revealed in all its pathos. She belongs to the public, body and soul. They have the right to fall in love with her but she must have no secrets from them. No matter how eagerly she craves

for love and affection she must for ever deny herself
and flit through life, storing in her mind a thousand
memories of what might have been. Then one day
Donata meets the young Swede Elj Nielsen, an adven-
turous, Viking spirit, and she falls in love with his
frank, spontaneous personality. For to Elj Nielsen life
is wonderful because it is for ever changing. Donata
under the inspiration of this love hopes to discover her
real self—the self that exists behind the mask she has
created in her acting. But Donata is doomed to
disappointment, for she finds that the very gestures she
makes, the caresses she gives Elj, are the same as those
which the public had noted in her acting. She must
be the same actress with her lover as she had been out
there upon the stage. When she tries to give up her
career to live with Elj she finds that it is too great a
sacrifice, for he only represents instinctive life and
nothing more. And so she sadly admits that she
cannot discover herself in the love for Elj. How can
she find herself when all the life in the universe is only
a desperate, struggling aspiration towards something
that cannot ever be achieved, because at the end there
is naught but death and destruction. Then she realizes
that only art enables her to find herself after her experience with her lover. Elj will not understand, for he
had wanted her all for himself, and so it is her destiny
to return to her lonely existence on the mountain peak.

As a pendant to *Trovarsi* Pirandello in 1933 composed
Quando si è Qualcuno (When One is Somebody), in
which he discusses Socratically the theme of literary
fame. The famous author is no less of a slave than the
great actress : his life is no longer his own : he is a
puppet who must jog on to a certain rhythm : everywhere he goes he is followed by the myriads of searching
eyes. And, as for his form and style, it must be reproduced with the regularity of a machine and stamped

with his impress. " Even my head," he says, " is owned by the public like the head on a coin." But the author does not submit willingly to this slavery. Behind the mask he suffers, because Life is for ever moving, whereas he wants to assume another fixed image. " At night in my study," he says, " I feel as if I were a puppet seated in part of my desk, in the light of the lamp, with wig, wax face, wax hands, lifeless eyes and motionless figure." The author lives in a musty library which smells like a church. When he is alone he tries to communicate with the four authors, Dante, Ariosto, Foscolo and Leopardi, whose pictures hang on the walls. They do not converse with him, for they are enclosed within the mould of tradition. All they can do is to adopt the typical postures which convention has given them. Dante with outstretched finger says " No " to Foscolo when the latter with upraised arm asks him to speak of new Italy. Leopardi shakes his head and opens his arms in a gesture of despair while Ariosto smiles indulgently. Then one day the old author meets a beautiful young woman, Veroccia, with whom he falls in love. He then dresses in youthful costume and enters life again. As a result of this love affair he writes passionate poetry which he publishes under the pseudonym, Delago. Delago is forthwith acclaimed as the great poet of youth, much to the discomfiture of the old poet, who feels that he has been overwhelmed by the puppet he has created. " What am I to do ? " he cries. " If I tell them that I am Delago, Delago would be ruined : he would become my mask—a mask of youth which I put on to mock the world." And as for the beautiful Veroccia with the auburn hair, she belongs to Delago— the short-lived creature of his dreams of past youth. He has then to face the cruel dilemma—either he must continue to live as Delago with Veroccia, or kill Delago and go back to his conventional family life and his glory as poet-laureate. He gives way to the entreaties of his wife, children and friends, who announce that the Italian Government intend upon his fiftieth birthday to confer upon him the title of count for his merits as poet. At the end of the play we see the official conferring of the title, and while the orator recites the laudatory speech, the poet listens, as it were, to his own funeral oration. He is dead : Veroccia had said so. She had left him for ever when she had discovered that Delago was only a joke, a hoax upon the public. Yes, he was truly dead, for Veroccia herself was the heroine of his spirit which was still youthful.

In this poignant play Pirandello tried to show the contrast between the old and the new generation of poets—a contrast which is rooted in a misconception. The moral of the myth is that the old writer, whose body is weary and worn, may yet have a youthful spirit longing to stretch its wings in flight after ideals that do not belong exclusively to either old age or youth.

Among the later plays of Pirandello none is of more interest to the student than *La Nuova Colonia* (The New Colony), which was produced in 1925, with Marta Abba in the principal part. Here the author discusses one of his favourite themes—the creation of a new society. In order to understand the scope of the play we should consider first some of the earlier " novelle " wherein he treats the same theme. In Sicily frequently new villages used to spring up in out-of-the-way places and it was possible to observe the growth of civilization from the pioneer stage. In a short story entitled " Romulus " from the collection *E Domani Lunedi*, Pirandello calls the old founder of such a settlement Romulus, because in him he recognizes the true founder of a city state. Romulus had not been suckled by a she-wolf, but if you looked into his eyes you would understand at once why men invented the legend that his mother was a wolf. And here Pirandello protests against the realistic historians, who like the scientists of the Positivist Movement put all their trust in documents and forgot all about the poetry of legend which is the true and eternal reality. In the process of explaining his myth Pirandello shows that humanity is divided into two categories—those who by instinct are nomadic, and those who are sedentary. Romulus is sedentary and so he halts in the deserted country and builds his house. Everything goes well until Remus arrives and builds another house directly opposite. Then straightway Avarice, Envy and Pride swoop down like three evil spirits. " For it is not true that men join together for mutual comfort ; they join to fight one another." And what is Civilization, says Pirandello at the end, but the knowledge that man in addition to possessing the war instinct has also the so-called gregarious instinct.

In *La Nuova Colonia* Pirandello sets his scene in a port in southern Italy, in a society of sailors, fishermen and whores. With grim, realistic touches he expresses the hopeless poverty of those poor wretches who have been ground down for ages by social injustice. But those smugglers and whores are not all completely degenerate : some of them long for better things and are eager to revolt. Spera the heroine is one of the rebels. She is a prostitute but she is in love with the fierce Currao, whose personality dominates all those waifs and strays. When Spera finds that she is pregnant by Currao she determines to escape from her life in the port and start afresh. Off the coast is an island which had been a penal settlement but had been abandoned because it was slowly sinking into the sea. Currao determines to escape to that island and start a new life with Spera. What odds if the volcanic island sinks beneath them? They could not sink deeper than they were doing in their present life. When Currao, Spera and their smuggler companions arrive in the island they vigorously set to work to create their society. Currao establishes a tribunal and distributes justice, and as for Spera she is queen and goddess of them all. As in the case of " The Sleeping Beauty " of Rosso di San Secondo, motherhood awakens in her the desire for purity, and the primitive life on the island redeems her. Spera, alas, is not fated to continue her idyllic life. As she is the only woman she awakens feelings of lust among the other men, who feel a grudge because she belongs to Currao. As long as all property was held in common the golden age could last, but then man's instinctive greed for ownership begins to assert itself. Some, too, refuse to co-operate in the society created by Spera and Currao and live by themselves apart. Spera alone preaches incessantly the gospel of sacrifice and renunciation. " We must," she says, " be nothing for ourselves and all for all." Crocco is the enemy, the anarchist, who tries to poison the minds of the men against Currao and disintegrate the state. Finding his plots of no avail Crocco leaves the island vowing vengeance. His plan is to secure the help of a rich fisherman, Padron Nocio, who possesses a fleet of boats. With the expedition he will sail back to attack Currao's new state and to help him in his task of conquering he will take with him wine and women— the two vices of the old civilization which will destroy the new. No sooner do the fishing-boats arrive with their sirens than the followers of Currao throw down their guns and rush to the shore calling out excitedly : " Women ! Women ! " As for Spera, she fears for the safety of her baby and she flees to the mountain peak of the island for refuge. She prays to the forces to engulf the island in the sea. Then comes a terrible earthquake which submerges the whole island in the waters, all but the peak where Spera hides. As the curtain falls we see Spera and her baby perched triumphantly above the ruin of the world. Amidst the wreck caused by the passions and instincts of humanity the love of the mother survives.

La Nuova Colonia is one of the most effective plays from a theatrical point of view. The character of Spera as impersonated by Marta Abba expresses Pirandello's idealism. As soon as she is removed from the corrupt influences of civilization she blossoms like a flower in primitive nature. Pirandello in those later plays incessantly turned his eyes back to a golden age when life was not so full of treasons, stratagems and spoils. With Wordsworth he held that :

> " Heaven lies about us in our infancy !
> Shades of the Prison-house begin to close
> Upon the growing boy."

Modern life with its corruption, frivolity and hatred is evil, but every now and then " our souls have sight of that immortal sea "—just enough to tantalize us and make us feel the sense of hopeless longing. In *The New Colony* Pirandello drew the moral that we must begin again from first elements, but we must remember the experiences which our forerunners had absorbed and forgotten. For no one can begin again unless he sees clearly around and takes account of the conditions achieved by human knowledge. It was owing to his desire for a " ricominciamento " that Pirandello supported the Fascist régime from the beginning, in spite of his pessimism and his hatred of politics. Even as far back as 1889 he gave expression to his disgust and disillusion with the political graft of post-Garibaldian Italy. Rome in those days was the Rome of Petronius —the Rome of decadence. It did not need the Great

War to awaken in Pirandello a profound longing for a revolution which would shake that ancient world to its foundations. In the long novel *I Vecchi e i Giovani*, which, by the way, was dedicated to " My sons—young to-day—old to-morrow," he painted on a big canvas that old world which was crumbling away.

Pirandello had the misfortune to appear on the scene at the end of the nineteenth century when the romantic world was in process of destruction. As he was in advance of his time he awakened but little response in a public that followed the ideals of D'Annunzio and his imitators. Before Pirandello the stage had represented a drama of clashing individualities. The plays of Ibsen, Strindberg, D'Annunzio, always describe a hero or heroine at grips with circumstance. Pirandello on the contrary, as one of his critics pointed out, just stuck his hand into a heap of humanity and pulled out a cluster of men and women. They belonged to the little bourgeoisie of the beginning of the century— bourgeoisie in dissolution. Pirandello took them as they were, without judging them, and showed the audience how they lived and died. Pirandello's drama, when we consider it in all its extension, is a drama of the masses. In a play such as *The New Colony* he observes the masses and observes how they are full of blind energy—a will which drives them onwards and gives them ever new laws and conventions. He felt genuine sympathy for them and he for ever said to his imaginary Socrates :

" What have we given those people to help them to live ? "

" We have given them God—a spirit of pessimism who preaches patience and reliance on God, whose scope is beyond this world."

" But," answered Pirandello, " God has been removed and people are now told that all is in this world. After death there is nothing. All is a dream and everyone is himself alone—*Uno, nessuno, centomila* (one, no one, a hundred thousand)." With those pessimistic thoughts in his mind Pirandello thrust his hands still deeper into the mass of humanity and set to work to study the specimens as a naturalist would in a laboratory. But instead of photographing the types he tried to get below the surface and understand the true cause of their suffering. It is not enough to say to them : " Social revolution will bring remedies to you, but you must not move until we tell you that the time has come." And so in Pirandello's theatre we do not find the struggle of a hero against his destiny, but of a mass of men—each one of whom is conscious of his own despairing loneliness. And all those plays are fragments of an immense drama in a hundred acts.

VI

Pirandello and Bernard Shaw

I. THE BANKRUPTCY OF THE SUPERMAN

AS WE HAVE NOW considered the majority of Pirandello's plays and the various manifestations of his genius, let us try to sum up our impressions of his theatre. His arrival on the stage, even though late in life, has been a great benefit to dramatic art, not only in Italy, but all over Europe. No art is so ephemeral as that of the dramatist : it is even truer to say of him than of the actor that he " struts and frets his hour upon the stage and then is heard no more." Each period of four or five years has its characteristic dramatist whose plays are either mirrors or expressions of the times during which he lives. In 1925 all London went to see the plays of Noel Coward, because in them society recognized its image—an image touched up with rouge and *poudre de riz* and deformed by jazz. In the years after the War, when for a while idealist notions of a redeemed world found favour, English audiences hastened to see the historical plays of Drinkwater, based on the lives of great and noble men such as Abraham Lincoln and Oliver Cromwell. Back in the early years of the twentieth and the last years of the nineteenth centuries dramatists preached the gospel of feminism. Each year has its dramatist of the moment, but, then, every twenty-five or thirty years there comes a big man whose plays take in a wider range of vision. Such was the titanic figure of Ibsen, who seemed to have sprung from the stock of Shakespeare. After Brand, Nora, Solness and Borkman drama could no longer slumber in the plain. It had to seek the mountain tops. Ibsen began ; then came Shaw to continue the master's lesson and open up new paths to drama. Ibsen created a new technique for the modern play ; Shaw abandoned this technique in order to give freer play to his individual talent. Shaw has taught the public of the world's theatre how to think on social questions. He has, with his normal sight, examined all the creeds, all the beliefs, all the systems of modern civilization and made them the butt of his malicious humour. Shaw is not only a destructive critic like many of the Futurists, he is also a constructor. He is a Utopian and an optimist whose religion is of the future. By will and creative evolution, according to Shaw, we shall reach the millennium. This optimism we can see in the theatre of Shaw if we study the noble part played by women in his plays. Every one of them, from Vivie Warren to Saint Joan, seems to have inherited the spirit of the Valkyrie heroines of Ibsen. And Shaw, who is supposed to play to the ten per cent of humanity gifted with normal sight, has given this sane normal gaze to all his heroines. They are all of them the apotheosis of the normal modern woman who wears no corsets, plays out-door games like a boy, lives her life unchaperoned and is not afraid to call her father a silly old ass when he is wrong in his views. Shaw is the next titan to Ibsen in the European theatre, and he looms gigantically because with the mass of his works he has erected a noble edifice based on sound foundations. Then we come to Piran-dello, who in the last few years has won a world position and has rapidly changed our notion of drama. Some critics have tried to impose the paternity of the Piran-dellian drama on Shaw, because one of the set phrases about Shaw is that he stands on his head, and Pirandello at times seems to assume that posture. But in spite of certain superficial similarities of talk and plot, no spirits are further apart. Shaw, an Irish Protestant, is a Puritan who wishes to see truth face to face, even though it should turn him to stone. His wit is Puritan, for it is painfully conscious of the final fact in the universe. The writers of the Italian grotesque school are the very opposite to Shaw : Shaw is a wit ; Pirandello is a humorist, and G. K. Chesterton defines the two terms thus : " The man who sees the consistency in things is a wit and a Calvinist. The man who sees the inconsistency in things is a humorist and a Catholic." No definition could give a better idea of the difference between the two writers. Pirandello sees nothing but inconsistency on all sides—his universe is ruled by the goddess of chance. We have seen in all his plays how the most absurd trifles cause mighty tragedies. There are no scenes of brooding calm leading up in gradual crescendo to a storm. The slightest hitch in the mechanism stretches the puppet useless at our feet. In *Il Giuoco delle Parti* the drama springs up owing to an egg-shell which the heroine throws out of the window and which hits two drunken men below. The fall from a horse during the performance of a pageant fixes Henry's mind. An earthquake destroys the records of Signor Ponza's marriage. We see the tricks of the goddess Chance in the technical construction of his plays. There is a direct reaction against the old well-made play originated by Scribe and developed by all succeeding authors. Nothing could be more untidy or inconsistent in its development than the Pirandellian play ; it all seems to advance with jerks and surprises. Some scenes are bursting with rhetoric, others are attenuated in the extreme. The characters seem to pant and stutter ; sometimes they pause for words, at other times they

overwhelm us by a torrent of speech. Then very often
the action is delayed while a character like Laudisi,
who has nothing to do with the principal action of the
play, discourses on the author's metaphysics and explains
his point with the aid of some image or myth. A good
example occurs in *Ciascuno a Suo Modo,* where we meet
another one of those friend-of-the-family mouthpiece
characters.

DIEGO.

" My dear lady, do you not think sometimes as it were
of a car drive over a country road on a fine sunny day ? "

DONNA LIVIA.

" A car drive ? What has that got to do with it ! "

DIEGO
(Angrily and seriously.)

" Lady, do you know how I found myself one night
when watching over my mother who was dying ? I saw
an insect before me, with flat wings and six legs ; it had
fallen into a glass of water on the table. Well, I never
noticed the passing away of my mother, so absorbed was
I in wondering at the faith which that insect had in its
two longer hind legs. It swam about frantically, obstinately believing that those two legs were enough to enable
it to jump out of the liquid, and yet feeling that something attached on to the end of them interfered with
its jump. As it found all efforts vain, it linked them
with the front legs and tried the jump again. I remained
for more than half an hour looking at its efforts. I saw
it die, but not my mother."

Pirandello has eliminated the rhetoric that we find in
the last vestiges of romantic pre-war drama, but he has
introduced a new type of rhetoric which he has drawn

from metaphysics and from psycho-analysis. Few dramatists are more difficult to translate than Pirandello, on account of his style. For this reason it was fortunate that Mr. Scott Moncrieff, the valiant translator of Proust, undertook the task of translating Pirandello. The difficulties can be appreciated if we remember that in its origins his style is Sicilian, with that tendency to jerkiness and incisiveness. Then to the Sicilian qualities must be added that complicated psychology of the author, full of reservations and subtle inferences. Finally we must infuse a good dose of metaphysics into the composition, and we have the Pirandellian style. The passion for metaphysical problems seems to be our author's only weakness. Whereas Shaw is for ever occupied with big social problems, Pirandello rarely touches them at all. No dramatist of European fame has devoted less time to the material problems of humanity than our author. In some of his short stories we meet the working classes of Sicily, peasants and miners from malaria-infested regions, but Pirandello does not cure their woes. He has no belief in progress, like Shaw ; rather does he seem to be a devotee of Dean Inge and Lucretius. We cannot imagine him writing a passage like the following, from *Man and Superman* :—

" The great central purpose of breeding the race, ay, breeding it to heights now deemed superhuman ; that purpose which is now hidden in a mephitic cloud of love and romance and prudery and fastidiousness will break through into clear sunlight as a purpose no longer to be confused with the gratification of personal fancies, the impossible realization of boys' and girls' dreams of bliss, or the need of older people for companionship or money."

Shaw gives his heroes and heroines a good modern education, but not at public schools or other places where tradition still holds sway. They all are students of psychology, and are able with admirable lucidity to control even their sexual passions. They are all men and women of the North, and will-power is their strength. Pirandello, being a man from the South, gives his characters the instincts of the Southerner. Nay, he gives them more than their share of instinct, and then, in addition, he makes them study psycho-analysis so that they may at any given moment project themselves outside and watch themselves live like the man in *E Due* who put his hat at the edge of the parapet in the same position as the hat of the dead man in order that he might watch himself in action.

II. STAGE DIRECTIONS

The precise details given in Shaw's stage directions concerning his characters have aroused much discussion among dramatic critics. William Archer attacks him for this habit of expanding these directions into essays, disquisitions, monologues and pamphlets. " This is a practice which goes far to justify the belief of some foreign critics that the English are congenitally incapable of producing a work of pure art." Must we therefore include Pirandello in this sweeping condemnation? Archer considered that when the dramatist steps to the footlights and begins to lecture, all illusion is gone. Owing to the habit of talking around his characters, he inevitably ceases to make them express themselves as completely as may be in their own proper medium of dramatic action and dialogue.[1]

It is interesting to compare Shaw's and Pirandello's method with Ibsen's, whose plays are always considered by dramatists as models of construction. Ibsen started where Scribe and Sardou left off. *Doll's House* might have been composed by Sardou—up to the moment in the

[1] W. Archer, *Playmaking*, p. 55. London, 1912.

last act when Nora and her husband sit down on opposite sides of the table to talk out their future relations. Ibsen gave as few stage directions to his characters as Sardou did, and that tendency has been continued by many modern dramatists like Jacinto Benavente, who hold that the dialogue of the play should be subtle enough to explain the character. Then, as a result of this tendency, we find post-war dramatists of the Expressionist school labelling their characters—The Woman with Blue Fox, the Man in Grey, and so on, just as if they wore masks.

With regard to Ibsen's curt stage directions, some critics say that this was the cause of the unpopularity of his theatre with the public. As they had no precise indications of the author's meanings, it was no wonder that they looked on his mystical titans as symbols of some obscure philosophy. It was Shaw who showed the world that Ibsen, with his drama of the individual, was the first great realist of suburban Europe. Shaw in his own plays was determined not to be misunderstood by his public. And so he follows Zola, who said that dramatists should follow the analytical method of the naturalist novel and describe all the physical and social as well as psychological influences which determine man's position in nature. Thus each play of Shaw becomes a kind of novel in dialogue like that famous sixteenth-century work, *La Celestina*. At the end of the nineteenth century many authors seem to have felt the same need to express their inspiration in this analytical form ; Galdós in Spain in 1892 commenced to produce his dramas, which were in most cases simply dramatizations of his novels. In the same year in France Marcel Luguet produced a piece, *Le Missionaire*, which was a fusion between play and novel. " The union between stage and novel," he said, " allows the author to describe his characters as he wants, in a positive way, instead of letting the other characters describe them at their own free will."[1]   In that play the action and dialogue were held up while a special actor read the descriptions.   In Shaw's plays the long stage directions are of the greatest interest and assistance, not only to the reader, but also the actors who study their parts.   They have helped greatly in creating a subtle modern school of acting which is the very antithesis to the old style followed by the actor-celebrity basking in the limelight.   Nowadays the actor is an artist who can study deeply the intentions of his author.   Pirandello in his stage directions seems to follow the same method as Shaw, though not with precisely the same object in view. There is none of the sociological essay, as Mr. Archer would say, about his stage directions.   They are often extensive, not for the purpose of amusing the reader, but of characterising exactly the individual presented. Pirandello even more than Shaw is anxious lest his meaning may not be understood by the public and the critics. As we saw in *The Six Characters in Search of an Author*, the characters of an author despair of finding actors to represent their mental processes, their personalities. And Pirandello, since he founded his " teatro d'arte " at Rome in 1925 set himself with enthusiasm to the task of creating a modern school of acting which shall rival in fame the traditional companies of the " Commedia dell' arte."   We have heard it said that he spends as much as five hours a day on the stage watching his company rehearse, and that he is inexorable in the demands he makes upon the actor in the matter of subordination to the author's will.

Sometimes in his plays the stage directions tell us more than the action of the play.   Pirandello hides himself in the wings, and by these directions conveys to us impressions that the stage, in spite of the interpretation

[1] A. Hamon, *Le Molière du XXe Siècle*, " Bernard Shaw," p. 204.   Paris, 1913.

of the actor, cannot render. At the beginning of the third act of *Henry IV*, when Frida from her niche calls out to Henry, Pirandello puts the following direction : " Henry IV (stopping suddenly on hearing the voice, as if he had been knifed treacherously in the back, turns towards the wall at the back and raises his arms instinctively as if to ward off a blow) : ' Who calls me ? ' (This is not a question, but an exclamation full of terror which awaits no answer from the darkness and terrible silence of that hall. It fills him all of a sudden with the suspicion that he is really mad.)" This example (and many others could be found in the Pirandellian theatre) shows us the limitations of his intimate drama, limitations of which the author himself is fully conscious. The consciousness of these limitations explains his restless energy as theatrical producer and stage-craftsman : he is ceaselessly tortured by the inadequacy of the modern stage to express the inner drama of his soul. Bernard Shaw in his stage directions adopts the functions of the Greek chorus : he comments and criticizes his own characters, and takes his reader and the actors themselves into his confidence, but he never lets these directions usurp the function of the stage itself, for he is always able to make his scheme of things fit into the conventional frame.

III.   PIRANDELLO'S ANTI-HEROES

Pirandello has no gospel for humanity ; he does not try to create a race of supermen. His philosophy is, as many critics have shown, a reaction against the philosophy of Nietzsche and the superman, which found its literary expression in Italy in the works of Gabriele D'Annunzio.

D'Annunzio explains his own tragedy in the words :—

> " Volontà, Voluttà,
>   " Orgoglio, Istinto,
>   quadriga imperiale."

His characters are at the mercy of Furies, who lash them mercilessly on to action. All life to them is a process of evolution towards the goal of the superman. But this struggle is at the beck of art, for they analyse the æsthetic sensations Victory gives. They are more preoccupied with the purple robe and golden crown and trappings of pomp than with the idea. They all have more than a small share of the spirit of Nero, who could fiddle while Rome burned, and cry out at death, " Qualis artifex pereo." Shaw, who has said in the Epistle dedicatory to *Man and Superman*, " For art's sake alone I would not face the toil of writing a single sentence," is nearer to the truth as preached by Nietzsche. He has studied deeply the doctrines of Evolution and Will which have moulded the nineteenth century. Following Schopen-hauer and Nietzsche, who in their turn founded their theories on Lamarck, Shaw raised Will from the plane of the individual to the plane of the race. In *Back to Methuselah* Man directs his will to extending human life and shows that creative evolution has become the religion of the twentieth century—" a religion that has its intel-lectual roots in philosophy and science, just as medieval Christanity has its intellectual roots in Aristotle." How different is the message of Pirandello ! His movement of reaction seems to be as much against Shaw as against D'Annunzio. The tragedy of Pirandello and of other modern Italian dramatists such as Rosso di San Secondo and Morselli is the tragedy of impotence and of the feel-ing of sadness at this destiny of man. To these writers man appears as a fallen god who remembers heaven of the past—an angel who has been driven out of Paradise and cast down into the darkest and smokiest abode of evil. There, rolling about in the mud and filth, he tries to con-quer that feeling of nostalgia for the azure heaven he has lost, by applying joyfully his subtle reason to cold and diabolical wickedness. We must therefore not expect to meet with heroes in these plays : the men are like soldiers who have been beaten in their first battle ; they have no belief in the future. Shaw in creating his men characters gives them a strong comforting dose of his optimism to carry them through the drama, but then he allows them to develop their own personality according to their own logic. Thus Captain Bluntschli symbolizes the astute Swiss professional soldier, the Reverend James Morell a self-satisfied reformer, Andrew Undershaft the hard-headed capitalist : Shaw's gallery of types is as brilliant as that of Molière. His psychology, as one of his critics says, is superior to that of Ibsen, for while Ibsen painted the individual only, Shaw paints the type. Pirandello finds it difficult to cut the leading-strings which bind him to his characters. Though he tries to allow them a definite logic of their own, they fatally sooner or later have to voice his metaphysical arguments. And there are very few normal creatures to be found in the Piran-dellian collection—they are all exceptional, abnormal beings. In nearly every novel or play we meet the same eccentric type, whether he be called Professor Toti, or Ciampa or Martino Lori. They are always grotesque and ridiculous in appearance, and Pirandello spares no pains in his stage directions to stress their peculiarities. Let us quote the stage direction of Ciampa to explain our point : " Enter Ciampa. He is a man of about forty-five years of age ; thick long hair brushed back in disorder. He has no moustache, but long side-whiskers spread across his cheeks. His eyes are wild-looking and piercing, and sparkle behind his big spectacles. A pen is stuck on his right ear. He is dressed in an old frock-coat." Or again, the father in *The Six Characters in Search of an Author* : " He is about fifty, his hair reddish in colour, thin at the temples, but he is by no means bald. His moustaches are thick and fall over his mouth, which often opens into a vacuous and uncertain smile. He is rather fat and pale, and his forehead is extremely wide. He has blue, oval-shaped eyes, which are very clear and piercing. He wears light trousers and a dark jacket."

This grotesque, ever-present type seems to draw its origins from Sicilian literature, for we meet it especially in the Sicilian works. In *La Patente* Chiarchiaro the *jettatore* is described thus :—

" He has allowed a stiff and matted beard to overrun his yellow, cavernous cheeks. On his nose he has perched a pair of horn-rimmed spectacles which give him the appearance of an owl. He wears a coat which is all glossy through age and much too big for him. In his hands he carries a bamboo cane with a horn handle."

We become in the end wearied by the monotonous succession of strange, lop-sided little men. The opposite type, and which we might call philosophic, is summed up in the person of Laudisi. He is a man of the world, about forty years of age, slim and elegant, though not loud in manner : he wears a violet smoking-jacket with black facings. Witty and chatty in conversation, he becomes irritable at the slightest pretext, but then he laughs and allows people to have their own way, for it gives him pleasure to watch the idiocy of others.

Laudisi and Leone Galla, the metaphysical culinary expert hero of *Il Giuoco delle Parti*, seem to be the author himself : they are the nearest approach we find in the Pirandellian theatre to a normal man. We could not but pity the world if we had many of the grinning and sarcastic Laudisi type amongst us. Pirandello's men characters very often strike us as caricatures in the style of Dickens. But they differ from Dickens profoundly owing to their inner struggles with themselves. For Pirandello is always seeking for hidden personality : he is not interested in the ordinary outside mask which men show the world, and so he often omits to observe that outer mask in all its details. His drama is the drama of uncertainty in contradistinction to the theatre of Bernard Shaw, which is certainty personified. Andrew Undershaft or John Tanner are very definite persons, and they live in a world of definite reality far removed from the insubstantial universe of Professor Toti. They are certain of their world and of their mission in it. Professor Toti, Martino Lori and other wan Pirandellians suffer from a perpetual sense of disquiet, which arises from the continual riddle which their personality propounds. They seek passionately for some clue to the enigma of their existence. They are puppets of logic, but the logic becomes a threadbare garment and ceases to cover their nakedness. No wonder, then, that Pirandello shows so many madmen and abnormal human beings in his works, for in such people logic follows a straighter and stronger course. They keep more rigidly and faithfully to their inner message. Such beings give Pirandello the opportunity of becoming a poet, not in the ordinary sense which we attach to the word, but in the sense which Croce gives to the word when he calls Guy de Maupassant a poet. Starting off with his metaphysical speculations, Pirandello, as he warms up to his subject, casts away abstractions and rises to the plane of fantasy. No character shows this quality better than Henry IV, who seems to have the same type of cold excitement as Pirandello himself. The Doctor is conversing with Donna Matilde and Belcredi about Henry's madness. Belcredi says that Henry used to be carried away by excitement, but in a curious way. It seemed to be a cold excitement that belied his passionate and eccentric nature.

" I am not saying that he feigned excitement, for, on the contrary, he often became genuinely excited. But I could swear, doctor, that he immediately saw himself from outside, in the moment of exaltation, just as if he had been a spectator. And this seemed to occur in the most spontaneous way possible. I am convinced that he suffered acutely on this account, for sometimes he used to break out into the most comical fits of temper against himself."

This analysis of Henry's personality fits Pirandello as we know him from all his works. Whenever his drama rises up in a crescendo, the author becomes more and more coldly precise and analytic, as if he wished to set down detail by detail his sensations. Whereas other dramatists would overwhelm their characters and the public in a flood of emotion, Pirandello becomes more and more precise, trying to achieve the exact truth of presentation.

Schlegel has spoken of the sublime coldness of Shakespeare—a sovereign spirit that has traversed the whole parabola of existence and has survived sentiment. Allowing for all the difference of degree, Pirandello shows a touch of this divine coldness in *Henry IV*. And this coldness becomes terrifying because it respects nothing in this world of ours. Against our will we are forced to doubt everything and dissolve all the shams to which we have become sentimentally attached. Bernard Shaw, with his normal gaze, has destroyed a great many of our petted illusions and conventions in order to bring us face to face with the truth. Pirandello starts where Shaw left off, and we might make him say, in the words of the latter, " I am greater than Shaw because I stand on his shoulders." The intellectual ideas that satisfy Shaw will not satisfy our author, for he refuses to look on them as a protection. According to him they are only the outer bark concealing the inner truth that he seeks ceaselessly. The plays of Shaw, with their sane, open-air morality, their brilliant comic spirit which acts as a corrective against our fads and fallacies, inspire us with a joy in life, a feeling of optimism and hope in the future ; the plays of Pirandello, with their fictions which are more real than men and women, fill us with terror as though the earth were crumbling away at out feet.   Let us take again Henry IV where he addresses his frightened attendants in the darkened castle: "Do you know what it means to find oneself face to face with a madman— with one who shakes the foundations of all you have built round you, your logic, the logic of all your con- structions ?   Ah ! lucky madmen who construct without logic, or else with a special logic of their own which flits about like a feather. . . . Beware of ever thinking, as I have done, on this terrible thing which really drives a man mad : that if you are beside another and looking into his eyes, as I looked one day into somebody's eyes, you might as well be a beggar before a door which can never be opened to you."

IV. PIRANDELLO'S HEROINES

It is when we consider the women characters of our author that we find the widest divergence from Shaw. Shaw's drama, like that of modern European playwrights since Ibsen, is decidedly feminist in its scope.   Ibsen created his heroines in order to escape from this world of sadness and suffering : they are all symbols of his aspir- ations towards a higher and more beautiful life.   They are gifted with the Valkyrie temperament, which makes them superior to man both in courage as well as in beauty.   Shaw's women are the sanest part of his world —they are the personification of common-sense.   Shaw through his heroines made a far greater attack on the conventional theatre than Ibsen had done.   He strips woman of all her romance and makes her look at life face to face. He delves deep down into the whole problem of sex. He shows that between man and woman there exists always a sex war, and it is woman who wins.   It is she who hunts man and secures him to be the father of her children, because in the world she is instinctively entrusted with the duty of perpetuating the race.   And this hunting is carried on in a subtle, treacherous manner, for man appears to be engaged in hunting for woman. In many of the Shaw plays men play the part of hunters, but in reality they are the hunted victims. They are defeated by the Life Force which is implanted in woman. As critics have shown, Shaw by dramatic exaggeration reduces the wretched man to a slave hunted by woman's devouring will to create. In *Man and Superman* John Tanner tries to evade pursuit, but he is powerless against the attack of Ann, his assailant. Shaw says, through the mouth of Tanner, that the devilish side of a woman's fascination is that she makes you will your own destruction. And Shaw makes this Life Force enter into married as well as unmarried life. All the wives of the Shavian theatre are maternal in their relations to their husbands. They are the stronger of the two, and they all, like Candida, recognize the faults in their husbands, but agree to stay on with them because they feel that the latter need protection. As Tanner again says, " They take care of their husbands as a soldier takes care of his rifle or a musician of his violin." They are always able to give a far more balanced judgment than men, for they are less swayed by prejudice and better able to use their powers of reason. Everything the Shavian girl does is calculated. Even Saint Joan was, Shaw tells us, in war as much a realist as Napoleon, and in fact, the very antithesis to a romantic young lady. In Pirandello the rôle played by woman is not a noble one. She is treated with all the disdain of one who looks on women as inferior beings. This, at any rate, is the impression we derive from perusal of the earlier plays and stories. As we showed in our introductory chapter on the *teatro grottesco*, the tendency to react against feminism was characteristic of the Futurists. In the pre-war dramatists in Italy like Roberto Bracco we find a great defence of woman. Bracco in plays like *Piccola Fonte, Notte di*

Neve and *Sperduti nel Buio* sets in antithesis the noble self-sacrifice of woman and the vile egoism of man. The tendency towards feminism was uppermost, not only in Italian, but also in European drama from the days of Ibsen down to the war. But then there began to be heard the voices of the Futurists proclaiming their revolutionary theories. One of their great battle cries was to banish the sexual obsession from literature. " Sex," they said, " tends to corrupt the life of the nation ; let us abolish the glorious conception of Don Juan and the grotesque conception of the *cocu*. Let us also abolish the nude from paintings and adultery from the novel, so that we may substitute the sublime male fury of creation of artistic and scientific masterpieces for all the sterile embraces of hedonistic eroticism."

These exaggerated theories did not achieve their purpose in those days, but they had the effect of causing a certain reaction against feminism, an attitude of *méprisez la femme* which we remarked in all the productions of the *teatro grottesco*. In Pirandello we see this tendency in still more striking light. Woman always seems to play an inferior part in his works, for she is always weak, capricious, frivolous, and sensual. There is no attempt in him to create idealised heroines who will act as balm to his tortured soul. In Verga and Capuana we find many pictures of the coquettish and capricious Sicilian woman who bears in her blood the subtle qualities of Greek, Arab and Spaniard. Pirandello has gone still further, and deformed the fair image. At best his women are tossed about in a sea of doubts, like Ersilia, the heroine of *Vestire gli Ignudi*, of Signora Morli. They have less consistence as characters than the men and less power. They are less imaginative because they are lower in the scale than men and sealed with the mark of inferiority. They might all be included in Verga's book *I Vinti*, that series of short novels which deal with the weak who have fallen in the contest of life and have lost all their courage. In the early novels of Pirandello we occasionally meet a Nora who is in revolt against the world. Marta, the introspective heroine of *L'Esclusa*, tries to raise her head against Society, which has handled her unjustly, but she is not the stuff that Valkyries are made of.

Luisetta, the *ingenue* young girl in *Si Gira*, who has been downtrodden by her family, one day breaks out into rebellion and casts all her accumulated hatred back at her parents. But the logical and ironic Gubbio withers her impulse with his frosty remark : " But you have endured all this despair for so many years—how are you now suddenly going to rebel fiercely ? " She belongs to the long line of contemporary Noras whose lungs are not strong enough for the heights. The Sicilian women, living in the keeping of traditionally jealous husbands, find it difficult to rebel. They are nearly all broken by the same destiny as Leonora, the poor young thing whom her husband shut up in a remote barrack of a house in Sicily and never allowed out into the world.

We do, on the other hand, find another type of woman in Pirandello, which we might call the Xanthippe type. In spite of the laws and traditions of Sicilian life, she manages to make life a misery for her husband. We find her in many of the short stories, and her husband is nearly always fat and philosophical by temperament. He likes his peaceful garden with its rose-trees and nightingales, and he listens unmoved to his wife's bickerings. Nay, he welcomes her lover because he knows that all her bad humour and capriciousness, all her hatred will be transferred to the lover. " She will join me here in the other world to-day or to-morrow," he says ; " her lover will kill her, I am sure—if only to avoid hearing that malicious laugh of hers." Such a woman would be certain to meet such a fate at the hands of any man except a fat man or else a Pirandellian husband like Leone Galla, who knows how to treat his wife Silia's lovers. Silia and her type appear very often in Pirandello's plays, so often that we are irresistibly drawn to compare them with Miss Julia of Strindberg. Silia, too, is neurotic, perverted and unashamed in her relations with men. She excites men's passion to gratify her own ; she is totally unable to control her sensuality. Pirandello, however, does not look on woman with the same feelings as the Northern master. Strindberg saw in woman the rival of man for power : he looked on feminist aspirations with all the distrust of one who feared for the downfall of masculine supremacy. As a critic has said, there are only two safe ways of treating sexual love in literature : as a fantastic jest of the gods against humanity, or in its proper place as one among the other human appetites. Strindberg, like Shaw, looked on sex as an elemental force ; Pirandello looks on it as a jest of the gods, and thus we do not find such towering examples of the vampire woman as in *Miss Julia* or *The Creditors*. Occasionally he sketches the exotic dangerous woman, as in *Si Gira*, where we meet La Nestoroff, the Russian film actress, or else in *Ciascuno a Suo Modo*, where the action of the grotesque play centres in Delia Morello, the actress for whom the sculptor committed suicide. They are only sketches and never crowd in upon our consciousness. Pirandello, with his spasmodic style, has not the exquisite subtlety of D'Annunzio for visualizing such beautiful women. He does not care to linger over details of description of their person or their surroundings, for he is eager to analyse their psychology. In D'Annunzio's art Venice in Autumn forms a flaming background to set off the declining beauty of La Foscarina. Line by line of his rhythmical prose unveils the languid graces of La Gioconda, and this power of description is the very life-blood of the poet. The following passage will show how coldly psychological Pirandello prefers to remain :—

DELIA.

" I see all these men before me—thus—dazzled by my eyes, by my mouth.   But not one of them minds me or pays attention to what I need most.   And so I punish them just in that which they are keenest about.   First of all I exasperate those longings of theirs which disgust me, in order to make my revenge the sweeter ; and my revenge is to sell my body to those who least expect it— just to show them how valueless I consider that part of me which they praise so highly."

These words are practically the same, word for word, as those uttered by La Nestoroff in the early novel.

If Pirandello lacks the artistry to describe exotically brilliant women, he shows greater power in his treatment of queer abnormal types that we meet in Sicily.   Whenever he brings on his stage queer grotesque women he fascinates us, and he spares no pains, by his minute stage directions, to make them live for us.   In the novel *I Vecchi e I Giovani* we see the models of later dramatic characters.   Donna Caterina Auriti-Laurentano, daughter of a princely house in Sicily exiled after 1848, has all the pride and steadfastness of the feudal aristocrat. We see her before us pale-faced, unbending in her attitudes.   Sufferings, both mental and physical, have so ruined her face that it appears as if she wore eternally a mask of agony.   She is like one petrified and fixed to her recollections of the past, and she stands bleak and desolate like a blasted oak.   She reappears often through the course of the short stories and the plays, and we take leave of her in the tragic play *La Vita che ti diedi*, where she refuses to admit the truth of her son's death.   In such works Pirandello shows all the pathos of such fixations, and there is genuine pity in his analysis.   On other occasions he is so pitiless in his description of the foibles and fancies of women that he nearly becomes a caricaturist.   In *L'Uomo, La Bestia e La Virtù* the stage directions of Signora Perella are as follows : " Signora Perella is modesty and decency personified, and yet she is unfortunately *enceinte* two months by Signor Paolino, the private tutor of her son Nono.   She is dressed in a ludicrous manner, for the duty of fashion is to make modesty seem ludicrous, and Signora Perella is constrained to dress according to the dictates of fashion ; God knows how much she suffers.   She speaks in a querulous undertone as if it was not she who was speaking, but the invisible puppet-man who moves her strings, imitating in a ridiculously inadequte way the voice of a melancholy woman."   And in the play when Paolino makes the unfortunate woman rouge her cheeks and lips, blacken her eyes and increase her *décolleté* in order that she may seduce her refractory husband, we are back in the old grotesque caricature of the " Commedia dell' arte," with the difference that the " Commedia dell' arte " had the good-humoured gross and combative laughter of the sixteenth century, whereas Pirandello in his laughter against woman seems to exhale all the bitterness of gall.   Nothing is sacred to his eyes—even maternity is made the subject of coarse jesting in the first act of the play.   Here we see the fundamental difference between Shaw and our author.   Shaw casts off the trappings of sentimentality which obscure our notions of the passion of sexual love, but he sets woman on a pedestal.   Maternity is held sacred because Shaw is ever preoccupied with his theories of evolution by which mankind must will itself up to the level of the superman.   All the Shavian women are maternal in their attitude towards men, because they feel that since they bear in themselves the Life Force they must treat their husbands with superior kindness and make allowance for their weaknesses.   Maternity is the subject of many Shaw plays, from *You Never can Tell,* where he exposes the right of children to self-expression to *Misalliance,* where he shows the new outlook of the Georgian girl. Pirandello has not glorified maternity like Shaw. In *La Ragione degli Altri* he allows Livia Arciani to triumph by her logic and carry off the child from its real mother. In *L'Innesto* he again exposes an irrational subject by attempting to prove that Laura, who has been brutally seduced by a stranger, can consider the child she bears as a result of that assault the true child of her husband. In another play, *Come Prima Meglio di Prima,* there is the same abnormal attempt to choke by logic the instinct of maternity. These plays show in its most exasperated form the contrast between reality and truth on the one hand and illusion on the other. It is here that we can accuse Pirandello of being cerebral and artificial. As critics have shown, Pirandello has not been able to impart a sense of humanity to these paradoxical situations which he himself feels so acutely. We are left with an arid sensation as if we had been reading about psycho-analytical experiments. Poor Pirandellian heroines : they seem for ever to be oppressed by some huge fatality, which sweeps them off their feet and scatters to the winds all that they have constructed with the utmost care. Even Marta Abba, the muse of the later myths, cannot make us forget Silia and Donna Matilde.

VII

Pirandello: Religion and Humour

I. PIRANDELLO AND RELIGION

IN READING MANY OF the stories of Pirandello we have
a haunting feeling of sadness, for we meet so many of
those poor desolate waifs.   Women who have had a
big position in the world during the life of their husbands,
but then after his death, when money fails, are abandoned
by their former friends.   Then again we meet young
girls afflicted with incurable disease whose whole life is
spent in the shadows of the sick-room—waiting, waiting
for death which never comes to deliver them.   No
modern story-writer since Guy de Maupassant has
such power as Pirandello to create this feeling of haunting
sadness.   Every story becomes a kind of monologue
which never ends, because the author ever questions the
enigma.   His characters, like those of Ibsen, express
thoughts that we usually keep hidden away in our subconscious mind.   They are in their relations with one
another like priest and penitent : not only do they hear
confession, but they also give comfort to one another.
In Guy de Maupassant we read the sad story of modern
man living in big cities.   We watch the arrival of the
spring of life for him, with its feverish, excited pleasures
of the senses.

But then we see the gradual drying up of the sap of life,
the slow approach of old age, with its wrinkles and

grey hairs—and death inexorable. At thirty years old man has read all the book and there is nothing else to hope for—nothing but repetition day by day and the reduction of life to a mechanism. It is this which causes these bored, sensitive men to think of suicide—" C'était fini. J'arrivais à la source et brusquement je me retournai pour envisager le reste de mes jours. Je vis la vieillesse hideuse et solitaire, et les infirmités prochaines, et tout fini, fini, fini ! Et personne autour de moi." Maupassant, man of great heart and subtle sensibilities, suffers, suffers with his characters. There is a great deal of that irreparable sadness that we find in some of the Greek funeral poems in the Anthology. As Croce says, his conception of reality is the exact opposite to the religious, which is the consciousness of union with all other beings and with God—Communion with the Whole.[1] God is absent from Maupassant's world of pleasure and pain. Pirandello, though he has not so sensitive a temperament as the French writer, and though his heart does not suffer for his characters in the same way, yet has the same despairing pessimism. When we penetrate through the maze of intellectuality in his works we reach the same desert solitudes. God too is absent from his work : there is no trace of that wonderful balm of mysticism, that sensation of union with all humanity and with God which we find in writers like Unamuno. " Nothing exists except that which exercises action, " said Unamuno, together with the modern philosophers of action. Pirandello's work seems at first sight the very opposite to the despairing invocation to action of Unamuno and his followers.

Unamuno in his *Life of Don Quixote and Sancho* and in *The Tragic Sense of Life* makes us look death the Sphinx in the face, until at last all its evil terror disappears and

---

[1] Croce, *Poesia e Non Poesia*, Bari, 1923, p. 311.

its aspect turns to kindliness, and we feel down in our core the hunger of immortality.

> " Cada vez que considero
> que me tengo de morir,
> tiendo la capa en el suelo
> y no me harto de dormir,"

Death immortalises us.   Nothing passes, nothing disappears into emptiness.   The smallest particle of matter, the weakest blow given is made eternal, and there is no Vision, however fleeting it may be, which is not reflected for ever somewhere.   Our life is a drama, a momentary lighting up of the dark substance, and when the passing flame dies down, its reflection descends to the depths of darkness, where it remains until a supreme spark will light it up again for ever one day. For death does not triumph over life with the death of the latter.   Death and life are mean terms which we use in this prison of time and space ; they both have a common root which stretches down to the eternity of the infinite, to God, the conscience of the Universe.[1]

Pirandello is more restless than Unamuno : he has not got the latter's severity and faith in the purpose that lies behind the Universe.   Unamuno, with his religion of action, is a mystic, and comes from the same province as Saint Ignatius de Loyola.   Pirandello, with his feeling for contrasts, is unable to lose himself, like the Basque writer, in his meditation and dreaming.   We feel all the time, when reading his works, that he wishes to follow the tumultuous forces of Verhaeren and say to himself :—

[1] M. de Unamuno, *La Vida de don Quijote y de Sancho*, Madrid, 1905, p. 323.

" Partons quand même avec notre ame inassouvie
puisque la force et que la vie
sont au delà des vérités et des erreurs.
Vivre c'est prendre et donner avec liesse
toute la vie est dans l'essor."

Pirandello longs to sing all the fullness of modern
European life with its steel and stress, its fevers, its
jarring complexities ! But he has not got the lungs of
Verhaeren, and his mind, full of doubts, does not allow
him to lose himself in the intensity of his emotions. He
watches modern man ceaselessly changing from minute
to minute, struggling against the victorious Life Force
which sweeps away the constructions, the forms in its
inexorable flood. There is no God to comfort humanity,
unless perhaps a negative God, for Pirandello seems to
say to us : " Open your eyes and contemplate the reality
of this world. Renounce the useless struggle against
Destiny and cease dashing on in your vertiginous course.
Abandon yourself consciously to the idea that your life
is a tiny spark kindled from that huge electrical Life
Force : it flashes for one second and then is gone. But
the force which produced that spark continues in its
course." We could imagine him saying to Ibsen :
" Your heroes belonged to the Romantic era of the
Superman and rose upon the wings of Wagner and
Nietzsche. They are set in gigantic mould, whereas
man as I see him is Lilliputian in size. With your
invulnerable belief in determinism, you regard Nature
as secondary and you set up your great individuals at
her expense. To me Nature, or as I call it the Life
Force, is so inexorable that it never allows the individual
to be consistent with himself, for he ceaselessly changes
and becomes someone else from minute to minute. You
said to Björnson, ' Your monument's inscription will be,
" His life was his best work." ' So to conduct one's life
as to realize one's self—this seems to me the highest

attainment possible to a human being. But how can a man consciously realise himself when he changes from day to day and minute to minute ? I cannot believe in the unconquerable will of man, for I have lived on into the twentieth century and seen the bankruptcy of the superman." Ibsen towers over the nineteenth-century dramatists on account of his courageous morality. His glorious sincerity was an example to the world, especially to those whose aggressive respectability made them unable to understand sorrow and suffering. " Life in Norway," he says, " has something indescribably wearisome about it ; it wearies the soul out of one, it wearies the strength out of one's will." Pirandello, living in the twentieth century, feels the same sense of the tedium of existence. Though his procedure is different, he has the same deep sincerity as the northern master. But he unfortunately lives in an age of crumbling creeds and faiths, and it is not possible for him to construct. Rather must he clear away the brambles and weeds from the earth before it is possible to set up the structure. There is a profound intimate tragedy underlying his works—a tragedy that arises form his sincerity. He seeks on all sides an answer to the riddle of life, and it is a proof of his sincerity that none of the facile answers which satisfy other writers can move him to conviction. Every play of Pirandello should be a tragedy in which the characters give expression to the inner struggle in the author's mind. But can he write tragedy ? The moment that he brings his character on the stage and makes him put on the buskin so that he may assume a kingly posture, then slinks in the malicious imp to poke fun at his kingly majesty. That imp makes the author see his king, if not naked, at least in his shirt. And thus every character of Pirandello dissolves into the air just at the point of being realized. Pirandello should be a lonely watcher like

Ibsen, viewing the world from the top of a mountain disinterestedly.   He should not descend to the humming life of the plain and enter the world of comedy, for comedy will not allow his folk to strike attitudes.   Tragedy shows the struggle of the individual with himself; comedy shows us the type, and Pirandello looks at his poor tragic puppets through the eyes of the comic.   It is the Pirandellian humour which destroys his characters, making them say, with Leone Galla : " When I have a sentiment I take it and nail it down."

II.   PIRANDELLO'S HUMOUR

When all the characters of the Pirandellian universe shall have faded into thin air, the author will nevertheless be remembered for his curious humour made up of contradiction.   In an exceedingly interesting volume on *Humour* he analyses his ideas on the subject and makes them fit into the scheme of Italian literature.   Every true humourist, according to Pirandello, is also a critic— a fantastic critic.   For in the conception of a work of art reflection becomes a form of sentiment, as it were a mirror in which sentiment watches itself.   And he gives many examples to show that reflection is like icy water in which the flame of sentiment quenches itself.   Thus we can explain the frequent digressions which occur in the novels and plays, digressions which are always due to the disturbing effect caused by the active reflection of the author.   The Pirandellian humour arises by anti-thesis.   In the mind of a man a thought cannot arise without at the same time causing a directly opposite and contrary one to appear, and so free, unfettered emotion or sentiment, instead of soaring aloft like the lark in the clear air, finds itself held back just at the moment that it stretches out its wings to fly.   Pirandello analyses the workings of Manzoni's mind when he was writing his book *I Promessi Sposi*, with its immortal humorous character, Don Abbondio, the priest. Manzoni had first of all an abstract ideal in his mind of the mission of the priest on earth, and he incarnates this ideal in Federigo Borromeo. But then reflection, which springs from his disposition towards humour, suggests to the poet that this abstract ideal is only very rarely to be found on earth, for human frailities are so frequent. And thus he creates the priest human in his faults. If he had only listened to his ideal he would have made Don Abbondio despicable and unsympathetic. But within himself he hears the voice of humanity and its weakness, and so the character wins our everlasting love and gratitude. The thought of man according to Guy de Maupassant turns around ceaselessly like a fly in a bottle, and according to Pirandello it is a demon who pulls to pieces the works of every image, every phantom set up by sentiment, to see how it is made. In our modern life of struggle we have to play many parts, like the actor in a huge repertory company. We have to appear strong when we are weak, we have to pretend that we are generous when we are really avaricious. The humorist like Pirandello, who is able to look from outside at our Vanity Fair, performs the functions of the producer of the play. He sits in the stalls and watches our attempts on the stage to play our parts, and he stops us every moment to point out our inability to assume completely the mask. However, as he is a humorist producer he never becomes angry. He knows that it is vain for us to attempt to play these parts for more than a fleeting instant, as Life is in a continual state of flux. Then in certain moments in our lives, when there is, as it were, silence in our minds, when our soul despoils itself of all its masks, its scenic trappings, and our eyes become more penetrating in their gaze, we see ourselves in life and we see life itself in all its nakedness. Then we receive a strange impression, as if in a flash we saw another reality different from the one we normally behold. And that reality terrifies us by its air of impassable mystery. All around us there seems to be a void, and our life seems to stop suddenly. Then, with a great effort, we manage to regain our normal consciousness of the world and connect our ideas, but all seems vain and fleeting around us, because we see how unstable the whole world is. There is always before us the sensation of that void into which a man may not gaze except at the cost of death or madness. These are the thoughts which seem to crowd up unceasingly in the mind of Pirandello, and whereas all of us see that terrifying void once in our lives in a flash, he seems perpetually to be gazing into it. It is this which gives that peculiar bitter flavour to his humour, so different in quality from the traditional humour of Italian writers[1] in the past. Alberto Cantoni, in an essay quoted by Pirandello, fantastically symbolises the ancient classical humour in the person of a fine, rubicund and jovial old man, and the modern humour in the person of a circumspect, slim little man with a bitter expression of countenance. Both meet together to argue. The old man is condemned by the young man, not only on account of the vulgarity and sensuality of his humour, but also because he always is the same in spite of his years. To this the old man answered, " And you, by dint of repeating that though you seem to be smiling yet you are in reality suffering, have brought things to such a pass that nobody knows what you seem or what you are in reality. If you could only see yourself you really would not know whether to weep or to smile." The modern humorist, though he has not got the rubicund joyful laughter of the ancients, and though, owing to the course of time, he has become all nerves, all sensibility, yet is well forearmed against many of the illusions of the past. And

[1] L. Pirandello, *Arte e Scienza, Un Critico Fantastico.* Roma, 1908, p. 62.

Pirandello is in the same position as the little nervy man : he has cast behind him the illusions that sustained the writers in the past, but he cannot help regretting the good old days.

We must confess, nevertheless, that the Pirandellian humour is a danger to humanity, because it makes such a frontal attack on our self-complacency and our pet illusions. It is better to laugh at the Pirandellian heroes, otherwise we may copy them and suffer from their disease of contradiction. All life would then seem grotesque—and Man would seem the most ridiculous of creatures, because every action he performs, looked at through the Pirandellian eye, is ridiculous in this most inconsistent of worlds. Let us laugh and say with Adam in *Back to Methuselah* when the Serpent laughs—" that noise takes away fear."

VIII

Pirandello's Fortunes after Death

GEORGES NEVEUX, one of the French avant-garde dramatists, in paying tribute to Pirandello as a great innovator in the modern theatre, recalled in 1953 the sensation in Paris in 1923 when Georges Pitoëff produced for
the first time the master's *Six Characters in Search of an
Author:* "Just thirty years ago today, an elevator came
down on the stage of the Théâtre des Champs Elysées,
and deposited on it six unexpected characters whom
Pirandello had conjured up. And, together with them,
dozens, hundreds of characters loomed up before us,
but we could not yet see them. In order to take shape
they awaited the breath of Giraudoux, of Salacrou, of
Anouilh, and of some others. And it will be impossible
to understand anything about today's theatre if one
forgets that little flying box out of which it stepped one
April morning in 1923."[1]

Pirandello, as Denys Amiel said, ". . . brought *liberty*
to the theatre, the possibility of attempting to search;
he stylized the mystery which roams through life and
which gives rise to so many hypotheses. . . . He appealed
to the collaboration of the public's intelligence, he took
the public for what it is: an advanced being and not a
child. . . ."[2] Many of the French authors were so dazzled
by Pirandello, especially by his subtle interplay of illusion and reality and by the technical virtuosity of the

[1] Quoted in *Théâtre de France,* no. 3 (1953), p. 125.
[2] T. Bishop, *Pirandello and the French Theatre,* p. 50. New
York, 1960.

"play-within-the play," that they went to extremes in imitating him. The result was not good theatre, but, as Silvio D'Amico said, "an external, mechanical, cheap Pirandellism." These poor imitations naturally brought discredit on the originals, and for some years in the early 'thirties Pirandello's popularity waned. Many Frenchmen considered him as no more than a clever craftsman. Then came the Volta Congress of the Drama in Rome, in October, 1934, which placed the Sicilian master again on a pedestal, for it was he who presided over the international gathering of dramatists to discuss the problems of the theatre. The meetings were held in the Campidoglio, in the Salone Giulio Cesare. There was a touch of pathos about the gathering, for it included many of the consecrated figures who had created the modern movement in drama at the end of the nineteenth century. We saw Maurice Maeterlinck, an Olympian figure, but a survivor whose veiled and subtle plays, such as *Pelléas et Mélisande* (1893), *Intérieur,* and *La Mort de Tintagiles,* had inspired the Irish dramatist Yeats at the beginning of his crusade for an Irish theatre. Next to Maeterlinck and Yeats at the Congress stood the third great pioneer of the modern theatre, Gordon Craig, whose influence as a designer had been paramount in the early years of the century. But he too in 1934 seemed a man of the dim past, and our attention was concentrated on the President of the Congress, Luigi Pirandello. What a clash of famous personalities there was at that historic Congress! What infinite possibilities of discord could have arisen between such personalities as Marinetti, the fire-eating Futurist; Paul Claudel, the sad-looking poet-dramatist of Catholic France; Antoine, the veteran creator of the Théâtre Libre in the 'eighties; Jacques Copeau, the austere Prior of Le Vieux Colombier; and Tairoff, the

Russian innovator![1] Nevertheless, in spite of the presence of those great pioneers, Gordon Craig's prophetic outbursts, and Pirandello's Socratic comments, we came away from the Volta Congress disillusioned and disheartened, and later, when we met Pirandello, he spoke sadly of the lack of unity among the theatre pundits. Marta Abba, the inspired interpreter of the master's work, quotes warnings he gave for the future: "If it is true that the theatre will never die, it is equally true that it must be helped in its competition with other forms of entertainment, which either have, as in the case of the lyric theatre, strong means of support, or else have, as in the case of sports and of the movies, popular success. Everywhere new stadiums are being built; a film because of its possibilities of mechanical reproduction can be performed many times a day. To-day as in ancient times, in the spring and summer months, out in the open, in old amphitheatres, the people are called together to witness extraordinary and magnificent productions. But these productions do not solve the problem of the theatre in its other shape, which it has come to have in every civilized country: the indoor theatre, where a play is given every evening. *The problem of the theatre is a problem of civilization.*"[2]

Alas, the problems that Pirandello strove so hard to solve remained unsolved and no pioneer has arisen in Italy to fill the void. His successors, such as Ugo Betti and Eduardo de Filippo, were called Pirandellians merely because they tried to escape from reality on the wings of illusions. The latter, whom Bentley, in a most perceptive essay, calls the "Son of Pulcinella," goes

[1] W. Starkie, *Les Institutions Internationales Européennes* ("Ritual in Theatre"), Strasbourg, July, 1952.

[2] L. Pirandello, *The Mountain Giants and Other Plays,* translated by Marta Abba. Introduction, p. 28. New York, 1958.

deeper than the Sicilian master into the traditional *commedia dell'arte*. This is not surprising, for he was born in Naples and imbibed traditions of the celebrated local dramatists Salvatore di Giacomo and Roberto Bracco. Indeed, in De Filippo's *La Grande Magia* and *Questi Fantasmi* we hear echoes of *Sperduti nel Buio* and *Don Pietro Caruso* by Bracco, and *Assunta Spina* by Salvatore di Giacomo.

In France the craze for Pirandello was followed by a movement of lassitude in the public, and the dramatist Lenormand, in his book about Georges and Ludmilla Pitoëff, comments as follows: "People no longer wanted to see in Pirandello anything but a shrewd conjurer, a superior entertainer who was supposed to have loaded his dice. Pitoëff never adopted this attitude, which seems wholly unjustified. He remained faithful to his conception of the Pirandellian production. What he scorned was Pirandellism, that disease of imitation, that chlorosis of copyists, a veritable epidemic of pale colours which the great Italian propagated among the literary youth at the same time as the public was becoming detached from him."[1]

In the 'thirties, however, among French playwrights there was a strong revival of Pirandellian influence, especially in Marcel Achard's plays, such as *Domino* (1932) which is strongly reminiscent of *Il Piacere dell' Onestà,* and especially *Le Corsaire* (1938) with its interplay of cinema art and life and its Pirandellian devices. Armand Salacrou, too, in his most striking play, *L'Inconnue d'Arras* (1935), and in *La Marguerite* (1944), reminds us, in certain details of the plot, of the Sicilian dramatist. In the latter play, the father, like the mother in *La Vita che ti diedi,* refuses to believe that his son died in a shipwreck, and so convincing is his faith that Marguerite, the son's widow, leaves her lover, to

[1] H. R. Lenormand, *Les Pitoëffs,* pp. 120–121. Paris, 1943.

wait for the husband who will never return. Many of Pirandello's ideas reappear in the most humanistic of modern French playwrights—Jean Giraudoux, who exploits double personality in true Pirandellian fashion in *Siegfried et le Limousin*. Forestier-Siegfried has two distinct personalities: as Forestier he is a mild-mannered Frenchman, who was reported missing in the war; as Siegfried he becomes an efficient leader of the new Germany. In other plays too, such as *Ondine, Amphitryon 38,* and *La Folle de Chaillot,* Giraudoux has taken some of Pirandello's original ideas and devices, but he transforms them in his own inimitable way and in a style which is the antithesis of the Pirandellian. The crisp, fanciful dialogue of *La Folle de Chaillot* is worlds apart from our Sicilian. Far closer to the Pirandellian theatre is Jean Anouilh, whose *Le Voyageur sans Bagage* (1937) and *Leocadia* (1939) resemble *Enrico IV*. In both plays amnesia creates the situation in which the multiplicity of a man's personality may be studied. Gaston, like Pirandello's Henry, reaches the moment in his life when his past discloses itself in direct opposition to his new self, thus revealing the split between the two aspects of his mind. In *Leocadia* the prince's mind became unhinged owing to the death of his beloved, but his aunt, a wealthy duchess, who looks after him, tries to preserve the illusion that the past still exists. She even schemes to bring him back to reality by dressing up Amanda, a seamstress, to impersonate the dead girl, hoping that the shock will cure him of his illusion. Although the methods are the same as those used in *Enrico IV,* the result is different. The prince falls in love with Amanda and thus succeeds in overcoming his passion for the dead Leocadia.

After the liberation of France in 1944 and the end of World War II there arose another great revival of interest in Pirandello in Paris, and in 1947 Marcel

Doisy, in his study of the contemporary French theatre, paid the following tribute to the Italian master: "The most important thing we owe Dante's homeland is Pirandellism. Surely no man since Ibsen has given Europe so totally renewed a conception of the theatre, a more violently original artistry together with so personal a technique. And it certainly seems as if his revelations are still far from exhausted. Indeed, Pirandello might easily remain one of the guiding lights of the period which is opening."[1]

During the "cold-war" period when anarchy was rampant on all sides, the moment was ripe for the spread of Existentialism, and as Umberto Cantoro says, "it is not difficult to recognize in Pirandello's thought the outlines of Existentialism from Kierkegaard to Heidegger, from Pascal to Gabriel Marcel, from Sartre to Abbagnano."[2]

Even Jean-Paul Sartre, the acknowledged leader of the Existentialist school and the foremost dramatist of the postwar era, was in no doubt about Pirandello's influence in France. When he was asked who was the most timely dramatist, the author of *Huis Clos* (1944) replied: "It is most certainly Pirandello." Thus, in *Huis Clos* (*No Exit*) Inés, the only one of the three characters to see clearly her own reality, echoes Pirandello's heroine of *Vestire gl'Ignudi*, Ersilia Drei, when, after unmasking the illusions of her two fellow-victims in hell, she exclaims: "Here we are stark naked." Indeed, as critics have shown, the victims in *Huis Clos* not only strip themselves naked but positively wallow in their anguish like the father and step-daughter in the *Six Characters*. In *Morts sans Sépulture* (1946) Sartre places his resistance fighters in agonizing situations wherein

[1] M. Doisy, *Le Théâtre français contemporain*, p. 272. Brussels, 1947.
[2] U. Cantoro, *Luigi Pirandello e il problema della personalità*, p. 191. Bologna, 1954.

they come face to face with their own inner selves for the first time, and we recall Pirandello's definition of his *Teatro dello Specchio:* "When a man lives, he lives and does not see himself. Put a mirror before him and make him see himself in the act of living under the sway of his passions: either he remains astonished or dumb-founded at his own appearance, or else in disgust he spits at his image, or again clenches his fist, to break it."

All through his works Sartre emphasizes the absurdity of life, and his example was followed by Albert Camus, though with a difference. The latter, as he shows in his essay *L'Homme Révolté* (1942), while accepting man's absurdity, is resolved to revolt against it and by that gesture of revolt he proclaims the solidarity of man-kind.

The absurd hero of Camus is Sisyphus[1] rolling his huge stone up the slope of eternity. He *is,* as much through his passions as through his torture. His scorn of the gods, his hatred of death, and his passion for life won him that unspeakable penalty in which the whole being is exerted towards accomplishing nothing. But Sisyphus has his silent joy, for his fate belongs to him. His rock is his thing. Likewise the absurd man, when he contemplates his torment, silences all the idols. Sisyphus, Camus says, teaches man the higher fidelity that negates the gods and raises rocks. When the truth bursts upon him he may like Oedipus cry out: "Despite so many ordeals, my advanced age and the nobility of my soul make me conclude that all is well."[2]

Within a framework of deep pessimism Camus, like Pirandello, succeeds in reaching a basic optimism about human life, and in the vision of both writers charity plays a preponderating part. For both authors the one

[1] A. Camus, *Le Mythe de Sisyphe,* Paris, 1943.
[2] W. Kaufmann, *Existentialism from Dostoevsky to Sartre,* p. 315. New York, 1956.

legitimate philosophical question is that of suicide or
life. The Absurd man (the man in whom the experience
of the absurd has occurred) forever abjures suicide and
death, whether through philosophical systems or at the
point of the gun.[1] Camus, too, like Pirandello, believed
in the bankruptcy of the Nietzschean superman, for the
Absurd man does not try to live on a loftier scale of
human or superhuman achievement. He possesses no
relationship to the totalitarian man, but seeks to enrich
his life by his experiences, which have all the deeper
significance for him because he is forever aware of his
mortality. In *Caligula* (1945), as in *Enrico IV,* we find
the same pessimism and the same denunciations of this
world, the same scorn for those who swim with the
tide, and the same awareness of the absurdity of
existence.

Finally we come to Samuel Beckett, the Irish dramatist, whose *En Attendant Godot (Waiting for Godot)* of
1953, with its heart-rending portrayal of absurdity as
the dominant aspect of life, reminds us in many details
of the dramas in which Pirandello laid bare his tormented soul. But though Pirandello, ever mindful of
his own case, moved his audiences all over the world,
because there is always pity with human suffering in his
plays, he never attempted to create a philosophy of
absurdity. Sartre and his followers, though they succeeded in dramatizing the absurdity of man's existence,
have left us abstract works that are completely devoid
of compassion for trapped humanity.[2] It was left for
James Joyce's disciple, Samuel Beckett, to write a
morality play with sympathy for mankind and a sense
of participation in its fate. This return of the theatre
to the humanistic tradition was of primary importance

[1] O. F. Pucciani, *The French Theatre since 1930,* p. 271. New
York, 1954.
[2] T. Bishop, *op. cit.,* p. 130.

in the postwar theatre which tended too much to the abstract. This will explain the clamorous success of *Waiting for Godot,* which burst upon the Parisian theatrical scene in January, 1953, like a bombshell, and made its author famous almost overnight. The account of the first night reads like that of the Pirandellian premières in Rome and Milan in 1919–1920. The first-nighters, who were expecting a different kind of play, were either perplexed, disgruntled, or thrilled. "The disgruntled left after the first act, the thrilled remained to applaud wildly at the end of the performance, and the perplexed sat on in puzzled silence. At the inter-mission the struggle between support and opposition was symbolically represented by a fist fight in the lobby."[1] Next day word had gone round and the people were forewarned, and the audience at the theatre was prepared for something "astonishing." Critics greeted the play with anathema or rapture, but of its original-ity there was no doubt. Jean Anouilh called the play a "music-hall sketch of Pascal's *Pensées* performed by the Fratellini clowns."[2]

And so *Waiting for Godot* marks an important date in the modern theatre, and Jean Anouilh again com-mented: "I think the evening at the Babylone Theatre is as important as the first Pirandello produced by Pitoëff in Paris in 1923."[3]

The essence of Pirandello's theatre is the marrow of contemporary ideas, of modern anxieties and pessi-mism. This is what the French playwrights admired in him. We can find elements of Pirandellism in the works of other modern dramatists, such as Unamuno, Crom-melynck, Kaiser, Herczeg, Molnar, and Priestley, and in America Elmer Rice and Thornton Wilder, but

[1] L. C. Pronko, *Avant-Garde: The Experimental Theater in France,* p. 22. Berkeley and Los Angeles, 1962.

[2] *Ibid.,* p. 33.

[3] T. Bishop, *op. cit.,* p. 132.

these are similarities rather than influence. It was France which was most receptive to Pirandello and which adopted him as its own. Thomas Bishop puts the case most succinctly, saying that the Italian, who had been most responsible for liberating his country's drama from simple imitations of French models, turned the tables by giving France bold new ideas and daring techniques.[1]

In conclusion, we might say that what Pirandello laid bare before us is not merely the work of the actors, nor that of the author, but something much more universal—the other side of ourselves.

[1] *Ibid.,* p. 148.

Epilogue

AFTER PLODDING THROUGH THE Pirandellian world it is a relief to pause at the end and create for ourselves a final vision of the master.

At first we saw him emerge out of the sunlit landscape of Sicily. Beneath blue skies he stood before us against a discordant background. On one side were the stately Agrigento's ruins of the Greek temples, through whose slender columns we watched the twinkling stars: on the other were the mean houses of Porto Empedocle, packed and squeezed together around the piles of sulphur from the mines. Pirandello soon lost sight of blue sky and Greek temples, while he gazed at the slave workers of the modern world, crawling barefoot towards the lighters, struggling to hold aloft the great loads on their shoulders.

We saw him next against the background of our machine-made world. A strident, cruel labyrinth of whizzing cog-wheels, through which he wandered in a daze. All the inhabitants of that world seemed to the sad-eyed islander to be frenzied puppets, gesticulating and writhing, as though Satan were pulling the wires for their infernal dance. Was it any wonder that the sensitive Sicilian, who had been pitchforked into the chaos of the modern world, would look upon it all as Dante did when he reached the second ring of the seventh circle of Hell, and saw in the pathless wood the souls of the suicides imprisoned in the trunks of trees.

Pirandello possessed one supreme virtue—sincerity.

His pessimistic nature, nurtured on Leopardi's poetry, could not submit to the hypocrisy of those who for the sake of so-called ultimate good refused to see the consequences of things. It was Pirandello's misfortune that he appeared at the end of the nineteenth century when, as Croce said in his famous essay, "insincerity was rife in literature."

All Pirandello's later plays are part of a gigantic sermon on the theme of "ricominciamento." In *La Nuova Colonia* (*The New Colony*), a social myth, he has postulated the creation of a new society, and he has drawn the moral that we must begin again from first elements, but we must remember the experiences of our forerunners.

Pirandello had welcomed the Fascist regime of Mussolini because, like the majority of the ex-servicemen who had returned to their homes from the front, he was disgusted with democratic chaos and wanted direct action. Even as far back as 1889 he had given expression to his disillusion with the political graft of post-Garibaldian Italy, when Rome was the Rome of Petronius—a city of decadence. It did not need World War I to awaken in Pirandello a profound longing for a revolution that would shake the world to its foundations. But under Mussolini and the Fascist State Pirandello was no happier than he had been before, in spite of all the honours the Government had lavished upon him. That is the moral of his autobiographical play *Quando si è qualcuno* (*When One Is Somebody*), where the author portrays the literary patriarch with pitiless irony: "he is nameless, and even his head is owned by the public, like the head of a coin." In his play *Lazzaro* (*Lazarus*) he creates another myth, this time of religion, but with social implications, for he indicts modern civilization as represented by the puritanical and ascetic hero Diego Spina, and Monsignor Lelli, who respec-

tively represent capitalism and obscurantism. The
author, in contrast, proclaims as the ideal a vague mixture of pantheism and Christianity. Pirandello identi-
fies God with the soul of man and considers the soul
merged with Him both during man's life and at his
bodily death. Pirandello in this play asks himself what
would happen if a man should die, and when brought
back to life by the aid of science, should realize that
there was nothing beyond? Science, he tells us, gives us
such a possibility since it has discovered that an injec-
tion of adrenalin into the heart will cause life to ebb
back into the body. Diego Spina, the Lazarus of the
play, is strictly orthodox in religion, and Christ is to
him the symbol of harsh and cruel suffering. When,
after he has died in a motor accident, the doctor brings
him back to life there is great excitement in the town,
and everybody looks upon Dr. Gionini as a sorcerer.
Diego Spina's reaction is more violent than the rest:
his faith gives way and he is appalled at finding himself
on the edge of the abyss of nothingness. His character
consequently changes as he becomes crazed by his
pessimism. The miracle of his return to life, however,
has the opposite effect upon his son Lucio, the priest.
Lucio's faith is thereby strengthened and by his serene
reasoning brings his father back to his faith. In spite of
its flimsy theology, the play illustrates Pirandello's
longing for a primitive pantheistic religion, personified
in Sara, Diego's estranged wife, and their son Lucio. If
Lazzaro is the author's myth of Religion, *I Giganti della
Montagna* (*The Giants of the Mountain*) is his myth
of Art. As Eric Bentley says in his introduction to
Naked Masks (New York, 1952), ". . . it would be either
a stupid or an over-ingenious critic who would stamp
these later works of Pirandello as fascist." They illustrate, at most, the plight of a playwright in a fascist
state, and show that, in some degree, he lived in an

"inner emigration like many German writers under Hitler." Certainly the impression produced by the unfinished play *I Giganti della Montagna* is that the players, the artists, and the people are the victims of the tyrannical giants who are bent on securing the strength and wealth of the earth for themselves.

Pirandello's eldest son Stefano, in a broadcast from Rome on December 10, 1938, the first anniversary of his father's death, described how his father during his last nights on earth remained wakeful hour after hour, with all his thoughts concentrated on his last play, with its setting on the border between fable and reality and its unearthly characters. This he meant to be his farewell to the stage, for even on his deathbed he was planning to return to narrative art and had high hopes of finding enough energy to terminate two vast "conclusive works," as he called them: his novel *Adam and Eve* and a strange work entitled *Informations of My Involuntary Sojourn on Earth,* which he had begun several times, and in which he wished to explore the more secret and direct way to reach the final truth about life. He also wanted to bring to completion his ambitious project of writing short stories for every day in the year (he had still a hundred to write). Stefano added that the dying author, in his dreamy evocation of all his life works, wished his dramas to be a parenthesis in his vaster output as a novelist, and he even expressed the wish that he might be granted enough time to return to the point whence he had started as a young man, and conclude his life's work as he had begun, by being a poet. *Adam and Eve* was to be a "mythical, humorous account of the beginning of human life after the huge earthquake in which all humanity perishes, except a man and a woman, who would begin again to build up civilization."

"I alone," said the ancient author, "have been fated

to tell how this all happens." He imagined that after the Cataclysm his wandering spirit, flitting through the starry spaces, would be permitted to return to see the earth emerge from the Flood, and with his miraculous vision as a disembodied spirit he would discover the solitary man survivor in that spot on earth which had been England, and the solitary woman in what had been Spain. And out of the silent desolation of the world these two solitary human beings, guided by their prodigious instinct, would cross seas, rivers, mountains, to reach one another, and he would chronicle their joyful meeting and mating. They would have one great advantage over their first parents, for they would remember the civilization that had perished. But would they avoid the mistakes their forerunners had made?

Pirandello died before giving us his conclusions, but all through his works he seems to say: "What have men been given to enable them to live? A God of pessimism, who told them to have patience and rely upon His mercy. But then God was removed, and mankind was told that heaven and hell were in this world, and beyond the grave there was nothing. And finally men were told that there was nothing here or there, for all was a dream. Every man is himself alone: he knows no more than all the rest."

Pirandello shrugged his shoulders resignedly and said in his mournful voice: "We can do nothing but draw closer to one another and create a religion of pity. Religion is an illusion, but a beneficial one if it curbs the wild beast within us. But we must not use it as an instrument of coercion and torture, killing one another for the love of God."

Pirandello himself died like one of the stoics of old. In giving his last instructions, he said: *"Il carro, il cavallo, il cocchiere e basta"* (the hearse, the horse, the driver—nothing more). He would allow no religious

ceremonies at his funeral, for he preferred to slip away
from life as one on a secret errand. His spirit departing
seemed to murmur the words from the unknown poet
in the Greek anthology:

> "Lay no offering of ointments or garlands on
>   my stony tomb,
> Nor make the fire blaze up; the expense is in vain.
> While I am alive be kind to me if thou wilt;
> But drenching my ashes with wine thou wilt
>   make mire,
> And the dead man will not drink."

Bibliography
of the Principal Works of Pirandello

(Arranged under the headings Poems, Novels, Collections of Short Stories, Plays, Critical Works, English Translations of Pirandello's Works, and Books on Pirandello)

Poems

1889. *Mal Giocondo.* Clausen, Palermo.
1891. *Pasqua di Gea.* Galli, Milano.
1895. *Elegie Renane.* Unione, Tip. Ed., Roma.
1896. *Elegie Romane* (Translations from Goethe). Giusti, Livorno.
1901. *Zampogna.* Soc. Ed., Dante Alighieri, Roma.
1912. *Fuori di Chiave.* Formiggini, Genova. (This is the best collection of Pirandello's poetry.)

Novels (Romanzi)

1901. *L'Esclusa.* Tribuna, Roma. (Contains dedicatory letter to Luigi Capuana.)
1902. *Il Turno.* Giannotta, Catania. (The author says it was written in his earliest youth, even before *L'Esclusa.*)
1904. *Il Fu Mattia Pascal.* Nuova Antologia, Roma.
1911. *Suo Marito* (out of print). Quattrini, Firenze. (Brit. Mus. 12471, r. 17. It is of interest because it contains the germs of the two plays *Se non Così* [1915] and *La Nuova Colonia* [1928]. The novel is now published by Mondadori, Milano, under the title *Giustino Roncella nato Boggiolo.*)
1913. *I Vecchi e i Giovani* (2 volumes). Treves, Milano. (Contains the dedication: *"ai miei figli giovani oggi, vecchi domani."*)

Bibliography

1916. *Si gira.* Treves, Milano. (Republished in 1925 under the title *Quaderni di Serafino Gubbio Operatore.*)

1925. *Uno Nessuno e Centomila.* Started as serial in *La Fiera Letteraria* (Milano), Dec. 13. Published complete by Bemporad, Firenze, 1926. (This novel had been announced nearly ten years before 1926. Pirandello was working at it in 1910. According to Stefano Landi, it refers to his own domestic life.)

The seven novels were published by Mondadori, Milan, in one volume in 1941.

Collections of Short Stories (Novelle)

Most of the earlier volumes of "novelle" were published by Treves & Co., Milan. In 1921 Bemporad & Co., Florence, began to issue a complete collection of the short stories under the title *Novelle per un anno* or *A Story for Every Day in the Year.* They have now been published by Mondadori & Co., Milan, in fifteen volumes, 1938. An "Omnibus" edition in two volumes was issued in 1944.

Pirandello had intended to issue the 365 stories in 24 volumes. Up to his death 14 volumes had appeared. The series includes versions of all the previously published stories plus many new ones.

1894. *Amori senza Amore.*

1902. *Beffe della Morte e della Vita.*

1902. *Quand'Ero Matto.*

1904. *Bianche e Nere.*

1906. *Erma Bifronte.*

1910. *La Vita Nuda.*

1912. *Terzetti.*

1913. *La Trappola.*

1914. *Le Due Maschere.* (Republished in 1920 as *Tu Ridi.*)

1915. *Erba del Nostro Orto.*

1916. *E Domani Lunedì.*

1918. *Un Cavallo nella Luna.*

1919. *Berecche e la Guerra.* (This volume is of particular interest because it describes the plight during World

Bibliography

War I of those whose education and sympathies had
been German.)

1919. *Il Carnevale dei Morti.*

The first volume of *Novelle per un anno* appeared in
1921. In the preliminary note the author said: "Each volume
will contain not a few new stories, and of those already published some have been reconstructed from top to bottom,
others recast and retouched here and there, all of them, in
short, re-elaborated with long and loving care."

Plays

Many of Pirandello's plays are dramatizations of "novelle."
The earlier plays, with the exception of *Liolà* and a few
short pieces, were published by Treves in a series entitled
Maschere Nude (1918; 4 vols.). In 1920 Bemporad & Co. began
to publish all the plays in a series also entitled *Maschere
Nude.* Mondadori & Co. have published the complete revised
works of the author in 1944. An "Omnibus" edition in four
volumes was published in 1949.

I.   *Tutto Per Bene.* Produced in 1920. From the "novella" in *La Vita Nuda.*

II.   *Come Prima, Meglio di Prima.* Produced in 1920.

III.   *Sei Personaggi in cerca d'Autore.* A play in the
making. Produced in 1921. From the "novelle" *La
Tragedia d'un personaggio* in *La Trappola* and
Colloqui coi personaggi in *Berecche e la guerra.*

IV.   *Enrico IV.* Tragedy. Produced in 1922.

V.   *L'Uomo, La Bestia e la Virtù.* An apology. Produced
in 1919. From "novella" *Richiamo all'Obbligo* in
Terzetti.

VI.   *La Signora Morli, Una e Due.* Produced in 1920 by
Emma Gramatica and in 1926 by Pirandello with
Marta Abba.

VII. *Vestire gl'Ignudi.* Produced in 1922.

VIII. *La Vita che ti Diedi.* Tragedy. Cf. the "novella" *La
camera in attesa* in *È Domani Lunedì.*

IX.   *Ciascuno a suo Modo.* Comedy in two or three acts

Bibliography

with choral interludes. Produced in Milan, 1924, by Niccodemi.

X.   *Pensaci Giacomino!* Produced in 1916. From "novella" in *Terzetti*.

XI.   *Così È (se vi pare)*. Parable. Produced in 1916. From "novella" in *È Domani Lunedì*.

XII.   *La Sagra del Signore della Nave—L'Altro Figlio—La Giara*. One-act plays. *La Sagra* was produced at the inauguration of Pirandello's Art Theatre in Rome, 1925.

XIII.   *Il Piacere dell'Onestà*. Produced in 1917.

XIV.   *Il Berretto a Sonagli*. Produced in 1917.

XV.   *Il Giuoco delle Parti*. Produced in 1918 by Ruggero Ruggeri. The reception accorded the play is referred to in *Sei Personaggi*.

XVI.   *Ma Non è una Cosa Seria*. From the "novella" *Non è una Cosa Seria* in *Terzetti*. It is dedicated to Emma Gramatica, who produced it in 1918.

XVII.   *L'Innesto*. Produced in 1917.

XVIII.   *La Ragione degli Altri*. Revised from the early play *Se Non Così*, which was produced in 1915.

XIX.   *L'Imbecille—Lumìe di Sicilia—Cecè—La Patente*. One-act plays.

XX.   *All'Uscita — Il Dovere di Medico — La Morsa — L'Uomo dal Fiore in Bocca*. One-act plays. *La Morsa*, which was produced 1912–13 was considered by Pirandello to be his earliest play. *L'Uomo dal Fiore in Bocco* was derived from the story *Caffè Notturno*, reprinted in *Novelle per un anno* as *La morte addosso*.

XXI.   *Diana e la Tuda*. Tragedy. Produced at Zurich in German, 1926; in Italian by Pirandello at Milan, 1927. Dedicated to Marta Abba.

XXII.   *L'Amica delle Mogli*. From "novella" in *Amore senza Amore*. Dedicated to Marta Abba.

XXIII.   *La Nuova Colonia*. Produced in 1928. The germ of it is to be found in *Suo Marito*. It is termed a *Myth, Prologue and three acts*.

XXIV.   *Liolà*. Had been produced by Sicilian actors in 1916.

Bibliography

Published by Formiggini, Rome, in 1917, with Sicilian and Italian text.

XXV. *O Di Uno O Di Nessuno.*

XXVI. *Lazzaro.*

XXVII. *Questa Sera Si Recita a Soggetto.* A play in the making. It is based upon the "novella" *Leonora Addio* in *Terzetti.*

XXVIII. *Come Tu Mi vuoi.*

XXIX. *Trovarsi.* Dedicated to Marta Abba.

XXX. *Quando Si È Qualcuno.*

XXXI. *Non Si Sa Come.* The German translation by Stefan Zweig was published before the Italian edition. It is based upon the "novelle" *Cinci* in Vol. XIV and *Nel Gorgo* in Vol. VIII of *Novelle per un anno.*

Pirandello also translated *The Cyclops* of Euripides into Sicilian dialect under the title *'U Ciclopu.* He also translated into Sicilian dialect his plays *Il Berretto a Sonagli* (*'A Birretta coi ciancianeddi*), *La Giara* (*'A Giarra*), *Lumìe di Sicilia, La Morsa,* and *Pensaci Giacomino!*

Critical Works

Laute und Lautentwicklung der Mundart von Girgenti. Halle, 1891.

A treatise upon the dialect of his birthplace Girgenti submitted for the doctor's degree at Bonn. The thesis is written in German but contains a short autobiographical note in Latin. Out of print. (Brit. Mus. 12901d. 36[8].)

Arte e Scienza. Modes, Roma, 1908.

Contains a very interesting article entitled *Un Critico Fantastico* on the work of the humorist Alberto Cantoni. It contains also, among other studies, articles upon the metrics of Dante and the sonnets of Cecco Angiolieri.

L'Umorismo. Lanciano, Carabba, 1908. Republished by Battistelli, Firenze, 1920.

Very important for the student of Pirandello's works. Discusses the Italian humorists and irony in early Italian poetry, and especially the characteristics of humour. It contains interesting pages on Don Abbondio and Don Quixote.

Bibliography

English Translations of Pirandello's Works

Three Plays of Pirandello. Dent, London; Dutton, New York, 1922. The volume includes *Six Characters in Search of an Author* (*Sei Personaggi in cerca d'Autore*), translated by E. Storer; *Right You Are* (*If You Think So*) [*Cosi È* (*se vi pare*)], translated by A. Livingston; and *Henry IV* (*Enrico IV*), translated by E. Storer.

Each in His Own Way and two other plays. Dent, London; Dutton, New York, 1923. The volume includes *Each in His Own Way* (*Ciascuno a Suo Modo*), *The Pleasure of Honesty* (*Il Piacere dell'Onestà*), and *Naked* (*Vestire gl'Ignudi*).

The Late Mattia Pascal (*Il fu Mattia Pascal*). Translated by A. Livingston. Dent, London; Dutton, New York, 1923.

The Outcast (*L'Esclusa*). Translated by Leo Ongley. Dent, London; Dutton, New York, 1925.

Shoot (*Si Gira*). Translated by C. K. Scott-Moncrieff. Chatto and Windus, London; Dutton, New York, 1926.

The Old and the Young (*I Vecchi e i Giovani*). Translated by C. K. Scott-Moncrieff. Chatto and Windus, London; Dutton, New York, 1928. 2 vols.

One-Act Plays. Translated by Elizabeth Abbott, A. Livingston, and Blanche Valentine Mitchell. Dutton, New York, 1928. The volume includes *Chee-Chee* (*Cèce*), translated by E. Abbott; *At the Gate* (*All'Uscita*), translated by B. V. Mitchell; *Sicilian Limes* (*Lumìe di Sicilia*), translated by E. Abbott; *The Imbecile* (*L'Imbecille*), translated by B. V. Mitchell; *By Judgment of the Court* (*La Patente*), translated by E. Abbott; *Our Lord of the Ship* (*La Sagra del Signore della Nave*), translated by B. V. Mitchell; *The Man with the Flower in His Mouth* (*L'Uomo dal Fiore in Bocca*), translated by A. Livingston; *The Vise* (*La Morsa*), translated by E. Abbott; *The Jar* (*La Giara*), translated by A. Livingston; *The House with the Column* (*L'Altro Figlio*), translated by E. Abbott; and *The Doctor's Duty* (*Il Dovere del Medico*).

As You Desire Me (*Come Tu Mi Vuoi*). Translated by Samuel Putnam. Dutton, New York, 1931.

A Horse in the Moon and twelve short stories (*Un Cavallo nella Luna. Dodici brevi novelle*). Translated by Samuel Putnam. Dutton, New York, 1932.

Bibliography

To-night We Improvise (Questa Sera Si Recita a Soggetto). Translated by Samuel Putnam. Dutton, New York, 1932.

One, None and a Hundred Thousand (Uno, Nessuno e Centomilia). Translated by Samuel Putnam. New York, 1933.

Better Think Twice About It and twelve other stories (Pensaci, Giacomino! e altre dodici novelle). Translated by Arthur and Henrie Mayne. Lane, London; Dutton, New York, 1933–1934.

The Naked Truth and eleven other stories (La Vita Nuda e altre undici novelle). Translated by Arthur and Henrie Mayne. Lane, London; Dutton, New York, 1934.

A Character in Distress (Tragedia di un Personaggio). Translated by Michele Pettina. Duckworth, London; Dutton, New York, 1938–1939.

Four Tales. Translated by V. M. Jeffery, with Italian text on the opposite page. Harrap, London, 1939.

Naked Masks; Five Plays. Edited by Eric Bentley. New York, Dutton, 1952. This American Everyman Library edition contains an excellent critical introduction by Bentley. The plays are *Liolà,* translated by E. Bentley and G. Guerrini; *It Is So (if you think so) [Così È (se vi pare)],* translated by A. Livingston; *Henry IV (Enrico IV),* translated by A. Livingston; *Six Characters [Sei Personaggi in cerca d'Autore],* translated by E. Storer; and *Each in His Own Way (Ciascuno a Suo Modo),* translated by A. Livingston. The volume also includes a translation of Pirandello's preface to *Six Characters,* and biographical and bibliographical notes by E. Bentley.

Books on Pirandello

To the following works I express my indebtedness:

Maria Alajmo, *Pirandello e il "suo Modo."* Girgenti, 1926. A short study based on a lecture given at the "Circolo di Cultura" at Girgenti.

Alvaro, *Luigi Pirandello* (article in the *Enciclopedia Italiana,* Vol. XXVII, 1935).

Andrenio. *See* E. Gómez de Baquero

Arcamone, *Il Personaggio Pirandelliano.* Napoli, 1938.

Bibliography

E. Gómez de Baquero (Andrenio), *Pirandello y Compañía*. Madrid, 1928.

Andrenio, one of Spain's most celebrated literary critics, describes Pirandello in Spain. He is an anti-Pirandellian.

Eric Bentley, *In Search of Theater*. New York, 1959.

Contains an excellent critical essay, "Pirandello; Joy and Torment" (pp. 279–295).

T. Bishop, *Pirandello and the French Theatre*. New York, 1960.

Bisson, *Pirandello all'Uscita*. Napoli, 1940.

Massimo Bontempelli, *Pirandello, Leopardi, D'Annunzio*. Milano, 1936.

G. A. Borgese, *Tempo di Edificare*. Milano, 1923.

Short study of Pirandello.

Umberto Cantoro, *L'Altro me Stesso (Il Problema della personalità nel dramma Pirandelliano)*. Verona, 1939.

A valuable study of Pirandello's personality.

Benvenuto Cellini, *Il Teatro di Pirandello*. Roma, 1934.

Benjamin Crémieux, *Panorama de la Littérature Italienne*, Paris, 1928.

Benedetto Croce, *Pirandello (La Letteratura della Nuova Italia*, Vol. VI). Bari, 1949.

Bottino Egle. *See* Puliatti Pietro

Silvio D'Amico. *Il Teatro Italiano*. Milano, 1933.

———, *Il Teatro dei Fantocci*. Firenze, 1940.

———, *Storia del Teatro Drammatico*. Milano, 1950.

Ettore Fabbri, *Luigi Pirandello*. Milano, 1921.

Luigi Ferrante, *Pirandello*. Firenze, 1958.

Important as a study of Pirandello's philosophy and relations with Catholicism, etc.

Francesco Flora, *Dal Romanticismo al Futurismo*. Milano, 1925.

An excellent study of the post-World War I movement in Italian arts written by one who was a disciple of Croce. A severe criticism of Pirandello's earlier works.

Petronio Giuseppe, *Pirandello Novelliere e la Crisi del Realismo*. Lucentia, Lucca, 1950.

Gino Gori, *Il Grottesco nell'Arte e nella Letteratura*. Roma, 1926.

Bibliography

A. Jannu, *Luigi Pirandello*. Firenze, 1948.

Lander McClintock, *The Age of Pirandello*. Bloomington, Indiana, 1951.

Federico Vittore Nardelli, *L'Uomo Segreto (Vita e Croci di Luigi Pirandello)*, Milano, 1932 and 1944.
> Indispensable to those who wish to know the secrets of Pirandello's life. It describes the master's youth, domestic struggles, and sufferings.

John Palmer, *Studies on the Contemporary Theatre*. London, 1927.

Ferdinando Pasini, *Luigi Pirandello (come mi Pare)*. Trieste, 1927.
> A valuable study which contains a useful bibliography.

Camillo Pellizzi, *Le Lettere Italiane del Nostro Secolo*. Milano, 1929.
> An important study of the modern movement in Italian literature.

Puliatti Pietro and Bottino Egle, *Lineamenti sull'Arte di L. Pirandello*. Catania, 1941.

Ramirez, *El Teatro de Pirandello*. Buenos Aires, 1927.

Pirro Rost, *Luigi Pirandello*. Milano, 1921.

Rosso di San Secondo, *L. Pirandello*. Nuova Antologia, Roma, 1916.

Slama, *Realismul in teatrul lui Pirandello*. Bucaresti, 1943.

Adriano Tilgher, *Voci del Tempo*. Roma, 1921.

———, *Studi sul Teatro Contemporaneo*. Roma, 1923.

———, *La Scena e la Vita*. Roma, 1925.
> Tilgher's books are of great importance to the student of Pirandello and the "teatro grottesco." These brilliant studies gave a metaphysical interpretation of Pirandello's theatre.

Luigi Tonelli, *Il Teatro Contemporaneo Italiano*. Milano, 1936.

M. Lo Vecchio-Musti, *Bibliografia di Pirandello*. 2d ed.; Milano, 1952.

Domenico Vittorini, *The Drama of Luigi Pirandello*. Philadelphia, 1935.
> An excellent study of all the plays written by one who is a decided Pirandellian. It includes a grateful letter from Pirandello to the author.

Index